BY FORCE OF ARMS

The Revolution at Sea Saga
Book One

James Nelson

CORGI BOOKS

BY FORCE OF ARMS
A CORGI BOOK : 0 552 14960 8

First publication in Great Britain

PRINTING HISTORY
Corgi edition published 2003

of [...] hor
[...]ns 77
[...]88.

In[...] are
e[...] are
us[...] ts or
l[...]tal.

Condition of Sale
This book is sold subject to the condition that it shall not,
by way of trade or otherwise, be lent, re-sold, hired out or
otherwise circulated in any form of binding or cover other than
that in which it is published and without a similar condition
including this condition being imposed on the subsequent
purchaser.

Set in 10½/12pt Galliard by
Kestrel Data, Exeter, Devon.

Corgi Books are published by Transworld Publishers,
61–63 Uxbridge Road, London W5 5SA,
a division of The Random House Group Ltd,
in Australia by Random House Australia (Pty) Ltd,
20 Alfred Street, Milsons Point, Sydney, NSW 2061, Australia,
in New Zealand by Random House New Zealand Ltd,
18 Poland Road, Glenfield, Auckland 10, New Zealand
and in South Africa by Random House (Pty) Ltd,
Endulini, 5a Jubilee Road, Parktown 2193, South Africa.

Printed and bound in Great Britain by
Cox & Wyman Ltd, Reading, Berkshire.

*To my parents, Selma and David,
and my sister Stephanie,
counselors who feelingly persuade me what I am*

And to Lisa, whom I love

Acknowledgments

I would like to express my heartfelt thanks to the following people: Richard Miles, who taught me how to take a risk; C. A. Finger, the best square-rig man I have ever known. Thanks to Tom Montgomery and Stephanie Nelson for their invaluable editorial input. Thanks to Bill Grose, Doug Grad, and most certainly to Peter Wolverton at Pocket Books. My deepest thanks to Nat Sobel, Andrea Harding, Dorothea Nelson, and all of the people at Sobel Weber Associates.

Thanks to my many shipmates of the past years. You are, in the words of Joseph Conrad, as good a crowd as ever fisted with wild cries the beating canvas of a heavy foresail; or tossing aloft, invisible in the night, gave back yell for yell to a westerly gale.

These Special Orders Shall be a full Warrant and Discharge to him, and all others on Board his Said Vessel and the other Vessels fitted out and employed as aforesaid under his Command, to encounter expulse expel and resist by Force of Arms . . . all and every such Person or Persons as Shall attempt or enterprise the Destruction, Invasion, Detriment, or annoyance of the Inhabitants of this Colony or Plantation.

—Instructions from the
Rhode Island Committee of
Safety to Capt. Abraham
Whipple, commander of the
armed sloop *Katy*,
June 15, 1775

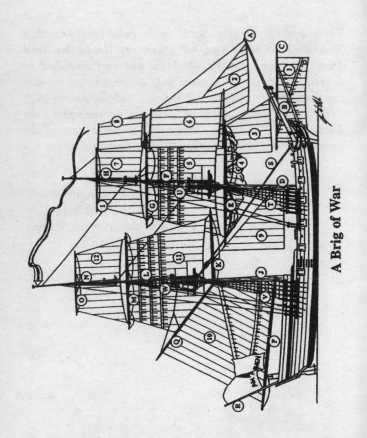

A Brig of War

Sails

1. Spritsail
2. Jib
3. Fore Topmast Staysail
4. Foresail (clewed up)
5. Fore Topsail
6. Fore Topmast Studdingsail (removable)
7. Fore Topgallant Sail
8. Fore Topgallant Studdingsail (removable)
9. Main Staysail
10. Mainsail
11. Main Topsail
12. Main Topgallant Sail

Spars and Rigging

A. Jibboom
B. Bowsprit
C. Spritsail Yard
D. Foremast
E. Foreyard
F. Fore Topmast
G. Fore Topsail Yard
H. Fore Topgallant Mast
I. Fore Topgallant Yard
J. Mainmast
K. Mainyard
L. Main Topmast
M. Main Topsail Yard
N. Main Topgallant Mast
O. Main Topgallant Yard
P. Boom
Q. Gaff
R. Ensign Staff (removable)
S. Mainstay
T. Fore Shrouds and Ratlines
U. Fore Topmast Shrouds and Ratlines
V. Main Shrouds and Ratlines
W. Main Topmast Shrouds and Ratlines

*For other terminology and usage see Glossary at the end of the book

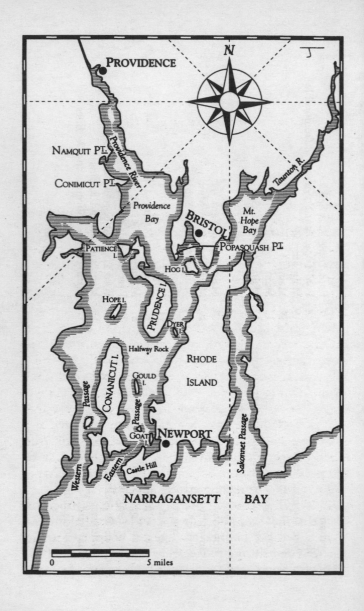

Chapter 1

Judea

Capt. Isaac Biddlecomb was carrying more sail than was prudent, more sail than was even safe, for the thirty-five knots of wind gusting from the south-southwest. It was a fact of which he was quite aware, but chose to ignore, hoping instead that the *Judea*'s thin spars would bear the strain for an hour more. An hour and a half at the most.

He pushed himself off the leeward rail and walked up the steeply sloping quarterdeck to the weather side, noting again, with some irritation, that such physical activity was not as effortless as it had once been. It wasn't his age – he was only twenty-eight – and while he no longer had the lean, tough physique that he had enjoyed as a foremast sailor and even as a mate, he could hardly be considered fat. Still, the work of a ship's captain and its concomitant lack of physical activity was spoiling him, and he made a vague resolve to do something about it.

Biddlecomb reached the weather side, grabbed on to the caprail atop the bulwark, and peered aloft. His long dark hair, bound in a queue, whipped around his head and stung his cheek like driving rain, and the tail end of his long wool coat beat against his legs.

13

His cocked hat was jammed into the binnacle box for safekeeping. He buttoned the uppermost of the silver buttons on the coat and flipped the broad collar up to keep the wind off his neck and to tame his flogging hair as he studied the sails and spars above.

In the light of the gibbous moon he could make out the fore and main topgallant masts, one hundred feet and more above the deck. They bowed dangerously to leeward, bending to the pressure of the yard and sail. He looked down at the water rushing along the ship's side and streaming aft in a long, straight wake before disappearing in the night. They were making eight knots at least, more likely eight and a half. Through the darkness he could just see the loom of the land ahead, the colony of Rhode Island. In an hour they would be safe in Bristol.

'Fall off a point, Rigney,' Biddlecomb said, turning to the helmsman.

'Fall off a point, aye,' replied Rigney at the wheel, easing two spokes to larboard.

Biddlecomb leaned over the weather rail and peered forward around the edge of the mainsail, staring into the darkness ahead. At last he saw it, a thin gray line, broad on the starboard bow.

'Rigney, there's Castle Hill. Do you see it?' Biddlecomb pointed toward the rocky slope that marked the entrance to Narragansett Bay, just visible in the moonlight.

'Aye, sir,' the helmsman said at last.

'And the breakers on the rocks?'

'Aye.'

'Good. We'll stand in as close to those rocks as ever we can. Plenty of water there, so don't be shy.'

In the glow of the binnacle light Biddlecomb

14

could see Rigney's face, and he did not look happy. 'Aye, sir,' was all he said.

The tip of Beaver Neck was now well astern and the *Judea* was charging down on Castle Hill. Biddlecomb drew a deep breath of the cold December air and grabbed hold of the mizzen topmast backstay. The rigging was hard as an iron bar, and Biddlecomb could feel it quiver under his hand, eight thousand square feet of canvas driving three hundred tons of ship and cargo. It was exhilarating and it made him deeply happy.

The ship raced through the short chop of Narragansett Bay, driven by the fresh southwesterly gale. The sails were full and hard; in the moonlight they looked as if they were carved out of marble. Considering how foul the *Judea*'s bottom was from the two months she had just spent in the Caribbean, Biddlecomb knew that no amount of additional canvas would make her go faster than she was at that moment.

He looked past the starboard leech of the mainsail. Castle Hill was bearing three points forward of the starboard beam and a quarter mile off.

'Bear up, Rigney!' Biddlecomb ordered. 'Right up to the breakers, head right for the breakers. I want to be in the shadow of the land. We don't need any prying eyes tonight.'

'Aye, sir,' said Rigney, grim faced, as he eased the wheel to starboard, turning until the *Judea* was sailing straight at the murderous rocks.

Biddlecomb kept his eyes fixed on Castle Hill. The rocks, black patches in the night highlighted by the white breakers beneath, appeared just at the edge of the foresail.

15

'Good. Steady as she goes. Hold her there.'

The *Judea* rushed down toward the rocks, one hundred yards, fifty yards. Biddlecomb gripped the backstay until his hand ached. He felt his stomach tighten, felt the soles of his feet tingling, like a limb that one has slept on wrong, his well-recognized signs of fear and exhilaration.

In contrast to his churning innards and his tingling soles, his face was stoical, his expression one of a man only vaguely interested in his surroundings. It was a trick he had learned from the better captains under whom he had served. As a young seaman he had thought them utterly fearless; as a mate he had discovered that they were simply good at hiding their anxiety. That was important.

The *Judea* charged down on the rocks, like something out of control. Biddlecomb recalled the chart in his mind's eye; he knew every ledge, every sounding, by heart, and he knew that there was deep water there. But looking at a chart was one thing, driving the ship he loved down on the rocks at night was quite another.

And suddenly the ledge was abeam, the breakers so close that the spray dashed Biddlecomb in the face where he stood on the quarterdeck. He heard Rigney suck in his breath. They hurtled past, the closest outcropping not fifteen feet away. And then the rocks were gone, and the East Passage of Narragansett Bay opened up before them.

'Good,' said Biddlecomb. 'Steady as she goes.'

It was worth the trouble to make certain that no one witnessed their landfall. Biddlecomb knew he was being cautious, perhaps overly cautious, sneaking into the bay at night and keeping in the shadow of

16

the land, but it was the cautious ones who grew old and rich, and he intended to do both. The chances of encountering a British revenue vessel were slight; in the two and a half years since the revenue schooner *Gaspee* had been run aground and burned by angry Rhode Islanders, the British had never seriously attempted to collect the import duties that they had imposed.

Still, Biddlecomb felt compelled to defend against the slightest possibility of the *Judea*'s being boarded and searched, as every corner of his ship was crammed with molasses smuggled from Barbados and destined for the distilleries of New England. As one-fifth owner of the *Judea* he would have made a handsome profit even if he had paid the duty. By ignoring the British tax his profit would far exceed *handsome*.

In the lee of Castle Hill the wind fell off and the *Judea* came down on a more even keel. Biddlecomb pulled his hat from the binnacle box and pushed it back into shape, then jammed it down on his head. He walked forward along the quarterdeck and stepped down into the waist of the ship. The watch on deck was standing by the leeward rail, talking softly, the men busy at various tasks. Biddlecomb's eyes moved automatically around the deck, noting everything. He was pleased with what he saw; *Judea* was a good ship with a good company. And that was what he had come to expect. In five years as a ship's captain Biddlecomb had acquired such a reputation as a savvy businessman, a fair captain, and a hard-driving sailor that more often than not he had to turn good men away.

'Where's the watch on deck?' he called out in the dark.

17

'Here, sir,' a voice called out.

'Take another pull in the weather mainsheet. The sail looks like a fishmonger's clothesline.'

'Aye, sir,' the seaman replied, but Biddlecomb was already past the foremast.

In the bow, with the courses no longer obstructing his view, Biddlecomb could just discern Bull Point and Point Adams in the moonlight. It was all so familiar to him, like the rooms of a house in which one has grown up.

Once past Point Adams the *Judea* skirted the entrance to Brenton Cove and Newport, hugging Goat Island and making careful use of the deep water that ran right up to the rocks. Biddlecomb conned the small ship through the shoals that littered the passage between Rose Island and the mainland. They continued northerly as their course wound its way through Narragansett Bay, quickly closing the distance to Bristol and safety.

Mr Sanders, the first mate, stepped aft.

'Happy New Year to you, sir,' said Sanders, and in response to Biddlecomb's confused look added, 'It's past eight bells, ain't it?'

'Yes, of course!' In their effort to remain unnoticed they had not been striking bells, and with all hands employed for the last few hours of the voyage and no change of watch, Biddlecomb had entirely over-looked the passing of midnight. 'Welcome to 1775, Mr Sanders. We will toast it proper when we're safely in Bristol.'

'I look forward to it, and I'll wish that 1775 is as kind to us as 1774 was.'

The mate turned and looked at the shoreline gliding past. 'We've knocked out what shoring that

18

we can, and once we're abeam Prudence Island, I'll break open hatches,' he said.

'Very good. We'll warp alongside tonight, and if we can get the help 'longshore, we'll start off-loading molasses. If we have someone aboard sober enough to be trusted, we'll send them to roust out some hands.'

Sanders cleared his throat. 'Sir, can I ask what kind of profit we'll realize this trip?'

'Fairly handsome, I should think. I bought the molasses from Glacous at eighteen sous per gallon.'

'Eighteen sous per gallon? From that thief? Sweet Jesus, sir, but how'd you manage that?' asked Sanders with undisguised incredulity.

'By convincing him I could buy molasses elsewhere for nineteen sous per gallon, rather than the twenty-five he was holding out for. Didn't you wonder why we spent that second day loading barrels of seawater?'

'Bless you, sir, I long since give up trying to figure what you're up to.'

'That might be best. Anyway, Glacous saw us loading barrels and he fairly panicked. I knew he hadn't any other buyers, so he sold to me at eighteen.'

'Eighteen sous per gallon! Sweet Jesus . . .'

The two men stood in silence watching the shore slip past and the water streaming down the hull. In the moonlight Biddlecomb could just see the buoy that marked Halfway Rock, lurking just below the surface. Sanders followed Biddlecomb's gaze.

'You were aboard the *Nightingale*, weren't you, when she went up on the rock?' Sanders asked.

'I was. I was third mate then. I was down in the hold breaking out shoring when she hit.' Biddlecomb

19

looked out in the direction of the submerged rock and thought back to that night, the men in the black hold knocked about by the rush of water, the sea rising above his chest as he drove the last frightened man up the ladder. It was one of the most terrifying experiences of his life. 'Stove in the whole starboard bow. The old man was drunk.'

Prudence Island was now visible on the larboard beam, a mile distant. 'I'll start breaking open the hatches,' said Sanders.

'Very good,' said Biddlecomb, and the mate started forward.

Biddlecomb stared out toward Prudence Island and thought about how he would spend the profits from this voyage. He would buy a house, to be certain, and buy a greater share of the *Judea*. At this rate it would be less than five years before he would be complete owner of his beloved ship, the finest vessel he had ever sailed. She would be the foundation of the fleet of merchant ships he intended to build.

From there his thoughts turned to Virginia Stanton. She was the daughter of William Stanton, the man who owned the major share of the *Judea* and the man who had practically raised Biddlecomb after his parents were gone. Biddlecomb had been shipping out on Stanton's ships since he was a boy, and between voyages he had stayed at Stanton House, where William had educated him, introduced him to the classics, to poetry and Shakespeare, had taught him navigation and taught him how to fence.

It was just in the past year that Biddlecomb had noticed that Virginia, William's scrawny, annoying daughter, was scrawny and annoying no more. She

20

was seventeen now, lovely and exciting, and Biddlecomb found his thoughts turning to her more and more. He wanted to court her, though his much vaunted nerve and eloquence often failed him in her company. That in itself was annoying; he had always had great success with women in the various seaports all over the Atlantic, but something about Virginia put him off his guard.

He couldn't imagine how William would react, but he was resolved this time to find out. He had made the same resolve before, he reminded himself.

Footsteps on the quarterdeck shook him from his dreams. He looked up, expecting to see Sanders coming aft to report some problem, but it was only the lookout.

'What is it?'

'I don't know, sir. Might be a ship. A big one. It's hard to see.'

'Show me,' said Biddlecomb, leading the seaman to the bow.

The lookout pointed into the gloom toward a spot just beyond Popasquash Neck. Biddlecomb saw it immediately, a dark shape moving against the darker background. It was a ship under two topsails moving slowly down the bay, close-hauled. On this heading it would pass well astern of the *Judea*. Biddlecomb looked forward past the *Judea*'s bowsprit. Popasquash Point was a mile away. They would close with it in less than ten minutes, and ten minutes after that they would drop the anchor in Bristol Harbor. He looked back at the strange ship. Who could it be?

'Well spotted. Keep an eye on her, let me know if she alters course.' Biddlecomb hurried back to the quarterdeck.

21

Who would be sailing at this time of night? Biddlecomb had good reason, but this strange ship was on a heading bound for sea, so she could not be a smuggler. Could it be a British revenue vessel? A vessel sent to stop smuggling? That was most unlikely. There had not been a revenue vessel on Narragansett Bay in years. Besides, Biddlecomb had never seen a revenue vessel larger than a brig, and this was a ship, and a big one at that.

And then the answer came with a flash of light and the roar of a single gun erupting from the ship's side. The muzzle flash, blinding in the night, revealed a single row of gunports, each one open, each gun run out.

'God damn me to hell!' shouted Biddlecomb, his practiced composure quite gone under the novel threat of gunfire. 'Clew up the courses! Clew them up!' he ordered, and he heard the men running for the gear.

The sails rose like curtains and now Biddlecomb was able to see in every direction. They were running down on Popasquash Point, would leave it just to larboard if they ran into Bristol Harbor. But there they would be trapped.

'Heave to! Heave to or we will fire into you!' a voice called across the water, metallic sounding through a speaking trumpet. Biddlecomb considered his options. Heaving to was out of the question. If they were boarded, they would be arrested for smuggling and found guilty. He would rot in prison and his men would be pressed into the British Navy, a miserable fate in either case.

The stranger fired again, the same gun, forward-most on their larboard side. The *Judea*'s fore

22

topgallant stay parted, and the jib, robbed of its support, collapsed and blew forward in the quartering wind. Biddlecomb heard a sharp crack aloft and knew that the fore topgallant mast had snapped. Looking up, he could just see the tangle of wreckage high above the deck.

Several of the Judeas flung themselves into the fore rigging, racing aloft to secure the damage.

'Avast there! Belay that!' Biddlecomb shouted. It was senseless to try to save the topgallant gear at that point, and he did not want anyone aloft.

Once again the voice came from across the water, demanding that the *Judea* heave to. Biddlecomb considered the *Judea*'s guns and dismissed the thought. She carried six absurd little four-pounders. Even if they could have done this enemy any harm, there wasn't the time to clear away the gear that was piled on top of them and to locate where their attendant rammers and sponges had been stowed.

Biddlecomb looked at the strange ship, and at Popasquash Point, both of which were now considerably nearer. He could tack right now, spin on his heel, and race back to sea. But this stranger with his fast gun crews would cut them to ribbons before they were settled on the new tack. He would not subject his men to that danger.

If they ran into Bristol Harbor, they could sneak around Hog Island and then head for the sea. No they couldn't. Not in this wind. He would be stuck in the harbor, windbound, and the man-of-war would follow him right in. The man-of-war will follow us in regardless, he thought. His stomach clenched like a fist. They were trapped.

He saw the men standing nervously in the waist,

23

waiting for orders, waiting for their captain to think of something.

'Lay aft!' he shouted. 'Everyone lay aft here!' In that instant he had come to a decision and he felt the tension abate. The men hurried aft, stumbling up the steps onto the quarterdeck and hurrying to the stern, eager for salvation.

Biddlecomb grabbed a fistful of Rigney's coat and yanked him from the wheel, grabbing the king spoke as he did. 'I'll take this, Rigney.'

Suddenly the night was illuminated by the man-of-war's broadside, twelve guns firing as one. The roar and shock made the *Judea* shudder. The longboat was cut in half and a section of the larboard bulwark disappeared.

'What are we—' someone began to ask, and was cut short.

'Silence!' shouted Biddlecomb, and the men fell quiet, the sound of the water and wind lost to their ringing ears.

Biddlecomb glanced aft at the man-of-war, tensing as he waited for the next broadside. He could smell the thick forest smell from the land mixed with the odor of expended gunpowder.

'Everyone, grab hold of something!' he ordered. 'Clap on to that taffrail there.'

The men obeyed, grabbing anything solid within reach. Biddlecomb could hear the squeal of the man-of-war's guns running out, a short pistol shot astern. He turned the wheel, three spokes to larboard. The rocky outcropping that made up the tip of Popasquash Point lay under their bow. It did not matter if the man-of-war fired now.

The *Judea* plowed into the rocks off Popasquash

24

Point at a little over eight knots. The stem collapsed on impact, and the planks ten feet aft of the bow sprung or were crushed, allowing the water of Narragansett Bay to flood unimpeded into the hold. The crew were flung to the deck and lay there, hands held over their heads in a useless attempt to shield themselves from falling debris.

The foremast broke off at the partners and tumbled over the bow, dragging the main topgallant and the topmast down with it. The main shrouds, twelve in all, seven-and-three-quarter-inch hemp, parted like spunyarn. The mainmast shattered eight feet above the deck and followed the foremast over the bow. The main top, weighing three tons, stove in a ten-foot section of the deck. The mizzen topmast snapped off at the doubling and crashed down through the main hatch.

For nearly a minute they lay on the quarterdeck as five tons of spars, rigging, sails, and blocks collapsed into so much garbage. Then it was quiet again. Biddlecomb scrambled to his feet and looked along the deck. The destruction was complete, absolutely complete. Already he could feel the ship settling lower in the water. But his men were stirring around him, and none of the wreckage had landed on the quarterdeck.

'Come on! Get up! Get up! Follow me!' Biddlecomb shouted, racing toward the bow. He tripped and fell over what had once been the mizzen topsail yard, then picked himself up and continued forward, his crew following close behind. They climbed over the fallen mainmast, kicking aside the tangled running gear, and rushed to the bow.

The *Judea*'s deck was steeply slanted, and

25

Biddlecomb guessed that she was not afloat at all, simply resting on the rocky ledge. If that was the case, she could slip off at any moment. The base of the foremast lay ten feet inboard of the bow forming a bridge between the wrecked ship and the shore. Biddlecomb looked down at the sea and the rocks twenty feet below, and then along the smooth, round mast. The fresh oil on the wood shone in the moonlight, and Biddlecomb cursed himself for having had the men oil it not two days before. This type of balancing act was not at all to Biddlecomb's liking, and it was worse that he was expected to lead his far more nimble men across this makeshift bridge.

He mounted the horizontal mast and carefully stood, his arms stretched out at his side, and stepped out along its length, first over the deck, then over the beakhead, and at last over the rocks below. His pace quickened and he was practically running along the mast when he began to lose his balance. His arms flailed in the air as he tried to take the last two steps, and failing that, he lunged out and twisted his arms through the futtock shrouds still clinging to the shattered foretop. He hung there for a moment, breathing hard and fast.

'Beg pardon, sir,' came a voice from behind, and Biddlecomb realized that the rest of the men were waiting, balanced on the spar, for him to continue. He pulled himself up and over the foretop, so familiar but for its odd angle, and stepped onto the doubling. From there it was a drop of five feet to the ground.

Biddlecomb turned and looked at the shattered vessel as one by one the men leapt from the doubling and formed up behind him. With a groan the *Judea*, his beloved *Judea*, and all that he had in the world,

26

settled lower in the water and then stopped, hung up on the ledge. Biddlecomb was overwhelmed with sadness, with loss and confusion. It was absurd, he knew, the *Judea* was just a ship, but he had not felt this way since he had watched them lower his mother's coffin into the frozen ground, sixteen years before.

Beyond the wreck of the ship, just visible in the moonlight, Biddlecomb could see the man-of-war was hove to and lowering a boat. In a few minutes they would be swarming over the wreck, the bastards, going through the personal papers left in his cabin, examining his contraband cargo. His name was on every manifest, every bill of lading. There would be no doubt about who had been master of that vessel.

After a moment of silence Sanders touched his arm. 'We best go, Isaac,' he said. Biddlecomb took a last look, then turned and followed his men into the night.

27

CHAPTER 2

Stanton House

The sitting room was all warmth and order, cast in the orange light that radiated from the oak logs in the fireplace and the first glow of dawn streaming through the huge bay windows. The light fell on the western wall, with its shelves of books, interrupted here and there by curios from South America and Asia and Africa. The walnut paneling fairly glowed, and the flickering light from the fireplace danced on the high ceiling and illuminated the intricate pattern of the Persian rug that lay across the polished oak floor. Everything about the room was shipshape, save for the muddy footprints that led to the overstuffed reading chair in which Isaac Biddlecomb was sprawled.

On the sideboard stood a model of the *Virginia Stanton*, a merchantman of five hundred tons, now under construction and destined to be the pride of the Stanton fleet. The father of the ship's namesake, Mr William Stanton, former ship's captain and now at sixty the owner of Bristol's largest merchant fleet, stood at the bay windows as the rays of the new sun washed over him, the light accentuating the lines carved in his face by years of standing a quarterdeck

28

from the North Atlantic to south of the Line. His hair, tied back in a queue, looked as white as if it were powdered.

'She is the frigate *Rose*, His Majesty's frigate *Rose*.' These were the first words that Stanton had spoken since Biddlecomb began fifteen minutes before his account of the destruction of the *Judea*. 'She mounts twenty-four guns, nine-pounders. But I imagine that I do not have to tell you about her firepower.'

'No, faith. I already know more than I care to.'

'I was afraid that this would happen, you know. The *Rose* arrived here in November, just a few days after you sailed, as luck would have it. I sent word to you by every means that I could. Obviously you didn't receive my warnings.'

'I did not.'

The two men were quiet, each lost in his contemplations. 'God, I'm sorry, William!' Biddlecomb said at last. 'Eighteen sous per gallon I paid for that molasses! We would have made our fortune off that cargo!'

'Your fortune, Isaac. My fortune was made some years ago, and you played no small part in making it. Hell, I built the new stables and tack room with the profit from your last voyage.'

'And the ship . . .' Biddlecomb's eyes wandered around the familiar room, toward the north wall, which he had been avoiding. He had to look, like a man unable to resist running his tongue over a sore tooth. He stared at the painting that hung there: the *Judea* as seen from three angles. Biddlecomb marveled again at how perfectly the artist had captured the spirit of his ship. His former ship.

'It's a shame about the cargo, and certainly about

29

the ship. Such are the fortunes of war,' said Stanton.

'War? What war?'

'The war for American independency,' Stanton said simply.

'No war has been declared. Has it?'

'It's only a matter of time now, and not much time, either. It's incidents like the *Judea* that bring the conflict closer.'

'Oh, come, William, let's not make a political issue of this.' Biddlecomb paused, gathering his thoughts, thinking through his anger. 'No one is more bitter about the loss of the *Judea* than me, but I can still be reasonable about it. I *was* breaking the law. I was . . . well, smuggling. Let's call it what it is.'

'Yes, you were smuggling. You were violating the law, English law, there's no question. The question concerns England's right to make such a law, to impose their taxes.'

'We've grown to be a rich colony under English law.'

'We've grown to be a rich colony despite English law. We've grown to be rich by flaunting English law. By smuggling.'

'Exactly. If the British didn't make molasses a scarce and expensive commodity, we wouldn't make so much money. More's the reason to preserve the status quo.' Biddlecomb was not in the mood for this discussion.

The two men were quiet for a moment, then Stanton spoke. 'Since you made captain, you've spent – what? – ten months total ashore in five years? There's been fighting already, you know. That revenue schooner the *St John* was fired upon, and then the *Maidstone*'s tender was burned, and then

30

the *Liberty* was burned. And of course you recall the *Gaspee* affair, do you not? That was just two years ago.'

'Of course.' There was no one in Rhode Island who did not recall the *Gaspee* affair. The *Gaspee* was a British revenue vessel whose captain, to the universal anger and resentment of the colony, had actually tried to collect the duties that were owed. She had been tricked into running aground on Namquid Point on a falling tide, and that night men from Providence and Bristol had rowed out to the stranded vessel and burned it to the waterline. Biddlecomb had often wondered at the extent of Stanton's involvement in that affair.

'The British are no longer willing to ignore these incidents,' Stanton continued. 'That's why the *Rose* and her captain, that damned James Wallace, are here. She was sent to stop all smuggling, and so far she has been bloody effective. Nearly choked Newport to death. Commerce there's practically come to a halt. The British are taking this very seriously, and so are the Americans. There'll be war soon, mark me.'

'Bah! War! We'd do well to stay out of any war we could never hope to win. Besides, Britain has the finest, freest government on earth. There are a lot of men in Rhode Island who've become rich under British rule. And I'd rather we didn't cripple the country just now, just when I'm starting to make some headway in my fortunes.'

'*Were* starting to make some headway. Need I remind you that the British just deprived you of every cent you had?'

Stanton was right, of course. The British had taken

31

everything he had. Why didn't he blame them? He was Biddlecomb the forgiving one, Biddlecomb the reasonable one, always able to see the rational argument underlying any situation. He felt himself growing angry, angry at himself.

The sitting-room door burst open and both men started as Virginia Stanton rushed in, still clad in her nightgown, her bare ankles protruding beneath, her long brown hair tousled, her breasts sharply defined under the garment.

'Captain Biddlecomb! I just heard! Are you all right?' she said, the words tumbling over themselves.

Biddlecomb stood and moved his gaze up to her face, the flash of her white teeth, her dark eyes, and the playful freckles that dotted her ruddy cheeks, and his dark thoughts were swept away. He loved to look at her face. He remembered that she had asked him a question. 'I'm, ah, fine. I'm fine. Virginia, thank you. How could you have heard . . . ?'

'Good God, Virginia!' Stanton interrupted. 'Go and dress yourself, child!'

'In a moment, Father. You are uninjured, Captain?' Virginia asked, her voice more controlled.

'I'm fine, as I said, and quite touched by your concern.'

'Don't be, sir. I am concerned with all Americans, especially when they are so ill-used by the British,' she said, flashing a quick smile that belied her disinterest.

'She follows in your wake, William,' Biddlecomb observed.

'I could wish that she would learn a bit of modesty from me,' said Stanton, sounding scandalized.

32

'Virginia, return to your bed or dress yourself at once!'

'Humph!' said Virginia, tossing her hair back over her shoulder in a way that Biddlecomb found profoundly enticing. 'Very well. I wished only to inquire after Captain Biddlecomb's health, after the rumors that I've heard.' She stepped from the room and Biddlecomb followed her with his eyes. She loved to pretend that she had no interest in him, he knew that. He was equally certain, save for those few dark moments of self-doubt, that it was an act. Now Stanton was talking to him, and he forced himself to listen.

'There is not a day goes by,' said Stanton after Virginia had taken her leave, 'that I do not grieve her mother's passing, but never so much as when I see that I am not able to educate her in the way a young woman should be educated. You know, Isaac, Virginia is not a little girl anymore, skylarking in the stables.'

'No indeed,' replied Biddlecomb, his eyes still fixed on the door through which Virginia had departed.

'I know what you're thinking, Isaac,' Stanton said, interrupting Biddlecomb's thoughts. Biddlecomb looked at Stanton. He felt his face flush. 'You're wondering if there's another command for you.' Stanton's eyes moved to the model that stood on the sideboard. 'You're the best captain in my fleet, Isaac, perhaps the best in Rhode Island.' Stanton paused. 'Eighteen sous per gallon! You're gifted, Isaac. I've never known a man who could talk his way through anything like you can. You've been the best in my fleet for sixteen years now.'

33

'That may be going it a bit high, William. For at least the first two of those years I was a cabin boy. Though a damn fine cabin boy.'

'Sixteen years from cabin boy to master. I intend to give you the *Virginia Stanton* when she's complete, but that won't be for ten months or more. I had hoped to keep you occupied with the *Judea* until she was launched, but now I don't know . . .'

'There's no ship for me now?'

'There is not. Things are very bad right now, with the British stepping down hard on our trade. There are dozens of captains on the beach.'

The silence was awkward. Biddlecomb began to speak, but Stanton cut him off. 'If it's money that you need, please, don't think on it.' Biddlecomb opened his mouth to protest but Stanton continued, 'Call it a loan, or an advance on wages, however you wish to arrange it. And of course you'll always have a home here.'

'Thank you, William. We'll add this on to the enormous debt that I already owe you.'

'Nonsense. But another thought occurs to me. It may not be safe for you to remain in Bristol. The British may come looking for you. You said the *Judea* hung up on the ledge; I have no doubt Wallace found your papers in the cabin.'

'Honestly, William, you're blowing this war thing all out of proportion. Surely the British have better things to do than—' Biddlecomb's words were cut short by a pounding, loud and insistent, at the front door.

Biddlecomb met Stanton's eyes, and the two men were silent for the forty-five seconds that the pounding continued. 'Perhaps now you'll see for yourself

34

how seriously the British are taking things,' Stanton said softly, then opened the door of the sitting room and stepped into the adjoining foyer. Rogers, the Stantons' butler, entered the foyer from the other direction.

'Rogers,' said Stanton in a low voice. Rogers was close to six feet in height, a somber man who reminded Biddlecomb more of a driver of a hearse than a manservant, but he was devoted to Stanton and had served him for years. He bent his lean body forward to hear better. 'Captain Biddlecomb and I are not at home for any stranger. Also, the household has not been informed of the incident involving the *Judea*.'

Rogers nodded, but his expression did not alter, as if he had not heard. 'Very good, sir,' he said, reaching out for the handle of the front door. He held it and waited while Stanton withdrew to the sitting room and shut the door.

In the sitting room Biddlecomb and Stanton listened as Rogers pulled the front door open.

'Rogers!' they heard an excited voice exclaim, accompanied by the sound of the front door swinging open and boots on the hardwood floor. 'Is Captain Stanton up yet? Have you heard? Surely you've heard?' the words spilled from the unseen messenger.

'I'm afraid that I don't know to what you refer, Mr Oray,' replied Rogers in a neutral tone.

'Why, it's the *Rose!* The damned *Rose*, sailing right into Bristol Harbor! And Captain Martin says they'll be landing the marines, and they'll tear the town apart until they finds Captain Biddlecomb!'

35

CHAPTER 3

Bristol

'It's Gideon Oray. He's a friend,' said Stanton as he swung the door open. He and Biddlecomb stepped into the foyer. 'Gideon, what brings you to our door at such an hour?' Stanton asked, extending a hand to the visitor. Oray took the proffered hand and shook it vigorously.

'Oh, Captain Stanton, odds my life, you can't imagine what's happened. Last night, or I should say rather this morning . . .' the farmer began, and as he spoke, his eyes wandered over Stanton's shoulder. 'But . . . why, there's Captain Biddlecomb now!' he exclaimed, and turned and looked at Stanton again. 'Well, damn me, sure he'd come here after . . . after what happened. So you know about the *Judea*?'

'Alas, I do, Gideon. The British are pleased to continue ill-using us.'

'Indeed, sir, I warrant they are. Them British bastards . . .' His voice trailed off, but then he looked up again, startled, as another thought occurred to him. 'Oh, and Captain Martin, he's turned out the militia. He sent me to tell you.'

'Indeed?' said Stanton. 'And why is that?'

36

'To what militia do you refer?' asked Biddlecomb, but the three men ignored him.

'First light the *Rose* was seen just south of Hog Island, standing into Bristol Harbor,' Oray explained. 'Captain Martin charged me to tell you he believes they intend to land their marines.'

'There, you see, Isaac?' Stanton turned to Biddlecomb. 'Here's further British aggression, like we've been seeing all along.'

'Now wait a minute, William,' Biddlecomb protested. 'We don't know that they're intending to land their marines. For all we know they're wooding and watering.'

'Do you believe that?' asked Stanton.

'No,' said Biddlecomb.

'Please, Captain Stanton,' Oray interrupted, 'won't you come down to the harbor with the militia? Your company needs you. Captain Martin sent me to fetch you!'

'Yes, yes, of course I'll come. Run along and tell Martin I shall be there in half an hour.'

'Half an hour, yes, sir!' said Oray, smiling in his relief. 'I'll tell him!' He gave a perfunctory salute and raced out the door, leaving Rogers to close it behind him.

'Your company?' asked Biddlecomb, but he received no reply.

'Rogers' – Stanton turned to the manservant – 'have the boy saddle the mounts, my horse, and we'll take Tempest and Pallada as well. You'll prepare the saddlebags?'

'Of course, sir.' Rogers turned and disappeared down the hall.

Stanton turned to Biddlecomb. 'Isaac, I think it

would be a good idea if you remained here.'

'If they're coming for me, which I still insist they're not, then I certainly don't care to cower here while others fight for me.'

'You could be in great danger. This Wallace, the *Rose*'s captain, is a very determined fellow. I'd rather you remained behind.'

'Then pray why did you tell Rogers to prepare three horses? But really, I've seen the Royal Navy operate in every port in America, and I know that they're not in the habit of landing marines and making war on Americans. You'll see. There's nothing in this.'

'Very well,' Stanton said at last. 'I'll go and shift my clothes,' and with that he turned and ascended the wide stairs that led to the second floor.

Biddlecomb returned to the sitting room, anxious to study the model of the *Virginia Stanton* that stood on the sideboard. She was a beautiful ship, certainly equal to her name, though he might recommend another fathom be added to the lower masts and the topsail yards be lengthened a bit. The mizzenmast could be stepped a bit further aft as well.

He got down on his knees beside the model and sighted down her keel, trying to assess the qualities of her underwater shape. So engrossed was he by the curve of the hull that he was not aware that the ship's namesake was standing in the door, and he was startled when she spoke.

'She's a fine ship, Isaac, to be sure, but I hardly think you should worship her.'

Biddlecomb looked up. Virginia was wearing a simple muslin dress, which she had apparently put on

38

in a great hurry. Her hair was even more mussed than before.

'I was just studying the shape of her bottom,' he said, wearing his deadpan quarterdeck expression as he regained his feet.

'Indeed?' Virginia smiled and then her expression turned serious. 'Honestly, though, I'm happy to hear you're uninjured. It's criminal how you've been treated.'

'How in the devil did you hear about the *Judea* so fast?'

Virginia smiled again. 'The men here are kept well-informed, with father as captain of the militia, and I see to it that Rogers keeps me informed as well.'

'And that's another matter.' The past twelve hours had been among the strangest in Biddlecomb's life. 'What's this militia that everyone's talking about?'

'They're local men, farmers and shopkeepers mostly, that have been training for war. There's a militia in Providence and Newport, and trains of artillery as well. All over New England, I understand.'

Biddlecomb was intrigued. He had no knowledge of any of this, so much of the past five years he had been at sea, and he wanted to question her further. But their conversation was interrupted by Stanton's coming back down the stairs, his arrival heralded by the thumping of his boots, loud on the hardwood stairs. He was not dressed in the clothes that he normally wore since quitting the sea, the elegant silks and linens and fine-tailored clothes that befitted a wealthy merchant. Rather, he wore wool stockings and a rough, homespun coat over leather breeches and a plain wool shirt. On his head was a battered

39

cocked hat. In each hand he carried a musket, and over each shoulder was slung a cartridge box.

'I've never seen you looking so rustic, William,' Biddlecomb said.

'The business that we'll be conducting is unlike my usual run-of-the-mill, and I'm afraid we're not yet so organized as to have uniforms, unlike some of our brothers in arms.' Stanton handed one of the muskets to Biddlecomb. 'Come, let's go to the stables. Good-bye, my dear,' he said, offering a cheek to Virginia.

'Good-bye, Father.' She kissed the proffered cheek. 'Please be careful. And you, Captain,' she said, smiling at Biddlecomb.

'Thank you, Virginia. Good-bye.'

The two men made their way through the back of the house, through the dining room, and onto the covered walk that led to the kitchen. Leaving the walkway, they headed across the lawn and toward the stables, their boots crunching on the brown, frozen grass.

The morning was cold and the men's breath preceded them in gray puffs. The bare trees and dead grass and high, brown reeds along the water gave a gloomy cast to the scene, despite the red glow of the sun in the clear winter sky. The commanding house, white clapboard, the picket fence, and the stables were amber in the light. Rogers emerged from the stable leading a saddled horse, and behind him the stableboy led two others.

Stanton slung his musket over his shoulder and took the reins from Rogers. He rubbed the horse's neck and then with practiced ease flung himself into the saddle.

40

Biddlecomb knew little about horses and cared even less. The two beasts being led by the stableboy seemed of very different temperaments. The chestnut brown horse flung its head from side to side, whipping its great black mane across its shoulders. Its breath shot from flaring nostrils in gray clouds. The other horse stood docile, following the stableboy's lead with not even a tug on the reins. Biddlecomb did not know if he was supposed to choose. His choice would have been to walk the mile to Bristol.

Rogers stepped up to the docile creature and took the reins from the stableboy, to Biddlecomb's chagrin, though he imagined that the feisty horse would have been preferred by any experienced horseman. He stepped over the chestnut horse, reaching a tentative hand for the reins.

'No, no, Rogers,' said Stanton. 'We'll give old Pallada to Captain Biddlecomb. You may ride Tempest.' There was mirth in Stanton's voice, but Biddlecomb was too relieved to care about any slight.

It was an easy ride to Bristol, and Pallada was as well behaved as one could wish a horse to be, but remaining seated and keeping pace with Stanton and Rogers called for all of Biddlecomb's concentration. Once during the ride Stanton turned to Rogers to explain Biddlecomb's discomfiture. 'You must realize, Rogers,' he said overly loud, 'that Captain Biddlecomb can maneuver a five-hundred-ton ship like it was a toy, but a half a ton of horse quite taxes him.'

'Indeed, sir,' said Rogers, and the two men turned back to grin at Biddlecomb.

They slowed the horses to a walk, much to Biddlecomb's relief, as they approached the outskirts

41

of the town of Bristol. Here the hard-packed dirt road grew wider, and the houses grew more numerous, here and there interrupted by a blacksmith's shop or a cooperage. Biddlecomb had not been back to his hometown for two months, but it appeared to him that nothing had changed. Nothing ever seemed to change. Except perhaps that the streets were deserted. Even at that early hour the citizens of Bristol were usually up and about.

They rode on, and the houses and buildings grew thicker and the dirt road became Hope Street, and above them the brown, square tower on St Michael's rose above the spindly trees. As Biddlecomb looked around, shifting uncomfortably in his saddle, he became aware of another sound that had joined the thumping of their horses' hooves. He listened and soon realized that the sound came from a crowd of men, and with it a squeaking and groaning, like an overloaded wagon.

They rode on toward the center of town, toward the intersection of Hope Street and Union.

And suddenly, stepping into the intersection from Union Street, the militia appeared. There were about thirty in all, dressed more or less the same in their rough breeches, coats, and cocked hats. Each carried a musket as well, not elegant hunting pieces like those carried by Biddlecomb and Stanton and Rogers, but the crude, dependable muskets found in every farmhouse in America.

Biddlecomb watched the men march forward in a ragged semblance of a file, and behind them came a horse, an enormous draft animal straining at its harness. It pressed on, pulling behind it a caisson and limber mounting a six-pound fieldpiece. On either

42

side of the cannon, and behind it, the gun crew marched as if lovingly protecting their charge.

At the head of this band a gray-haired man walked beside the boy leading the horse. He was dressed much as the others, save for his brown coat, which, with its red facing and cuffs and single gold epaulet on the left shoulder, Biddlecomb took to be some sort of uniform. His hat was unlike any Biddlecomb had seen before. It was made of leather and fit neatly over his head with a small red tuft on the top. A frontpiece was attached, a flat piece of leather shaped like a cresting wave with an anchor painted on it. The man glanced over at the mounted party and his face lit with recognition. 'William!' he said, breaking stride with the others and hurrying over to Stanton's horse. 'Thank heaven you received my word. I'm betting we need you today, no lie.'

'Thank you, Captain Martin. I see the militia and the train of artillery has done itself credit in turning out right away. May I introduce—'

'Captain Biddlecomb! You are Captain Biddlecomb, ain't you?' asked Martin enthusiastically. Biddlecomb saw that above the anchor on Martin's cap were the words *For Our Country*. He could smell the rum on the artillery officer's breath.

'Aye, I'm Biddlecomb. I am certainly sorry about all of this.'

'Damn me!' said Martin. 'You sure taught old John Bull a famous lesson last night! No one tries to stop an American ship! And now we'll finish your good work!' He grinned broadly.

'Aye, I guess I showed him,' agreed Biddlecomb without enthusiasm.

With the grin still planted on his face Martin took

43

his leave of the three men and hurried back to his place with the gun crew. Biddlecomb, Rogers, and Stanton wheeled their horses in behind the shuffling minutemen and followed them through the town.

The armed band marched through the center of Bristol, past the merchants' offices, the bank, and the chandlery and toward the waterfront with its stone quays and warehouses. The sun was well up by now, revealing a brilliant blue sky. The wind was light from the northwest, the usual morning offshore breeze.

A low stone wall ran along the waterfront separating the docks and quays from the heavy traffic of Thames Street. The minutemen clustered around the wall, military discipline quite forgotten as they chattered and pointed out toward the water.

From his vantage point high on the horse Biddlecomb looked over the men's heads and beyond Bristol Harbor. A mile and a half distant, looking like an intricate toy and fairly glowing in the morning light, was the HMS *Rose*, standing toward Popasquash Point. Just at the moment that Biddlecomb thought they might go aground, he saw the frigate's bowsprit begin to swing, her sails begin to flutter, as she came about for the long tack that would take her into Bristol Harbor. She turned smartly, despite the light airs, and hauled her mainsails at the same moment that Biddlecomb, watching the evolution, mouthed to himself the words *mainsail haul*. She hung there, like a crippled bird, then continued to turn, her main and mizzen sails filling and her foreyards bracing around, and she became a thing of perfection once again, gathering momentum as she headed into Bristol Harbor, her jibboom pointing straight at the gawking militia.

44

Biddlecomb was impressed and he doubted that he himself had ever tacked a ship as quickly, though he reminded himself that the *Rose* must have over one hundred and fifty men aboard, while he had never had a crew number above twenty-three. Still it had been well done, and Wallace was displaying some nerve standing into an unfamiliar harbor with courses, topsails, and topgallant sails set. Biddlecomb hoped for a moment that the frigate might run aground on the muddy shallows that extended far out from Hog Island. He looked over at the island, and its position relative to the *Rose*'s course, and realized with disappointment that they would be well clear of the mud. He saw a figure crawl out in the frigate's fore-chains to heave the lead. The fore and main courses flogged and were clewed up, and like magic men appeared on the yards to stow the sails.

'You know, Isaac,' said Stanton, who had watched the evolutions with Biddlecomb's appreciation and expert eye, 'there's some talk, mostly out of Providence, of starting a navy of our own. But I must admit that seeing the *Rose* put through her paces disheartens me a bit.'

'She's well handled,' admitted Biddlecomb, never taking his eyes off the ship. The topgallant sails came down on the run and they too were swiftly furled, and the frigate stood on under fore and main and mizzen topsails, fore topmast staysail, and mizzen. 'I don't see how Rhode Island, or any colony, could build or man anything as powerful. And to the British she's nothing, a sixth rate, the smallest ship in their navy to warrant a captain in command.'

'Do you know the *Katey*?' Stanton asked. 'John Brown's sloop *Katey*?'

45

'Yes, I do. A fine little sloop. He's using her to hunt whale, is he not?'

'He is. There's some talk of buying her and arming her for war.'

At that Biddlecomb took his eyes off the frigate and looked at Stanton. 'What in the world do they think a sloop could accomplish?'

Stanton shifted uncomfortably. 'She could harry shipping. She could take prizes, force the British to use their frigates to convoy merchantmen,' he said in a defensive tone.

Biddlecomb considered the argument. 'She could do that. It would be David and Goliath.'

'Let's hope,' said Stanton, and the two men turned their attention back to the *Rose*.

The frigate was well into the inner harbor by now, not more than a quarter mile distant. She was magnificent in the morning light. Her hull was a deep yellowish brown, a black stripe at the gunwale and another just above the waterline. Her masts were buff up to the tops, and the standing rigging and yards gleamed black. There was about her an ominous and beautiful symmetry.

Biddlecomb's gaze was drawn to the crowd of men on her foredeck, and he imagined that they must be clearing away the anchor. He caught a motion out of the corner of his eye, and turning, he saw Stanton raising a telescope to his eye. He wanted desperately to borrow it.

'Rogers packed the glasses,' Stanton said, never taking his eye from the telescope. 'Bloody man never forgets a thing. If he ever leaves me, I shall be quite lost as I have forgotten how to remember anything. There's a telescope in your saddlebag as well, I fancy.'

46

Biddlecomb twisted in the saddle and dug through the saddlebag, found the telescope, and brought it to his eye. Now he could see every detail of the activity on the frigate's deck. The forecastle men were indeed clearing away the anchor, and as Biddlecomb watched, the best bower swung out and hung from the cathead, ready to be let go. In the fore-chains the leadsman continued to sound the depth. Biddlecomb knew that there was a steady three and a half fathoms there, but of course Wallace did not.

'Captain Martin,' Stanton called out, lowering his glass. 'Perhaps it would be best to prepare the fieldpiece now, while there's time.'

Martin, who had been standing with the gun crew and staring at the frigate, readily agreed and began issuing orders for the deployment of the gun.

'Gun crew!' he shouted with military bearing. 'Lay out your gear! Balls and cartridges!' The gun crew broke from their reverie and swarmed around the caisson and limber like ants on an overturned anthill. Biddlecomb turned his attention back to the *Rose*.

The frigate was far up the harbor now. She must let go, or sure she'll be aground, he thought. He could hear the splash of the lead as it hit the water, could hear the monotonous chant of the leadsman: 'And three and a half, and three and a half . . .'

Biddlecomb watched the magnificent man-of-war glide past, silent but for the man in the fore-chains. Then suddenly, and with no orders that Biddlecomb could hear, the ship's company flew into activity. Her bow swung away from the waterfront, up into the gentle wind, and her fore and main topsails came flying down the masts as the mizzen came aback and checked her headway. She hung motionless for a moment, then gathered sternway and the anchor plunged into the blue water. The topmen were already stationed in the tops, and as the yards settled in their lifts and the topsails were clewed up, Biddlecomb strained to hear the shouted order from the deck that would send the men out along the yards to stow. No order came that Biddlecomb could hear, but nonetheless the topmen raced out along the yards and began to fist the canvas, like a flock of birds taking flight, each somehow knowing without being told when it was time to go.

Capt. James Wallace of His Majesty's frigate *Rose* stood by the taffrail, hands clenched behind his back, and observed the town of Bristol. It was charming, as so many of the small New England towns were, with its evergreens and ruddy brick buildings and smoke wafting from chimneys hidden among the trees. A part of his mind acknowledged this charm, while another part, the more active part, considered the strategic aspects of the town and the *Rose*'s position relative to it.

He felt the ship snub up against the anchor cable and ease to a stop, so gently that it would have been missed by one not so intimate with the ways of his vessel. They had finished stowing topsails, he knew that as well, for he could feel the vibrations of the shrouds in the taffrail as the topmen raced back to the deck, and he could hear the heavy footfalls of Lieutenant Leighton, the first officer, coming aft to report. No orders had been shouted, no conversation of any kind had taken place since the *Rose* had first raised the entrance to Bristol Harbor. That was how evolutions were done aboard a taut ship, and Wallace ran a very taut ship. He turned and faced Leighton just as the lieutenant was opening his mouth for a 'Beg pardon, sir.'

'All sail stowed, sir, and the anchor is holding in four fathom of water,' Leighton reported.

'Very well.' Wallace held Leighton in his stare, watching him fidget as he considered the orders he would give next. Wallace was young for his rank, well shy of thirty, but his taciturn manner and granite expression made him appear much older. His officers were unnerved by his frequent silences, those moments that he gave himself to consider a situation. He knew that, and he did not care. Careful consideration led to good decision making, and that in turn had led to his achieving post rank at his age.

'I want to rig a spring,' Wallace began at last, 'larboard side so that we may bring the starboard battery to bear. There are some fools behind that stone wall near the quay, and I believe they have some sort of fieldpiece. Let's hope for their own sake they are not foolish enough to use it.'

'Indeed, sir. I'll set Norton to work on the spring and—'

'No, not Norton. I have need of him. Set Michaelson to work on the spring. I want you to take command of the starboard battery. I'll send a midshipman with my orders. Now, please pass the word for Norton.' Saying that, Wallace turned his back on the first officer, indicating that the interview was over.

It took Michaelson and the men under him less than fifteen minutes to wrestle the spring line, five tons of unwieldy cordage, out of the cable tier, across the deck, and out an after gunport. From there the

49

bitter end was carried by boat to the anchor cable, where it was seized in place, while at the same time the end still on board the ship was made fast to the capstan. It was an impressive display, but Wallace expected impressive displays, and he ignored the work going on around him, focusing instead on the preparations taking place behind the low stone wall.

Idiots, he thought, but no more idiots than the Admiralty, who refused to deal with this treason in an appropriate manner. His presence on Narragansett Bay was meant to be a show of force, he knew that, but he knew as well that any overt use of force would be frowned upon. If these colonials wish a war, we should damn well give them a war, he thought, not for the first time. But he knew that he would order Leighton to fire at the rooftops. Initially, at least.

He heard the squeal of blocks and the stamping of feet and knew that the longboat was going over the side. He turned and looked down the length of the deck. The boat's crew was waiting in their clean, matching outfits for the boat to settle in the water. Lieutenant Norton stepped aft and gave Wallace a formal salute.

'Here is the letter, Mr Norton,' he said, handing the lieutenant a sealed note. 'It is a formality, nothing more. Keep your eyes open, learn what you can about this Biddlecomb. I want him, but if he is there, don't try to apprehend him in the face of a mob. We shall bring the persuasive powers of the ship and the marines to bear.'

Wallace was being more loquacious than was his custom, but he liked Norton and saw in him the makings of a good officer. 'Carry on,' he said, and

50

Norton saluted again and hurried forward. Wallace turned to a midshipman at the larboard rail. 'Once the longboat is clear, please pass the word to Mr Michaelson to take up on the spring. I want the starboard battery to bear on the town. When it does, you may tell Mr Leighton to load and run out.'

CHAPTER 4

HMS *Rose*

Biddlecomb watched as the officer – a lieutenant, he believed – clambered down the frigate's side and settled in the stern sheets of the longboat. The bowman pushed off with his hook and the two banks of oars came down as one, and the longboat turned and headed for the quay.

The moment the boat left the frigate's side, the steady clack clack clack of the capstan's pawls drifted across the water, and the spring line rose dripping from the harbor and stretched out until it was nearly straight. The frigate seemed to hesitate, hanging between the pressures of the wind and the spring, then it yielded to the increased pull of the hawser, and slowly, silently, the stern swung away from the watching Americans and the long yellow side and the terrible gunports came to bear on the stone wall and the town beyond. Before the ship had come to rest again, twelve gunports opened together and twelve heavy guns were run out.

'Your Wallace is quite the showman,' commented Biddlecomb wryly.

The militia was so transfixed by the sight, so silent and ominous, that they failed to notice the longboat

52

until it ground up against the stone quay and the bowman leapt ashore, the painter in his hand. Then the spell was broken, and with a shout the Americans leapt over the low stone wall and marched in a ragged mob toward the quay.

'Come, Isaac!' said Stanton, dismounting. 'We must see that they don't do anything untoward.' Biddlecomb swung his leg over the saddle and slid to the ground, then hobbled toward the stone wall, his sinews protesting the unnatural shape forced on them by the horse. He hopped over the wall and raced to catch up with Stanton, who was pushing his way through to the front of the militiamen.

Stanton at last managed to halt the rush of the mob. Biddlecomb pushed his way through the crowd to Stanton's side, and together they stared at the British ten yards away. Blue-jacketed, pigtailed seamen held the bow and stern lines of the long-boat. The lieutenant, already ashore, stood facing the militiamen. He was not a big man, but well proportioned, and Biddlecomb guessed that they were about the same age. His expression was all business and he seemed not the least disconcerted by the presence of an armed and angry mob.

He stood on the quay and glanced around, then stepped toward the crowd of Americans. Biddlecomb heard a low murmur, a restless shifting from the militia.

'I am Lieutenant Norton, third officer of His Majesty's frigate *Rose*.'

'God save the king!' yelled a voice from the crowd, and the Americans laughed, a bit louder than was necessary. Norton stood expressionless until the laughter subsided.

'I am carrying a letter from Captain Wallace—'

'Stick it in your arse!' another voice called, and again the Americans roared. Stanton held up his hand and the laughter died away.

'I am carrying a letter from Captain Wallace,' Norton began again, 'to Mr Isaac Biddlecomb, late of the merchant ship *Judea*. I would like to know his whereabouts.'

'You go to hell, you . . .' began a man in the crowd, but Biddlecomb cut him off by stepping forward. He glanced toward the longboat, wondering if the seamen might be readying for a fight. The boat's crew were grinning broadly, evidently enjoying the abuse being hurled at their superior officer.

'I am Captain Biddlecomb.'

Norton looked surprised, just for an instant, and then the stolid expression returned to his face. 'Good day to you, sir. This letter is for you.' He handed the folded and sealed paper to Biddlecomb and bent stiffly at the waist. Biddlecomb took the letter with a nod of his head.

'Read the letter, Isaac!' someone shouted. Biddlecomb tore open the seal and unfolded the paper. The writing was cramped but neat.

His Majesty's ship *Rose*
Rhode Island
January 1, 1775

Sir:

On the morning of January one my frigate did run the merchant vessel *Judea* aground on Popasquash Point, of which ship you were in command.

54

Biddlecomb read aloud. Behind him the militia was quiet.

As an investigation of the wreckage revealed that the cargo consisted of contraband items, you are hereby requested and required to accompany the officer bearing this note aboard His Majesty's frigate *Rose* and account for your actions of the night above.

I am, sir, your most humble and most obedient servant.

Jas. Wallace

Biddlecomb looked up at Lieutenant Norton, but the man's face was still without expression, as if he were still waiting for Biddlecomb to read the letter.

'You cannot possibly go aboard the frigate, Isaac, it would be the last we ever hear of you,' said Stanton, just loud enough to be heard above the howling patriots.

'Of course you're right, William,' Biddlecomb muttered. He felt stunned, as if he had been hit on the head. The *Rose* had come for him. Addressing himself to Lieutenant Norton, he said, 'I'm sorry, sir. Please express my apologies to Captain Wallace, but I feel it would be . . . healthier . . . if I were to forgo his kind offer.'

Norton considered this for a moment. 'Be aware, sir, that Captain Wallace is prepared to take extraordinary measures to see his wishes complied with.'

'And so are we, sir,' interrupted Stanton. 'Do not for one moment doubt that.'

55

Behind them, the militiamen began to raise loud questions concerning the virtue of Norton's mother, though the lieutenant seemed to take no notice.

'I am sorry that this is your decision, sir,' he said at last. 'Captain Wallace will be most put out.'

The frigate's first broadside came even before the longboat had settled back on the booms. The black and yellow hull disappeared in a gray cloud of its own smoke, and the thunder of the great guns was joined with the sound of over one hundred pounds of iron striking the town of Bristol. Three jagged holes appeared in the brick tower of St Michael's three blocks inland from the quay. A chimney on the blacksmith's shop disappeared, and the storefront of Webster & White, ship's chandlers, was reduced to wreckage.

The minutemen, those few who had not leapt for cover behind the stone wall, stood gaping at the frigate. Biddlecomb imagined that none of them, farmers and shopkeepers all, had ever seen a man-of-war firing her broadside, and it was a terrible and frightening sight. Stanton was the first to recover his wits.

'Gun's crew! Load and fire at will! Captain Martin, please see to your gun's crew! Militiamen! To me! Form up!' The minutemen broke into a disorderly run, each man racing to his assigned position. Powder, wadding, and shot were handed along to the loaders and rammers, who forced the charges down the barrel of the ancient gun. To his left Biddlecomb saw the militia form up in reasonable lines, the front row of men on bent knee, the back row erect, each feverishly loading their weapons.

The still air exploded with another broadside,

56

and several men jumped with surprise. Round shot screamed overhead, followed instantly by the crushing and shattering sounds of the fusillade striking the town.

'Front ranks, fire!' Stanton called, and the crouching men fired, but the muskets seemed pathetic and insubstantial after the broadside of the ship. Biddlecomb watched Captain Martin thrust the priming wire down the touchhole and, satisfied that the cartridge was broken, withdraw the wire and pour loose powder down the hole. The *Rose* will get nearly three broadsides to our one shot, thought Biddlecomb, wishing that the gun's crew could move faster and with greater coordination.

'Run up!' shouted Martin, and the gun was pushed by the grunting artillerymen up to the stone wall.

'Back rank, fire!' ordered Stanton.

Martin sighted down the length of the barrel. 'Handspikes here!' he shouted, and the spikemen trained the gun around. Martin twirled the linstock in his hand and the slow match glowed brighter. The gun's crew stepped back and Martin shoved the slow match into the powder in the touchhole. There was a flash and the gun went off with a terrific roar, leaping back eight feet with the recoil. Biddlecomb kept his eyes on the frigate, as did the others. The aftermost deadeye on the main channel exploded into slivers, and the topgallant backstay swung loose.

'We hit her! We hit her!' cried Martin, capering, as the others took up the cheer. The *Rose* fired again, her broadside more ragged as some guns were worked faster than others, but the artillerymen did not seem to notice, and Biddlecomb could not see where the shots had struck.

57

Biddlecomb turned to Stanton. The minutemen were firing continuously, though small arms at that range would be of questionable effect.

At last the gun's crew left off their cheering and turned to reloading. Biddlecomb watched as they swarmed over the gun. 'For God's sake, stop your vent!' he shouted as the enthusiastic swabber began to shove his dripping sponge down the barrel. The force of the sponge would blow any burning embers out of the touchhole, then suck them in again when the sponge was withdrawn, possibly igniting the cartridge while the gun was being loaded. Biddlecomb knew little about artillery, but he knew that much. He had once seen a man's arm blown off at the shoulder that way. Captain Martin placed his thumb over the touchhole and the sponge was rammed down the barrel again.

'Would you like the glass, sir?' asked Rogers, who appeared at Biddlecomb's side, the telescope in his hand.

'Indeed I would, thank you, Rogers.' Biddlecomb took the glass and brought it to his eye. The frigate swam in the lens. On the quarterdeck the captain, Wallace, stood in solitude on the starboard side. On the larboard side stood the other officers, lining the rail. All faces were turned toward Bristol. He moved the telescope down and swept along the side of the ship. The better-served guns were beginning to emerge from the dark gundeck, their muzzles gleaming in the sun as they came like dragons from their caves.

The first of the *Rose*'s guns fired and Biddlecomb turned and looked at the town behind him. With each gun he could see wood and brick fly from various rooftops. The British were firing high, and Biddlecomb hoped that they would continue to do so.

'Run up!' shouted Martin, and again the old fieldpiece was pushed to the wall. Martin squinted over the barrel and, satisfied, stepped back and fired.

The gun leapt back, and this time the crew could see splinters flying from the frigate's bulwark, but the activity of loading and the steady fire from the ship had sobered them and they fell to reloading without so much as a cheer.

Biddlecomb brought the glass to his eye again to inspect the damage to the frigate. There was a piece taken out of the bulwark, though that amounted to an afternoon's work for the ship's carpenter, no more.

He moved the glass to the quarterdeck and saw the captain turn toward the officers behind him. A midshipman scurried across the deck and the captain addressed him, pointing toward the stone wall, seeming, to Biddlecomb, to be pointing right at him. The midshipman nodded and raced forward, disappearing down a scuttle.

Biddlecomb could guess what orders the midshipman was carrying to the gunnery officer below. He moved his glass down to gaze at the empty gunports. Number-three gun was being run out, and number five was following quickly. Biddlecomb waited for the shot, but it did not come, and he imagined that the gun crews were receiving new instructions. The rate of fire would slow, of course, as the gun crews tired, but Biddlecomb suspected that the *Rose* would always maintain an impressive level of gunnery. And they had twenty-four guns to the Americans' one.

He whipped the telescope up to his eye again. Nearly all of the great guns were run out, and it seemed to Biddlecomb as if he were peering straight down each of the gaping muzzles.

'Get down!' he yelled to the surprised patriots. 'Get down, all of you!' Biddlecomb leapt for cover behind the stone wall and the others followed.

Another broadside exploded from the frigate's side, and the air was filled with the deafening sound of grape and round shot passing scant feet above their heads. The stone wall shuddered with the impact of iron, and stone chips, as lethal as grape-shot, flew in all directions.

And then it was quiet again and the Americans leapt to their feet, the artillerymen running the fieldpiece up to the wall and the militiamen continuing their hail of musket balls.

Martin sighted down the barrel of the gun. He jammed the quoin further in, lowering the elevation, and called for the handspike to train the gun around.

The gun's crew leapt clear as Martin brought the slow match down on the touchhole. The gun went off and Biddlecomb saw a section of the quarterdeck rail crumple and noted with satisfaction that Wallace jumped clean off the deck in surprise. He swept the glass over the officers, but no one on the quarterdeck seemed to have been injured, either by the ball or the splinters from the rail.

Then Biddlecomb heard another sound and realized it was a man sobbing in agony. An artillery-man was lying on the ground, hands pressed to his face. Blood was already seeping through his fingers. The others stood looking at the man, unsure what to do.

60

'What happened here?' demanded Biddlecomb.

'I think a stone chip got him,' one of the other men offered.

'Here, you two, help me move him aside,' Biddlecomb ordered, getting hold of the man under his arms. The two others grabbed his legs and they dragged the wounded soldier as gently as they could to one side. The man screamed in renewed agony at the handling.

'Get back to the gun. I'll take care of him,' said Biddlecomb. He knelt by the man's head and slowly began to pry his fingers away from his face. In sixteen years at sea Biddlecomb had seen his share of horrible accidents, and he had learned a great deal about treating them. He pulled one hand back, gently, like taking a dangerous object from a baby's grasp, uttering soothing words as he did. He could see torn skin under the mass of blood, and the gleam of white bone.

And then he stopped, seized by panic. When had the frigate fired last?

He grabbed the telescope and was halfway to his feet when the broadside shattered the morning, grape and round shot sweeping through the standing knot of soldiers and tearing a bloody path. Three feet away, Biddlecomb saw a man lifted off his feet and flung to the cobblestone road, torn to bloody ribbons. The man holding the rammer dropped the tool and grabbed at his face, screaming, blood spurting from between his fingers.

Stanton! Biddlecomb whirled around. The neat lines of militia were now a shambles. Five men lay dead or dying. The others attended them, their muskets discarded on the road. At the far side of the

61

ruined square, Stanton lay prone on the cobble-stones, another man flung across him.

'William!' Biddlecomb cried, racing to his friend, pushing others aside. The man that lay across Stanton was dead, his chest torn apart. Biddlecomb pulled the corpse aside. Stanton lay motionless, covered in blood.

'William!' Biddlecomb cried again.

Stanton stirred and opened his eyes. 'Isaac, are you all right?'

'Yes, I'm fine. I thought you were dead.'

'No,' said Stanton, struggling to sit up. 'I'm un-hurt. This poor fellow took the shot for me, dear soul,' he said, indicating the broken body at his side.

'But, the blood . . .'

'It's his. How are our losses?'

'Bad, I fear.' And then Biddlecomb remembered the *Rose*. He peered over the wall, bringing the glass to his eye.

The first of the great guns was emerging from the depths of the gundeck, and he could see the others following close behind. 'Get down, they're firing again!' he shouted, and stunned though they were, the Americans crouched in the shelter of the wall.

The sound of the iron flying overhead and slamming into the wall was joined by another sound, iron striking iron, a dull ringing like a broken bell. The ancient six-pounder lifted up and spun in the air, seeming to hang there, and then crashed to the ground ten feet from its shattered carriage. The muzzle was splayed open and the barrel cracked clear back to the trunnions.

The gun's kneeling crew stared at their ruined charge. No one spoke.

62

Biddlecomb peered over the wall at the anchored ship. The frigate's launch was lifting off the booms once again. It swung outboard and settled in the water, and the boat crew swarmed over the side. Biddlecomb could see cutlasses dangling from their waists and the occasional pistol shoved in a belt. He held the glass to his eye and swept the deck. In a row stood the marines, their scarlet coats and white crossbelts seemed to glow in the morning sun. They began to climb down the side, encumbered by their gear and awkward in comparison to the nimble sailors.

'They are sending a party of marines!' Biddlecomb shouted. He turned and looked anxiously at Stanton.

'We can't fight the marines,' Stanton concluded.

'We most certainly cannot,' agreed Biddlecomb. He swallowed hard, then forced the next sentence out. 'I'll surrender myself while you and your men fall back.'

'A noble gesture, but a wasted one. I won't let you do that. Besides, they're no longer interested in you alone. I imagine they've not taken kindly to the way we've used them.' Stanton turned his head to address the soldiers crouching behind the wall. 'All right, you men. Get the wounded up, those that can walk with help. Carry the others. The dead as well. We're falling back to the prison yard. Let's move!' Stanton bellowed orders with the authority he had learned on a quarterdeck years before, and the militia hurried to obey.

Biddlecomb peered over the stone wall. The launch was shoving off from the *Rose*. Once again the banks of oars came down in perfect unison.

63

'Rogers!' Biddlecomb shouted. 'Bring those horses over here! We'll carry the dead men on them!'

The two men, Biddlecomb and Stanton, stood twelve hours later in the darkened upper room of the Blue Goose Tavern surveying High Street below. The lights from the tavern windows on the lower floor illuminated the street sufficiently for the men to see the British patrols as they passed.

'Listen, William,' said Biddlecomb. The two men were silent, separating in their minds the different sounds of the night. Boots beat against the cobblestones in a regular cadence, more than a few pairs of boots.

'It's another patrol,' said Stanton as the two men took a step back from the window, receding into the dark.

The cadence grew louder, and into the circle of light stepped a uniformed midshipman, and behind him a file of eight marines. Their breath made little clouds that reflected the tavern light as they stopped just below the window, the tired marines leaning on their muskets. They had been searching the town and the surrounding countryside for the past ten hours and, despite offers of generous rewards to informers, had found not one man that they could be certain had participated in the morning's fight.

The midshipman below peered into the tavern, then glanced nervously up and down the dark street. He hesitated, as if wrestling with indecision, then beckoned to the file of marines and stepped out of sight into the tavern below. Biddlecomb heard the raucous sounds from the floor below taper off, then die.

64

'They're searching the tavern again,' Biddlecomb observed.

'They didn't find us there the last three times, I don't know why they think they'll find us now,' said Stanton.

Three minutes later the midshipman reappeared on the street, followed by the marines. In the tavern the noise swelled again as the last of the soldiers stepped out into the night. The midshipman led the way down the street and the marines fell in behind him, and one by one they left the circle of light and were gone.

'Do you know Ezra Rumstick?' asked Stanton.

Biddlecomb was surprised by the question. Rumstick was a seaman, a great jolly bear of a man and an old friend of his.

'Why, yes, I do,' said Biddlecomb. 'But how do you know him? I don't imagine that you two move in the same circles of society.'

'I didn't meet him at the Governor's Ball, this is true. But we have friends in common, and business. Anyway, I think it would be best if you left Rhode Island for a while.'

'I agree. If there are no berths open for a master or a mate, I suppose I'll have to sail before the mast.'

'I am afraid so. Which leads us to Rumstick. If any man can get you a seaman's berth, he can. He's in Providence now. We'll get you to Providence, and Rumstick will find you a ship.'

'It might not be so simple to get to Providence. I would be surprised if the roads aren't being patrolled.'

'Have no fear for that, I've arranged everything.'

65

Stanton looked out the window once again, searching up and down the street as far as he could see. 'I suspect Rogers will be here any minute to tell us the way's clear.'

Biddlecomb joined Stanton at the window just as another figure lost in a long, hooded cloak stepped into the tavern lights and disappeared inside.

'That wasn't Rogers, was it?' Biddlecomb asked, and before Stanton could answer they heard the sound of shoes on the rough wooden steps outside their small room. The door swung open, and in the dim light from the tavern below, Biddlecomb could make out the proprietor, and behind him Virginia Stanton, peering out from under the hood of the cape.

'Virginia! Good God, where's Rogers?' Stanton asked.

'He's at home, Father,' Virginia said, her arms emerging from under the cape, a pistol held in each of her small hands. 'I couldn't allow him to come. He would have been stopped the moment he set foot in town and certainly would have been arrested when they found these on him.' She handed the weapons to the two men.

'It's hardly safe for a young woman, walking around in the middle of the night,' Stanton protested.

'No one is safe today,' Virginia said, 'but I had a better chance than Rogers. The way is clear to the wharf. I've spoken with Captain Higgens and he says there's less than half an hour till flood.'

'Humph,' Stanton said, sounding resigned to, if less than pleased with, his daughter's behavior. In the dim light Stanton and Biddlecomb checked the prime

66

in their pistols. 'Well, we best be off,' Stanton said, leading the way down the stairs.

The two men, with Virginia between them, walked down High Street toward the water, careful not to step loudly or draw attention to themselves, listening above their own faint footfalls for the sound of the marines' boots. They kept to the storefronts, in the shadows, peering around each corner before they turned. In this manner they made their way down to the stone quay where the merchant ships groaned against the docks and the water could be heard lapping against their hulls.

They moved past the silent ships, keeping to the shadows, and arrived at last at a trim sloop, the *Nancy*, the Stantons' packet that plied Narragansett Bay. The dock lines were singled up and the sails ungasketed and hanging in their gear.

Stanton paused at the gangway and looked furtively around before climbing over the side and dropping to the deck below. Biddlecomb followed, and as his feet struck the planking, a harsh, low challenge broke the stillness.

'Who goes there?' The voice was a whisper but carried menace nonetheless.

'Stanton,' the older man hissed.

Boots sounded on the deck and a man emerged from the shadows, a cutlass in his hand. It was Captain Higgens, master of the *Nancy*. Biddlecomb recognized him in the pale light.

'Glad to see you, sir. We almost missed the tide,' said Higgens, sliding the cutlass into the scabbard hanging from a leather shoulder strap. 'And Captain Biddlecomb! Welcome aboard!'

'The British were more thorough than I had

67

expected,' said Stanton. 'Have the patrols been by here?'

'They came by once. They kept to the street and didn't stop. We should have no problems getting under way.'

'Good. Then I shall not keep you,' said Stanton. Higgens turned and issued a series of orders in the same harsh whisper, and four men emerged from the shadows and prepared the small ship to sail.

Stanton turned to Biddlecomb and put his hands on the young man's shoulders.

'A few months, Isaac. A few months and then you'll come back and have command of the finest merchant ship in Rhode Island.'

'The finest in America,' said Biddlecomb.

Stanton smiled and squeezed Biddlecomb's arms. 'Godspeed, Isaac.' With a nod to Captain Higgens, Stanton jumped back onto the dock and was gone. Biddlecomb watched his figure moving silently down the quay, watched Virginia step out of the shadows and join him. Virginia. He wanted to say good-bye, wanted to say something, but he dared not call out.

CHAPTER 5

Boston

Winter brings with it a clarity of light to the cities of New England, and Boston and neighboring Charlestown on that day were not exceptions. The wide harbor that the cities share, churned into a pea green during the busy summer months, was deep blue and as unmarred by wave as the sky was by cloud. The cities seemed vivid after the humid summer, and the brick warehouses and the tangle of masts and yards on the ships tied to the wharves stood out in sharp relief.

Boston Harbor was quiet in the opening days of 1775, quieter than it had been for half a century, and the only vessels moving in the harbor were those of the Royal Navy on the North American Station. Eight months earlier a Parliament incensed by the rebellious act of a Boston mob had enacted the Boston Port Bill, which stopped, without exception, all waterborne commerce in Boston Harbor. Since then Parliament and the king had waited for the crippled city to pay for the tea that had been dumped in the harbor, waited for the other maritime centers of America to vie for Boston's lost commerce, like a wolf pack devouring a fallen leader. But neither had happened yet, nor did it seem likely that it would.

And James Pendexter, making his way as quickly as he was able toward the waterfront, cared not in the least about any of it. He was James Pendexter, and not Lord Pendexter, due to the bad luck of being the second of three sons. But at least he had the satisfaction of being, at twenty-one years of age, Lieutenant Pendexter, R.N., with every reason to believe that he would end his years as Adm. Sir James Pendexter, or perhaps Adm. Sir James Pendexter, M.P. It could have been much worse; his younger brother had been made to enter the Church. And Lieutenant Pendexter still held out hope that his older brother would die young.

He pushed his way down King Street, between two officers of the Royal Regiment of Artillery, ignoring their cries of protest as he barged past. The blue and red uniforms of the artillerymen were far more elaborate and colorful than Pendexter's modest blue coat with white facings, white breeches and waistcoat, the trappings of a mere lieutenant. This despite the fact that Pendexter's uniform had been made by London's most fashionable tailor, and the gold buttons on the coat and the gold buckles on his shoes were worth more than any ordinary sailor in His Majesty's service could expect to collect in two years of wages and prize money. Still, Pendexter was just a lieutenant, of average height and unremarkable brown hair and pinched, aristocratic features, virtually indistinguishable from any of a thousand lieutenants in the Royal Navy. The fact that he was the nephew of the admiral in command of the North American squadron did not change that.

70

He did not stand out on the streets of Boston.

King Street turned into the Long Wharf, leaving the city behind and jutting out half a mile into the harbor. Pendexter hurried along, peering over the edge of the wharf as he walked. He was to have met the flagship's gig forty-five minutes earlier, and now he found himself in the familiar position of having to rush to an appointment while simultaneously concocting an excuse for being late.

And then he remembered, and the realization was so startling that he stopped in his tracks. A sergeant of the Fourth Regiment of Foot bumped into him from behind, muttered an obscenity, and continued on, but Pendexter did not even notice. A smile spread across his face, and it turned into a laugh. Why was he rushing? He was not trying to catch a boat that would take him to a ship aboard which he was serving, there to be lambasted by some idiot first officer about being late. He was rushing to meet the gig from the flagship *Preston*, his uncle's, Admiral Graves's, flagship, and the boat was taking him to his own command. He had no need to rush, they could wait for him.

He continued on, still smiling, strolling at a leisurely pace. He stopped to inspect the wares of a pie cart stationed on the wharf, but the offerings were rubbish, as was most American fare. He crossed over to the edge of the wharf and looked out toward the anchored men-of-war, trying to pick out the *Icarus*, the brig *Icarus*, his first command. He had not been down to the harbor in three days, not since the interview with his uncle aboard the *Preston*, and he was unable to identify the *Icarus* among the many small vessels at anchor. It did not matter. The

71

midshipman in the *Preston*'s gig would know which vessel it was.

Pendexter thought back over the interview with his uncle in the *Preston*'s spacious day cabin. His uncle had served Madeira, a fine Madeira that he had insisted, in his philistine way, on calling 'blackstrap.'

'There is a brig, just come in from the West Indies with dispatches,' his uncle said. They had been discussing the military situation in the colonies, and Pendexter found the subject an absolute bore, but now they were moving on to considerations of his career, and Pendexter once again gave the admiral his full attention. 'She's the *Icarus*. Have you seen her?'

'I haven't been down to the harbor in almost a week, Uncle, so I am afraid that I have not had the pleasure.'

'Her commander, Bleakney, a most able young officer, is to be made post. I have a mind to promote you as commander into her.'

Pendexter smiled, quite involuntarily. 'That would be most agreeable.'

'Now, there are some things that I wish to discuss with you,' said the admiral, spinning his glass between his fingers and staring into the red wine. 'I know that for most of your time as midshipman you were carried on ship's books while you were in school. Now, I'm not saying that there's anything wrong with that, most mids do it, but you don't have a great deal of time at sea.'

Pendexter snorted. 'Please, sir, you act as if you were posting me into a first rate! I should think that I can handle a silly little brig!'

The admiral's eyes narrowed as he stared at

Pendexter, and the lieutenant felt suddenly uncomfortable, afraid that he had gone too far. 'Don't mistake me,' said Graves, 'I do believe that you're ready for this command. But bear in mind the great responsibility that command carries. Even the command of a "silly little brig." '

Pendexter saw that it was time to mollify his uncle. 'I apologize for that, Uncle, and I am aware of the responsibility with which you're entrusting me. Please be assured that I will always endeavor to do my duty.'

Graves leaned back and his expression softened. 'Very well. The *Icarus* has on her a very experienced sailing master, a Mr Charles Dibdin. Knows the West Indies as if it were Piccadilly. A good man, we sailed together back in '62. Turned down more than one offer of a commission.'

'I shall most certainly call upon his expertise, Uncle.'

'Now of course we can't give you a lieutenant with more seniority than you. This might be a problem as you've only been passed for lieutenant for a year . . . No doubt my clerk can find someone with sufficient experience to be your first officer.'

'That would be of great benefit, indeed.'

Graves sat for a moment, looking at Pendexter, then stood and extended his hand. 'Congratulations, James. This is the first real step up the ladder to flag rank. I have no doubt that you will do our family great honor.'

'I thank you, sir, and I pray that I shall live up to your expectations.'

'You will, son, you will . . . Greenhurst!' This last was directed toward the small office partitioned off

73

on the starboard side. A harried clerk stuck his head out of the door.

'Sir?' he said, but Admiral Graves ignored him and continued to direct his words to Pendexter.

'Greenhurst here has your orders and will see about getting you a first officer with some experience. I would like to invite you to dine with me, but I fear that you won't be in port long enough. Good luck, James.' With that Graves stood and shook Pendexter's hand, then turned and walked aft into the great cabin, the meeting over.

Pendexter stepped over to Greenhurst's tiny cubicle where the clerk was shuffling through a stack of papers, searching, apparently, for Pendexter's orders.

'Greenhurst,' said Pendexter in a low voice, 'I am going to write down a name for you.'

He reached across the desk and pulled Greenhurst's pen from its stand and scrawled a name on a blank sheet of paper. 'Lt John Smeaton,' he said as he wrote, 'currently fourth in the *Asia*, an excellent seaman and a gentleman of the highest breeding. I would be most obliged if you could see that he is posted to the *Icarus* as first officer.' Pendexter blotted the ink, laid a five-pound note on the page, and folded it in two, handing it to Greenhurst. 'Do you think that that could be arranged?'

Greenhurst tucked the paper and the banknote into his pocket. 'I am certain that something can be arranged, sir.'

And indeed it was. Pendexter continued his stroll down the Long Wharf, his eyes still on the anchored ships. John Smeaton was already aboard whichever of those vessels was the *Icarus*, making the ship ready for her new captain.

74

Twenty yards down the wharf Pendexter saw the *Preston*'s gig bobbing at the base of the stairs that led from the wharf down to the water. The men at the oars were in matching shirts and tarpaulin hats, and a midshipman slouched in the stern sheets. Pendexter was considering whether he should make them wait a bit longer when, to his dismay, the bowman shoved off and the gig began to move away from the wharf.

'I say! I say, *Preston*'s gig!' Pendexter shouted. Several people turned to look at him, and he could feel his face turn red. '*Preston*'s gig!'

The midshipman held up his hand and the bowman hooked on to the steps once again as Pendexter came running up breathlessly. '*Preston*'s gig? I am Lieutenant Pendexter.'

The midshipman looked at him with annoyance. 'You were to meet the boat an hour ago, sir. We were just heading back to the flagship.'

Now that he was certain that he had not missed the gig, Pendexter's attitude of superiority reasserted itself. 'I'll have none of your peevish mouth, do you hear me? What is your name?'

'Thornbird. Sir.'

'Well, Thornbird, the reasons that I am late are related to interests of the service and are not for the ears of a midshipman. Now get me out to the *Icarus* before I have you disrated and packed off to the forecastle.'

'Humph. Cast off forward there,' the midshipman said in a tone that implied that he knew Pendexter had no authority to carry out such a threat.

The oars came down and the gig gathered way.

75

Thornbird held the tiller over and the boat curved away from the dock. 'All right, sir, which is the *Icarus*?' Thornbird asked.

Pendexter felt the panic that attends potential humiliation. He stared at the midshipman, trying to guess if this was insubordination or genuine ignorance. He struggled for a reply. 'As a midshipman aboard the flag, you should know what vessels are where, Thornbird,' Pendexter said at last, his haughty demeanor masking his uncertainty. 'I suggest you find her, and we shall see if you can find her without my help.'

Bloody Wilson and Israel Barrett sat side by side in the main top of His Majesty's brig *Icarus*, legs dangling in space and hands wielding heavers and marlinespikes as they clapped round seizing on the freshly set-up lanyards. Their dress was almost identical: square-toed leather shoes, wide trousers, wool shirts, and well-worn blue jackets, all products of the man-of-war's slop chest, the closest the British navy came to a uniform for the lower deck. They worked quickly, steadily, and though their height above the deck might make a landsman shudder, they were quite oblivious to it.

Wilson was thirty-two and had already spent more years in the navy than out. His long queue, clubbed and tarred, and his face, which was weathered beyond his years, were testaments to his time at sea. His body was lean and sinewy, the result of a surfeit of hard work and the navy's standard ration of food, which was adequate and no more. Barrett was twenty years his senior, and except for the bushy gray and black whiskers that ran down his cheeks and stopped at the

76

level of his mouth, he looked for all the world like an older version of Wilson.

The two men coveted the job that they were doing. It was a clean job, and one that required little physical effort, both rarities aboard a man-of-war. It was a job best accomplished from a sitting position, something rarer still on a vessel where the closest that a foremast hand could get to relaxing while on duty was pushing a holystone across the deck on hands and knees. Fifty feet above the deck the loquacious Wilson was able to indulge his love of long, usually one-sided conversations, as long as his voice was low. But none of these was the chief reason for loving their current occupation.

It was not the weather, either, though the unseasonable warmth made their task even more pleasant. The main top commanded a spectacular view of the harbor and the city beyond. From where they sat, Wilson and Barrett could see all of Boston, the dockyards, and those ships on the North American Station that were anchored there. There was the mighty *Boyne* of seventy guns, her crew of some five hundred men laboring to send up her top-hamper. A half a mile away lay the *Asia*, and in the intervening stretch of blue water lay the *Mercury*, *Glasgow*, and a half dozen of the sloops, brigs, and schooners that constituted a preponderance of the squadron. And beyond the dockyards lay the lovely city itself with its neighborhoods of ruddy brick buildings nestled on the peninsula, and beyond the city loomed Breed's and Bunker Hill.

A crack, like a whip striking flesh, sounded on the deck below them, interrupting the flow of Wilson's story, and was followed by a suppressed cry of pain.

77

The two men glanced over the edge of the top, down to where McDuff stood.

'He's at it again, the bastard,' muttered Wilson.

'Again? He ain't ever stopped,' said Barrett, cutting the tail end off his seizing. Mr McDuff, the *Icarus*'s boatswain, was the reason that the two men were thankful to be aloft.

On the deck below, a majority of the crew labored, under McDuff's eye, to perfect the appearance of an already perfect vessel in preparation for the new commander's arrival. McDuff was stout and powerful, the size and shape of a hogshead cask, but lacked even a hogshead's spark of human kindness. He encouraged the men's efforts with blasphemies, kicks, and lashes with his rattan cane, known in the service as a starter.

His solitary boatswain's mate, Edward Longbottom, was thin and hollow chested, a weakling who kept his sadistic streak in check only when McDuff was not around. Longbottom idolized the boatswain and emulated his behavior to the extent that he was able. Enforcing discipline was a large part of the duties of a boatswain and his mate, but McDuff and Longbottom went about these duties with a zeal that was remarkable, even by Royal Navy standards.

A cane cracked again and Longbottom cursed a man working by the bitts.

'Christ, he's enjoying himself. How come that new lieutenant don't put a stop to this?' asked Wilson. 'And how come they didn't keep Jackson as first lieutenant? He was a bully officer, took no slack, but he was fair. How come we got this Smeaton, all the way from the *Asia*?'

78

At the mention of the lieutenant's name the two men glanced down toward the quarterdeck. The *Icarus*'s new first officer sat there, straddling a bench borrowed from the sailmaker, his coat and hat tossed casually over the binnacle box. He had not moved in an hour. Smeaton was working with his head down, and Wilson and Barrett could see only the blond hair that covered his head and not the fine, almost delicate features of his face. Smeaton had a face that would have looked more in place at a fox hunt, or a ball in London at the height of the social season, than on the deck of a man-of-war.

Laid out before him were a pair of dueling pistols broken down into their component parts. Carefully, lovingly, as if he were handling religious artifacts, Smeaton polished and oiled and reassembled the guns. With the officer of the watch thus engrossed, McDuff and Longbottom were free to run amuck.

'You know how it goes in the navy, Bloody Wilson, interest and all that. We had a bosun, bad one like McDuff there, aboard the *Caesar* back in '58.'

Wilson wrapped the riding turns around the seizing, waiting for Barrett to continue, but the older man did not.

'Well, Israel, what became of him?' Wilson said, containing his exasperation.

'Don't know. We was on deck in the middle watch. It was blowing like snot, a real howler in the Bay of Biscay. Sun came up and no one knew where he was. Just sort of disappeared. Course we have our ideas what happened to him.'

'Bleeding McDuff's too clever to let himself get shoved overboard in a blow. Might get Longbottom that way.'

79

'You just stop that kind of talk, Bloody Wilson. When you've been in the navy as long as I have, you'll see there's no good ever comes of it.'

'I've been around too and seen some things. You think no one's ever been in the navy as long as you, Israel. You think you're father bloody Neptune.'

'I ain't that old, Wilson. I could still kick your arse,' said Barrett, but there was humor, not anger, in his voice.

Wilson pulled his knife from its sheath and cut off the tail end of the seizing. As he slipped the knife back in its sheath, his eyes scanned the harbor and stopped on a small boat pulling for the *Icarus*.

'Is that Dibdin, coming back?' he asked, directing Barrett's glance toward the boat. 'Ain't that the master there, in the stern sheets?'

Barrett scrutinized the boat, then shook his head. 'No. Dibdin took the jolly boat over with the purser. That ain't the jolly boat.'

'That's too bad,' Wilson said. Dibdin was the *Icarus*'s sailing master. He was almost sixty, the oldest man on the brig, and with his long gray hair and lined face and quick smile, he oftentimes seemed more like a benevolent grandfather than a warrant officer. He was the best disciplinarian aboard because the men liked and respected him and wanted him to be pleased with their work. 'That's too bad,' Wilson said again. 'Dibdin would have set that bastard McDuff straight.' The two men continued to watch the boat, which grew closer with each stroke of its oars.

'I believe,' said Barrett a moment later, 'that's the new captain, coming out to take command of our *Icarus*.' The two men watched the boat draw nearer

80

and considered the significance of this moment.

'Think we should sing out?' asked Wilson. They looked down at the deck below. Smeaton continued to clean his guns, and McDuff and Longbottom were concentrating their efforts on one unfortunate soul on the starboard side. No one had noticed the approaching boat.

'Ain't our watch,' observed Barrett, and the two men returned silently to their work, glancing up now and again to catch the developing action below.

The boat disappeared from their sight behind the great stern section of the *Boyne*, then soon emerged from under her counter and pulled straight for the *Icarus*, with only blue water intervening.

'Wonder how long it'll be before someone sees them,' said Barrett. The two men looked down again. Smeaton was wholly engrossed in adjusting the flint in the cock of one of the pistols, and McDuff and Longbottom had moved toward the bow and were inspecting the flemished train tackles on the bow chasers. The boat was just two hundred yards, a cable length, away. In half a minute there would be no time left to properly man the sides to receive a commander.

A half a minute passed, then a full minute, and the boat had drawn to within fifty yards before the oarsmen stopped, expecting a hail. When none came, the bowman in the boat hailed the brig.

'*Icarus!*' he shouted, indicating that he had on board the brig's commanding officer. Three heads, Smeaton's, McDuff's, and Longbottom's, snapped up at that cry, and all three began shouting at once. Aloft Wilson and Barrett tried to suppress their laughter, giggling like children at the chaos below.

81

McDuff was the first to move, running over to the forward scuttle and shouting down below. 'Side boys!' he roared. 'Side boys, man the sides!' He pushed Longbottom toward the gangway, still shouting for the ship's boys below.

On the quarterdeck Smeaton had overturned the sailmaker's bench in an effort to grab his coat and hat. He was on hands and knees collecting up the bits of the one still-disassembled gun and shoving them into the mahogany case that normally housed them. McDuff ran up to the entry port and stood beside Longbottom just as the boat bumped alongside. Smeaton abandoned his attempt to collect the components of his gun and ran across the quarterdeck and down to the gangway, pulling on his coat as he ran.

Pendexter had already set one foot on the boarding steps when the four ship's boys emerged from the forward scuttle. They were all quite young, the oldest of them twelve years of age, and none of them were overly bright. To make matters worse they had been cleaning the limber holes in the bilges, a job for which their size made them well suited. Each of the boys was covered with the filth associated with a ship's bilge; they were black from head to foot and stunk horribly.

Pendexter's head appeared above the level of the deck, and McDuff and Longbottom began the traditional salute with their bosun's calls. This, the first lieutenant struggling with his coat, and four confused boys, stinking and squinting in the sun, was the sight that greeted the captain as he stepped aboard his new command. Wilson bit down hard on his fist to contain his laughter.

82

'Welcome aboard, sir,' he heard Smeaton say on the deck below.

'How very kind of you to notice, Lieutenant Smeaton,' said the new commander. Wilson and Barrett peeked through the slats of the main top, watching the action below. The new officer ran his eye over the ship, fore and aft, then looked aloft. He looked directly at the main top, but long experience told Wilson and Barrett that save for their legs they could not be seen.

'Assemble the men aft,' the new commander said.

'Bosun, assemble the men aft!' shouted Smeaton to McDuff, who was standing two yards away. McDuff and Longbottom put calls to their lips and blew like demons, interspersing the notes with shouted orders and curses.

The crew of the *Icarus* gathered quickly, and soon all that were aboard, sixty-four men, almost the entire company, stood gathered in the waist or clinging to the lower shrouds, staring at the new commander. After years under Captain Bleakney's command they had a new master whose whims would dictate every aspect of their lives. Wilson looked over the men, with their expectant gazes, and then over toward the quarterdeck.

The new commander was leaning on the rail that lined the forward edge of the quarterdeck. Behind him, Smeaton had regained his coat and hat and stood in a stiff approximation of attention. Just as the new commander straightened to speak, Mr Midshipman Appleby burst like a startled pheasant from the scuttle in the break of the quarterdeck, shoving his hat on his head as he jumped up the steps and took his place beside Smeaton. Appleby was fourteen and had the maturity of a boy that age. The new commander shot him a look that spoke ill of the midshipman's future, then turned and addressed the men.

'Hello, men. I am Comdr James Pendexter.' He paused. 'I shall read myself in,' he said, as if he were speaking to himself. He broke the seal on his orders and held them before him like a town crier. 'From Adm. Samuel Graves, commander in chief, North American Squadron, to Lt James Pendexter, R.N. Sir: You are hereby requested and required to proceed on board . . .'

Wilson had heard it before, many times. The same tradition-bound phrases that each captain read as he took command of his ship. The younger men might be awestruck, or afraid, but Wilson regarded it with the fatalism that any man develops when he spends his life at sea. Any man who does not first go mad.

Pendexter came to the end of his orders and folded them again. This was Pendexter's first command, Wilson knew that without being told. He relaxed his stance and waited for the speech that would follow.

'Ahem,' Pendexter cleared his throat. 'Men, I am Captain Pendexter, your new captain. I look forward to a successful cruise aboard the *Icarus*, and I know that together we can confound the king's enemies.'

Wilson wondered briefly to whom Pendexter referred, as England had not been at war for over a decade.

'Now, I am a fair man, but I will tolerate no slackness in my command, do you hear? I am no lover of the cat, but by God I am not afraid to use it either!' He paused, looking over the men, then

84

began again. 'But I trust that you will all do your duty and we shall have no trouble. Bosun, carry on.'

'Three cheers for Captain Pendexter!' cried McDuff, and the Icaruses, anxious to make a good first impression, gave lusty cheers for their now beaming captain. Wilson joined them, hoping at the same time that these men would still be cheering as loud in a year's time. A good officer would develop a sense for firm but just discipline during his first command. A bad officer might become a tyrant, and a weak officer might be manipulated by a man such as McDuff. Wilson wondered when Dibdin would be back on board.

The *Icarus*, formerly the *Bordeaux* and the pride of the French naval shipyard at Brest, was as fine a brig as was ever launched. Even Pendexter, with his limited knowledge of naval vessels, could appreciate the workmanship that had gone into the brig. He looked fore and aft at the backs of the retreating ship's company, and a smile began to spread across his face. Then he remembered that as a captain he should look stern, and he scowled again.

Pendexter stepped down the two steps that led from the quarterdeck to the waist, then stepped around to the scuttle in the break of the quarterdeck. He pushed the door open and stepped through, feeling with his foot for the steps that led down to the deck below. He was anxious to look over the little ship. Most important, he wished to see his great cabin.

The lower deck was utterly black after the bright daylight above, and Pendexter stood for a moment, letting his eyes adjust. He reached a cautious hand

85

above his head to feel for the deck beams. He was surprised to find that he could almost stand upright, then realized that the raised quarterdeck would give more headroom below.

'God love the Frenchies,' he muttered to himself.

As his sight returned, Pendexter saw a long table in front of him and small cabins to starboard and larboard.

This must be the wardroom, he thought. The gunroom, I should say, he corrected himself, remembering that a brig would have only a gunroom, and that would be on the same deck as the great cabin. This was unlike a ship of the line, whose great cabin was on the main deck with a wardroom for warrant officers a deck below and a gunroom for petty officers elsewhere. On the *Icarus* Pendexter would have to endure having his officers live and eat just outside his own cabin. 'Damned nuisance,' he said out loud, hoping that it would not be long before he had a larger command.

Pendexter stepped around the table and walked aft to the great cabin door. He flung the door open and surveyed his private domain. He was disappointed, though not surprised, by what he saw. The cabin had the same headroom as the gunroom, not quite enough to stand upright, and it extended from the bulkhead about ten feet aft to the transom. The space was brilliantly lit by the windows that ran the full length of the transom and the light that came in from the small quarter galleries on either side. The deck was covered with the traditional black-and-white-checked canvas, and though it appeared to be freshly painted, it showed signs of age.

86

Bleakney had left most of his furniture behind, no doubt thinking he was doing the next captain a favor. Pendexter laughed at the thought of it. The furnishings consisted of a rough table and chair that occupied most of the cabin as well as a sideboard of heavy oak and painted with the same buff paint used for the *Icarus*'s hull. The furniture had probably been built by the ship's carpenter, and Pendexter did not consider it fit for a servant's quarters.

He had just begun to consider the placement of his wine rack when Smeaton knocked on the doorframe.

'Come,' said Pendexter, never moving his eyes from the bulkhead.

Smeaton stepped into the cabin. 'The hands are employed about the ship, sir.'

'Very well.'

'James, I am dreadfully sorry about not being ready for you. I know it is inexcusable, but I was so distracted with preparing the ship for sea. I'd a world of things on my mind—'

'Damn it all, man!' shouted Pendexter. 'It was a damned embarrassment, that's what! How in God's name am I supposed to command the respect of a bunch of Billingsgate villains when I do not receive it from my own first officer?'

'You're right, of course,' said Smeaton, avoiding Pendexter's gaze. 'I can do no more than apologize.'

Pendexter stared at the lieutenant, and at last Smeaton met his gaze. There was a cold silence, and then Pendexter grinned and shook his head, unable to remain angry in the presence of his old friend.

'It's done now, John, so let's put it behind us. Besides, I flatter myself that my little speech struck a

87

chord with the men. I believe that we're starting out on as fine a foot as we could hope.'

'Indeed we are, James! And I've not had the opportunity to congratulate you on your promotion, so please let me do so now.'

'I thank you. And as you see, I'm not one to forget old friends as I move up.'

'I can't adequately express my gratitude for your recommending me to this position. I don't believe I could have tolerated one more cruise aboard that damned *Asia*. The captain was a philistine; not a gentleman to be found abroad. We were more civilized in our first year at Eton than the whole damn wardroom is now.'

'Well, we'll not have that problem aboard the *Icarus*.' Pendexter held out his arms and looked around the great cabin. 'She's mine, John! Just as we've always imagined. And with me as captain we'll have no one telling us what we shall and shall not do aboard her!'

'She'll be our own version of the king's yacht.'

Pendexter sat on the small table that took up most of the cabin. 'Give me your impression of the brig's company.'

'The men seem the usual sort. Leftovers from the last war, no doubt once the dregs of Newgate, but now tolerably good seamen. Some are quite new to the navy, running from debts or some pathetic love affair I should imagine, but they can be trained, you know. This Appleby is as useless as midshipmen are wont to be. The gunner, Hickman, and the carpenter seem up to their duties, as does the purser, who's ashore at the moment. I am not so certain about this Dibdin, the master.'

'What's wrong with him?'

'Damn morose man. Complains about bloody everything. The men seem to like him, though.'

'I am always suspicious of an officer who's too well liked by the crew. It could well mean that he's pandering to them. What of the boatswain?'

'Ah, Mr McDuff! He's a man worthy of his warrant. Takes no guff from the men, and by God he does keep them hopping. He knows his business, and I have been quite satisfied in leaving him to oversee the men's efforts. His mate seems competent as well, though he lacks experience.'

'Good. We seem to be reasonably well manned, and those that are not up to snuff we'll bring up to our standards or we'll leave them on the beach. Now, the first order of business is to turn this deplorable den into something fit for a gentleman. If you trust this McDuff to handle affairs, let us, you and I, take the launch ashore and select some furnishings. Perhaps a trip to the wine merchant might be in order as well.'

'Excellent, James. But, if I might be so bold . . .'

'By all means, what?'

'Well, I was curious as to what our orders might be.'

Pendexter's face lit with surprise. 'Oh, quite right! I had all but forgot, you know!' He pulled the orders from his coat pocket and broke the seal. He read the sheet quickly, then read it again, and his expression turned to one of bitter disappointment.

'What is it, James?'

'We are going to the West Indies. Barbados.'

'Barbados! Why, that's capital! The weather is warm there, and the girls are quite starved for

89

companionship. I know the governor, and his daughter, and the admiral and his daughter as well.'

'Yes, that's fine, but the orders are to fetch dispatches from the flag and proceed to sea as soon as we are ready. What's our state of readiness, John?'

'Our wood and water is all laid in, and most of our food. We're waiting on powder and shot. Bleakney, who had the *Icarus* before you, seems to have found any excuse to fire off the great guns, and it has become a great nuisance. I'm surprised that he was made post, after such waste. Anyway, with some prodding of the navy yard we could sail on the morning tide.'

Pendexter frowned. 'This is damned inconvenient,' he said at last. 'Damned inconvenient. You see, I had planned a bit of a party aboard for tomorrow night. I've invited some damned influential people, and some very eager young women. It would never do to cancel now.'

Smeaton smiled. 'I know just the thing that will answer. As I said, it's only with great prodding that we would be ready tomorrow. It's hardly our fault if the shipyard fails to respond to a standard request, and if we follow proper channels, it could take us a fortnight to get to sea. And none of the fault our own.'

'Excellent. We'll have the chance to show off our brig after all. All the more reason why we must get into the city and secure some civilized furniture.'

'I'll see the launch swayed over immediately,' said Smeaton, stepping out the door.

'Very good. And pass the word to the carpenter that he is to break up this abominable furniture for kindling, and I don't give a damn if he made it himself.'

90

CHAPTER 6

Providence

Tea
Destroyed by Indians

Ye Glorious Sons of Freedom, brave and bold
That has stood forth . . . Fair Liberty to hold;
Though you were Indians, come from distant
  shores
Like Men you acted . . . not like savage Moors
Boston's Sons keep up your courage good,
Or Dye, like Martyrs, in Fair Free-born blood.

Biddlecomb read, with some difficulty, the weathered broadside. The wheat paste that made the sheet an almost permanent fixture on the wall to which it was plastered had preserved the paper, though it had been posted the better part of a year ago. Biddlecomb wondered if the patriots of Boston, Hancock and the rest, felt quite so brave and bold now, with their harbor sealed tight and their livelihoods dying of atrophy.

The packet *Nancy* had warped alongside the Providence waterfront on the first of the flood tide that morning after an uneventful run upriver.

91

Biddlecomb had paid his respects to Captain Higgens and begun his search of the Providence waterfront for his old friend Ezra Rumstick. The activity that surrounded the merchant fleet of Providence flowed around him in a hundred different directions. The breeze carried with it the smell of tar and paint, and from aboard the ships came the shouts of mates and seamen and the groaning and creaking of blocks and tackle as cargo went on and off. The longshore-men added their voices to the confusion, as did the merchants, who kept watchful eyes on their interests. This was Biddlecomb's world; he loved it, and it gave him security and strength.

And Isaac looked as much a part of that world as he felt, dressed as he was in the most ubiquitous outfit on the waterfront. His clothes were those of a foremast jack: square-toed leather shoes, loose trousers liberally spotted with tar, a blue jacket trimmed out with brass buttons, and on his head a wide-brimmed tarpaulin hat, cocked just so to one side, a black ribbon trailing astern. The outfit had been provided by Captain Higgens from various articles that had made their way into the *Nancy*'s slop chest. It had been eight years, from the time he made third mate, since he had worn similar clothes.

Biddlecomb found no one along the waterfront who knew of Rumstick's whereabouts, but it was universally assumed that he was to be found at 'the hanging.' And though Biddlecomb had no knowl-edge of any hanging, it was clear from the hushed tones in which people spoke of the event that such ignorance was best kept secret. At last he managed to obtain directions, and he turned onto High Street and made his way up the steep hill toward the center of town.

The farther he walked the more unlikely it seemed that the directions he had been given were correct. The neighborhoods, as Biddlecomb climbed, turned from respectable to affluent, from tradesman and artisan to wealthy merchant and government official. The attention paid to paint and windows and gardens of each house made them look as if they were all new built, and only the ivy climbing halfway up the brick walls belied this impression. This was not where one would expect to see a public execution.

He was almost to the top of the hill when he became aware of the noise. At first it sounded like a rustling, like wind in the leaves or the rush of water. He walked on, and soon it was clear to him that the sound was voices, perhaps hundreds of voices. They rose and fell together, stimulated by some unseen occurrence, and the distance and the buildings made them sound as one. A smell was in the air as well, a familiar smell but one that was out of place among the odors of cooking and horses and of the marshy tidal flats. And though he was certain that the sounds came from a mob of people, Biddlecomb was still surprised when he rounded the corner and stepped into the public square.

Perhaps four hundred people were in the square, which was of no great size. There seemed to be no uniformity in the crowd; Biddlecomb could see sailors and cobblers and men and even women whose clothes indicated wealth. The rich merchants stood shoulder to shoulder with apprentices and laborers, and all were lending their voices to the din. Several people held flaming torches aloft, and muskets as well

93

were in evidence. Biddlecomb turned to look in the direction that the mob was facing, and his eyes opened wide and he gasped at the grisly sight that confronted him.

The body that hung from the tree was well dressed in immaculate white breeches and a green coat trimmed out in gold. It hung with its back to the crowd, and Biddlecomb could see the expensive, coiffured wig that crowned the head. In a circle around the body stood a group of men. They each held long cudgels, and as Biddlecomb watched, they alternately struck the hung victim. The body jerked and twisted under the blows, and Biddlecomb wondered whether the unfortunate wretch was dead. Then the body swung round and Biddlecomb started at the grotesque canvas head and painted face and realized, to his relief, that it was an effigy that hung from the tree and not a man at all.

One of the men circling the straw victim stepped forward and delivered it a terrible blow. The body jerked and a cloud of powder exploded from the wig. The delighted crowd roared again, and Biddlecomb smiled as he recognized the man who had delivered the blow. It was Ezra Rumstick.

Biddlecomb wondered that he had not noticed him immediately. Rumstick stood six feet two inches tall and weighed two hundred and fifty pounds. He towered over the men around him. He wound up with his cudgel and struck again, this time ripping the canvas head half off the shoulders. Biddlecomb was not at all surprised to find his friend at the center of this action. Rumstick was a natural leader, and Biddlecomb had been listening to his cries for independence for five years and more.

A sailor standing beside Biddlecomb began to shout. 'Burn him! Burn the rascal!' he yelled, and the rest of the mob took up the cry. Rumstick looked up at the crowd, gesturing to the torchbearers, and looked Biddlecomb square in the face. His expression turned to surprise and recognition and his great face split in a grin. He raised his arm to beckon Biddlecomb over, but the torchbearers were on him, igniting the effigy. The dry straw that filled the dummy caught quickly and the body erupted in flames, which climbed up the halter and threatened the tree above. The crowd went wild, screaming and throwing clods of dirt and rocks at the burning corpse. Biddlecomb looked for his friend again and saw that he had withdrawn from the flames and stood by a knot of men well back from the crowd, clustered around an older man who wore only his smallclothes and an expression of anger and embarrassment. His hair was sticking out in every direction, and the clothes that he retained were torn and dirty. Biddlecomb guessed that he was the original owner of the fine clothing that was now burning on the back of the straw man, and that the straw man was meant to represent him. Biddlecomb wondered what offense he might have given to warrant such a display.

The smoke from the burning effigy drifted down on the crowd, and Biddlecomb caught again the familiar smell that he had noticed blocks from the square, and he realized that it was Stockholm tar.

Biddlecomb looked past Rumstick and the knot of men who detained the wretched victim and noticed for the first time the cauldron that hung from a tripod over a small flame. And just as he realized what

95

was about to happen, Rumstick's voice roared out above the crowd.

'Fetch the tar, lads!' he cried. 'Let's do him right!' And with that command half a dozen boys dipped buckets in the cauldron and pulled them out filled and dripping with the steaming tar. The men that had been restraining the victim now tore off what few clothes he had remaining. Biddlecomb could see the man's mouth moving, forming curses and screaming protests, but he could not hear the words over the mob. The halter holding the burning effigy parted and the body fell in a mass of burning embers. The crowd surged forward over the still-burning straw and circled the victim, now half-covered in tar.

The mob seemed crazed, and Biddlecomb wondered if they would turn on the man and hang him in actuality as they just had in effigy. But the man was unharmed, save for the buckets of tar that were being poured steadily over his head. Already the unfortunate man was quite black, white showing only when he dared to open his eyes or mouth.

Rumstick held up his huge hand and the tarring stopped, and a group of women stepped forward with half-filled pillowcases in each hand. The women, laughing and encouraged by the shrieking mob, poured feathers over the thrashing victim. The more the poor man flailed his arms, the more widely the feathers were distributed, and within a moment he looked like a macabre chicken with a vaguely human form. The look was comical in the extreme.

The crowd was now beyond the control of Rumstick or anyone else. They laughed and shouted insults and pelted the man with dirt and mud. A dozen men pushed through the crowd bearing a split

96

log rail over their heads. They dropped the log to the ground and bound the victim's hands behind his back. Then they forced the victim to straddle the rail and lifted it again, none too gently, with the now silent chicken-man riding it like a horse. The crowd parted for them as they jogged down a street that opened onto the square, and the onlookers followed at a trot, their shouting not in the least diminished. Biddlecomb stood as the crowd flowed around him, watching the weird carnival disappear down the block.

'Isaac Biddlecomb, you great whoremonger!' he heard. He looked up and saw Rumstick rushing toward him. Rumstick threw his arms around him and squeezed, in much the same manner that a bear would crush someone to death.

'Rumstick, good man! How are you, friend?' asked Biddlecomb when he had regained his breath.

'I'm well, my friend. Quite busy, but well.'

'Aye, I can see that you are busy indeed. Who might that poor unfortunate have been?'

'He is the Royal Customs officer, the Billingsgate villain, and an infernal Tory. And far too zealous he was in carrying out his duties.'

'Indeed. Well, I'll take my lesson from that and never do a job but by half whenever I'm in Providence,' said Biddlecomb, and Rumstick laughed his deep laugh.

'I have no objection to a man doing his job, depending, of course, on what that job is. Have you come to join the fight?'

'Which fight is that, Ezra?'

'Why, the fight for independence, of course. When I saw you in the crowd, I thought, "Now here is my

97

good friend Isaac Biddlecomb come to forgo his avarice and ambition and join the Sons of Liberty." '

'Independence? Is that what you're fighting for? I thought you fought just because you liked to fight,' Biddlecomb said, smiling, though he was not entirely joking.

'There might be something in that, I ain't adverse to a good fight. But at the heart of it is independence. Have you come to join us?'

'No, Ezra. As sweet as independence might be if it's given, I doubt it can be taken. Besides, independence would ruin my business, just when I'm coming into my own.'

'I heard John Bull already ruined your business. You had all your money tied up in the *Judea*, didn't you?'

'Yes, I did, and, yes, it's gone.' Biddlecomb felt the despair sweep over him again. It was so unreal, the events of the past days, like a wild dream, like someone else's life, that he had actually forgotten that the profit of five years at sea had, in five minutes, been swept away.

'I'm sorry, Isaac, really. But if this means you'll come to see how British rule is threatening our natural rights and liberties, well, then maybe it's for the better,' Rumstick said, smiling, and before Biddlecomb could make an angry retort he continued, 'Another thing. If you don't see the need of independency yet, that's your business, but I reckon it's best if you kept it to yourself here in Providence. I pray you'll remember what you just witnessed and keep a mind of what you say.'

Biddlecomb could see that his friend was not joking. 'I'll be silent as a corpse on that subject.'

98

'A fine plan. Come, we'll go to Sabine's and you'll buy me some beer. Or a sling. Yes, Sabine makes a fine sling, rum or gin, well to the northward.' The two men stepped off toward Church Street, just as the sun disappeared behind the elegant houses on the hill.

Biddlecomb remembered Sabine's from previous visits to Providence as a crowded and raucous establishment. Seamen, newspapermen, merchants, rich or otherwise, all crowded into Sabine's. It was a place for those who held strong opinions and were not shy in their expression. Sabine's was the center of unrest in Providence, and the unrest, like ink on a blotter, was spreading out quickly in all directions.

By the time Biddlecomb and Rumstick arrived at the tavern, every bench was jammed with men and nearly all of the standing room as well. Biddlecomb recognized many faces from the crowd in the square, and the excitement from the tarring and feathering of King George's customs man did not seem to have diminished. The men yelled at each other, calling over the din to make their points heard, and the occasional cries of 'Liberty!' and 'Death to parliamentary rascals!' made Biddlecomb shake his head and wonder at such open treason. Around and about through the crowd the potboys scurried with their wooden trays, spilling ale in the trampled sawdust on the floor, and the barmaids skillfully fended off the ribald suggestions of the men.

'So, my friend,' began Rumstick when the two had seated themselves at a table whose occupants had deserted it in order that Rumstick might sit, 'I had other reasons, you know, to hope that you had come to join the Sons of Liberty. That was

99

something, what you did with the old *Judea*. Deprived that blackhearted Wallace of his prize. Showed him what was what.'

'Oh, yes, I showed him all right. Plowed a beautiful ship up on the rocks, threw away a fortune in molasses, not to mention every penny I was worth. I have no doubt that Wallace rues the day he crossed my wake. How on earth did you hear of this so soon?'

'I hear things. But don't you see? This is why we must fight for independence.'

'Ezra, please. I was breaking the law. I was smuggling. I'll own up to that. Wallace was simply doing his duty.'

Rumstick took a long pull on his sling. 'Those days are long over, Isaac, the days of flitting around the British law like some French dancing master. We can't live like that, the country can't. There'll come a time, and soon, when everyone will have to take a side.' He paused and looked Biddlecomb in the eye, his countenance more serious than was his custom. 'Having the British in our country's like . . . like having a mad dog around the house, and everyone just trying to avoid it and hope it'll be good or go away. But that don't work. You have to shoot the dog.' He took another pull on his sling. 'Sometimes you have to put personal interest aside and fight for what's right.'

'That's how my father felt. He died at Quebec in '59, fighting for what was right.'

'I didn't know that. I have no doubt he died proud, fighting for what he believed.'

'I can't speak to that. He didn't seem too proud to me, lying in my arms, blood everywhere. I had come with him to Quebec, you see, after my mother died.

100

I ran away that night and went to sea. That's how I ended up as a sailorman.'

'I'm sorry . . .'

'It doesn't matter now. He was trying to keep from thinking on my mother's passing as much as fighting for any cause. In faith I owe more to William Stanton for my upbringing, wretched though my state might be at this moment. But listen, I must beg your assistance.'

'You need only ask, my friend. Any assistance I can provide, humble man that I am, is yours.'

'Humble indeed. As humble as . . . never mind. I must leave Rhode Island for a while.'

'Yes, so I understand. Captain Wallace isn't taking things lying down as the others did. It may happen that his *Rose* goes the way of the *Gaspee*.'

'Unless you're planning on putting the frigate to the torch tonight, I think it would be best if I were to leave the country for a while. I'm looking for a berth before the mast.'

'Ah! I was wondering why you was dressed like Jolly Jack Tar himself. Why are you shipping before the mast?'

'I couldn't find a mate or master's berth quick enough, and even if I could, word would get out. I think I could disappear in a forecastle easier than a quarterdeck.'

'But do you remember what ropes to pull on, or how to use a paintbrush? It's been a long time since you've done an honest day's work. Aren't your hands too soft now to sweat a line or fist a sail?' Rumstick was enjoying himself.

'I was hoping that you could teach me,' said Biddlecomb dryly.

'Your luck still holds. It happens that I'm shipping as boatswain on the *William B. Adams*, and we're short an able-bodied seaman, which I imagine you could still pass for. The cargo is aboard and stowed down, so there's no fear that you might blister your lily-white hands, and we've already warped out and lay at anchor waiting the morning tide. And the *Adams* is as sweet and fine a ship as one could ask.'

'The *William B. Adams*? Not that great slab-sided apple crate with a bow and stern nailed in place that I saw half-sunk in the tideway?'

'One and the same. The finest little merchantman out of Rhode Island. The mate is a whore's son bastard, an infernal tool of the British, but the old man is a fine gentleman, Abraham Peabody. Do you know him?'

'No, which under the circumstances is for the best.'

'I have no doubt that he will be glad to sign you aboard. We are bound for Jamaica. General cargo, beef, rum, barrel hoops, the usual lot.'

'This is perfect, Ezra, thank you. I was afraid that you had swallowed the anchor.'

'This'll be my last trip for some time. In fact, if I weren't beholden to Peabody for this voyage, I would be staying ashore. The time has come for my brothers and I to be taking up arms.'

'I wish you the best of luck in your good fight . . . One other thing. I think it would be best if I were to sign aboard under a false name. It seems I've become somewhat famous over these past days, and masters and mates don't take too kindly to a foremast jack who has sailed as master of his own

102

vessel. You understand, afraid a former master will be second-guessing them, criticizing each order.'

'As indeed you would do, you arrogant rascal. But to be perfectly honest I believe you are a better master than Peabody, and that's no criticism of Peabody.'

Biddlecomb smiled, embarrassed by the offhand compliment.

'But I agree with you,' Rumstick continued. 'So tomorrow you shall be, say, Jack Nastyface.'

'There's a name they'll certainly believe I was born with. Please be serious, Rumstick.'

'Fine, fine. You'll be Jack Woodhead.'

Biddlecomb snorted. 'Fine, I'll be Jack Woodhead, before you think of something worse.'

'Good. Then you'll buy me another sling or two and then we go aboard the ship.'

The din in the tavern did not lessen with the opening of the door, and the raucous shouting continued until the first of the red-uniformed marines stepped inside, musket at bayonet charge, a file of marines following him in. In a wave the tavern fell silent, all eyes on the soldiers. At the head of the band stood a dark-haired man in the uniform of an officer of the Royal Navy. Biddlecomb shuffled across the bench and pressed himself against the wall, peering around Rumstick. The officer searched the room, his face expressionless, his eyes searching the crowd. Biddlecomb stared at the impassive face, unable to accept his cursed luck. It was Lieutenant Norton.

Norton's search turned to the end of the room where Rumstick and Biddlecomb sat. Rumstick was turned in his seat, staring at the lieutenant. Their

103

eyes met and Norton stepped across the room, the marines never more than a few feet behind.

'Ezra Rumstick, in the name of King George the Third I am placing you under arrest for your part in the cowardly destruction of His Majesty's revenue schooner *Gaspee*. Sergeant . . .' he began, and his eyes moved across the table. He hesitated and then broke into a grin. 'And Capt. Isaac Biddlecomb! It appears that this is my lucky day!'

CHAPTER 7

Orders to Sail

It was midmorning on the intended day of the party that Pendexter felt his first pangs of terror. The ship's company was scouring the berthing deck, trying to remove the smell that inevitably accompanies close-packed men. Pendexter stood on the quarterdeck, looking down along the line of guns to the bow. He pictured eighty or so of Boston's elite parading around the deck and realized that there was no room to parade. The cramped deck space only accentuated the insignificance of his command.

Everything else was in perfect readiness. His foray ashore to furnish and provision the great cabin had been entirely successful, though the British blockade of Boston Harbor had adversely affected the selection at the local wine merchants and he had been forced to visit four shops before he was able to procure the quality and quantity he needed. In the end there had even been time to purchase, on Smeaton's advice, a red silk dress that might be used to win the favors of some reluctant girl on the West Indies station.

He was at least gratified to see, upon his return to the *Icarus*, that McDuff and Longbottom were still hard at it, driving the crew to clean and paint the brig to a perfection not previously known. It was almost midnight when the sailmaker and a dozen hands, working by lantern light, finished stretching the new-built awning over the waist and quarterdeck.

But that was last night. Pendexter knew that decisive action was needed now to avoid the humiliation of having his guests tripping over themselves on the crowded deck. If only there was still time.

'Pass the word for the bosun,' he said to Midshipman Appleby, who stood on the leeward side. As Appleby ran forward, Pendexter resolved to be firm. He would give his orders and take no back talk.

McDuff stepped up to the quarterdeck, knuckling his forehead.

'I'm sorry, bosun, but we must strike all of the guns into the hold,' Pendexter said, indicating with a sweep of his arm the *Icarus*'s battery of fourteen six-pounders.

McDuff looked down the line of guns, then squinted up at the awning overhead. Pendexter braced for an objection, but the bosun only nodded. 'Guns in the hold, sir, aye. I'll set the sailmaker to striking the awning whilst I clear away a space below,' and with that he ran forward, silver call shrieking.

It had not occurred to Pendexter that the awning would have to be struck in order that the stay tackle could be used to strike the guns below, but then he had not really given the matter any thought. His anxiety mounted as he began to comprehend the enormity of the task ahead and the real possibility that his guests would arrive to find the work half-done. He paced the quarterdeck, trying to calculate the time that it would take to clear the guns away, finally admitting to himself that he had no idea.

106

'Just leave the train tackles,' he called to McDuff, 'but see the falls are flemished just so,' and then resumed pacing.

It was very late in the afternoon, with the hands working straight through dinner and 'up spirits,' when the last gun sailed down through the hatch and the hatch was battened down once more. McDuff had again proved his worth, driving the men like savages, and though one man had managed to crush his hand and another had fallen down the hatch and knocked himself senseless, the operation had gone quite smoothly.

It was two bells in the evening watch when the sailmaker and his mates began to drag the heavy awning out again.

'No, no, you can belay that!' said a greatly relieved Pendexter. 'There's no time for the awning, and besides, I don't believe it will rain.' That said, he disappeared below to see to his own preparations.

'Mr Dibdin,' said Pendexter when he emerged on deck an hour later. The master, who for most of the day had worked sullenly on his charts, now stood, sullen, on the quarterdeck. 'I intend to give the hands a run ashore tonight, say until four bells in the morning watch, save for the ones that we feel do not deserve liberty or those whom we may require aboard.'

'You are giving the hands liberty? Overnight?' asked Dibdin, incredulous. 'Are you certain that's wise? I thought we were sailing soon.'

Pendexter bristled at this. 'I am not in the habit of discussing my decisions or my orders with my subordinates, and frankly I am being quite generous now. I have every intention of giving most of the

107

crew a night ashore. They've worked hard and earned it. And further, this brig is small enough and will be quite crowded with my guests. These are important people who are attending tonight, you know. It would do your career no harm to be pleasant to them.'

Dibdin coughed. 'I'll tell off the liberty men and the boat's crew, sir,' he said, and walked off forward.

It was well past midnight, with his guests mingling in groups about the deck, before Pendexter was able to relax and quietly survey all that he had accomplished. From his vantage point on the quarter-deck the deck looked positively vast with the guns stowed below, and the lanterns strung fore and aft cast a warm yellow glow on the scene. Most of the guests were still aboard. The elegant dresses and the men's finery and powdered wigs gave the *Icarus* a cosmopolitan air that Pendexter found pleasing.

It had been, nonetheless, an exhausting evening. Despite McDuff's urging the men had been slow and inept at laying out the buffet and preparing for the guests' arrival. The boat's crew was carefully fitted out in matching shirts and slop pants and tarpaulin hats, with instructions to return the clothes to Dibdin the next day. And despite emphatic warnings to Appleby to keep the boat crew sober and respectful as they ferried his guests out to the brig, Pendexter did not feel at all relaxed in the knowledge that his orders were being carried out.

A squeal of female laughter drew his attention to the larboard side. Smeaton and two of Boston's gentlemen were entertaining a knot of young women. One of the women had relieved Smeaton of his uniform hat and now had it balanced precariously

108

atop her own high-piled hair. She twirled around, displaying her new fashion to the laughter and encouragement of the onlookers. The gold lace of the hat, a bit more than was quite proper for a junior lieutenant, glittered in the lantern light.

Pendexter was trying to think of something witty to call out when the young woman caught her toe on a ringbolt. She staggered, dropping her wineglass as she fell. Smeaton and the two gentlemen around her threw their wineglasses aside and lunged forward, catching her before she struck the deck. She lay inclined in their arms for a moment, confused, then broke out in gay laughter and the others joined in.

Pendexter looked down at the deck. The wine, the good Bordeaux from four broken glasses, pooled together, making a dark stain as it seeped into the deck. It recalled to Pendexter's mind the time when as a midshipman he had seen such a stain left behind after a new-pressed hand had fallen from the main topgallant yard. He imagined the results of a naval battle were similar to this. Now Smeaton was kicking the broken glass into the scuppers, leaving streaks of wine like dark fingers across the deck. Pendexter looked out across the harbor, uneasy about the stain on the white deck planks. It was hardly the first bit of wine spilled that night, he reminded himself.

Beyond the larboard rail of the quarterdeck Pendexter could just make out the few lights still glowing in Boston, but the brightly lit deck of the *Icarus* prevented him from seeing any other detail in the night. He stared out into space, recalling again the pleasures of the evening. He had made great advances on the affections of Colonel Williams's daughter. Certain she was watching now, he decided

109

to act the aloof captain for a few moments longer, then seek her out and continue the campaign.

His eyes caught a light, actually a rectangular block of lights, at the far edge of town. It appeared too large to be a window, and anyway the *Icarus* was anchored too far out to distinguish any window that clearly. He could not imagine what it was.

And then he realized with a start that the light was not from the town at all, but came from the windows of the *Preston*'s great cabin, where apparently the admiral was still at work. He had noticed the lights earlier, just after the sun had set. What the hell's the old man doing still up at this hour? he thought. He shifted uneasily under his uniform coat.

'I say, old man!' Smeaton called out. Pendexter turned around. Smeaton and his crowd were at the break of the quarterdeck. 'I say, old man, you may come and join the party. You are the host after all.' The observation evoked laughter from the young women. Pendexter caught a waft of perfume. The scent mixed oddly with the smell of tar and hemp and scrubbed wood. He smiled and stepped down to the waist.

'Whatever were you looking at, James?' Smeaton asked.

'There are lights still in the flagship's great cabin. I was wondering what the old curmudgeon was up to this late.'

'Bloody man won't let up, what? You'd think we were fighting a proper war, not just a mob of bloody colonials. No offense, sir.' Smeaton directed the last comment to the clique of Bostonians.

'None taken,' replied one of the young gentlemen with a quick bow.

110

'Still and all,' Pendexter continued, 'one wonders what so occupies his mind.'

'It would behoove you, James,' said Smeaton in a low voice, 'to more concern yourself with what occupies Miss Williams's mind. You've ignored her this past half an hour and more.'

'You're right, John, to be sure.' Pendexter cast one last look over the larboard rail, but the lights from the *Preston* could not be seen from the *Icarus*'s brightly lit waist. 'Ah, Miss Williams!' he called out, then made his way forward to a group of partygoers by the bitts.

Pendexter slept through the striking of four bells the next morning, slept through McDuff's and Longbottom's shouts of 'Out or down!' as they roused the ship's company. The sound of the pumps being rigged and manned brought him around at last.

'Bolton, God damn your eyes!' he shouted, swinging his legs over the edge of his cot.

Bolton, his servant, came running at the call. He was a short man, and hunched over as well, which gave him the advantage of not having to stoop beneath the deck beams, his bald head with its fringe of brownish hair never coming within six inches of the overhead.

'Where in the hell is my coffee?' Pendexter demanded.

'Beg pardon, you didn't say you wanted no coffee, sir.'

'Stupid man. I have coffee every morning, do I not? Must I order it every morning? Don't answer, just go and get me some damned coffee, and make it strong this time!' These last words were shouted

111

through the doorway at Bolton's retreating back.

It was two bells in the forenoon watch before Bolton had served out Pendexter's coffee, laid out his uniform, and helped him dress. Pendexter stepped out of the great cabin and crossed the dark gunroom. He could hear voices, Dibdin's and McDuff's, on the deck just beyond the scuttle.

'Mr McDuff!' he heard Dibdin say in a quiet, hissing voice. 'I have told you before that you are too free by far with your starter. You must lead the men, not drive them like animals!'

'Lieutenant Smeaton says I's to put the men to work however I sees fit,' protested McDuff.

'I am the officer of the deck and shall remain so until such time as the captain or first lieutenant emerge from their cabins, and I do not wish to see the men beaten!'

It was time for the captain to intervene. Pendexter threw open the door to the scuttle, catching the brilliant winter sun square in the face. He blinked and squinted, holding a hand up to shield his eyes. He felt his eyes water and a tear run down one cheek.

'What seems to be the problem here, Mr Dibdin?' he asked, blinking more tears from his eyes.

'The bosun is being far too liberal with the use of his starter, once again. I do not wish to see the hands beaten like animals, sir. Commander Bleakney—'

'I am not in the least interested in Commander Bleakney, Mr Dibdin,' said Pendexter, cutting the master short. The sunlight had renewed the pounding in Pendexter's head and exhausted his spirit of confrontation. 'Mr McDuff, pray be less liberal with the use of your starter,' he said, and hurried aft to the sanctity of his quarterdeck.

The first scrubbing in the predawn hours had eliminated most of the evidence of the night's bacchanalia. The sweepers had found the broken glass, and holystones applied to the great splotches of red wine had returned the planking to all of its former snowy whiteness. Now the remarkable quiet of the morning was broken only by the steady clank-clank-clank of the capstan pawls, the curses of McDuff and Longbottom, muted now in deference to Dibdin's wishes, and the crisp orders of the master as he coordinated the swaying out of the fourteen guns, each of them weighing in excess of twenty-four hundred pounds.

As Pendexter watched, number-four gun, starboard side, emerged through the hatch, hanging in midair beneath the twelve-inch block of the stay tackle.

''Vast the capstan!' shouted Dibdin, and the men at the bars froze.

'Haul away your yard tackle!' Dibdin called. A party of seamen hauled away at the tackle that hung from the mainyard. The gun began a slow arc outboard, rising and moving across the deck, seeming to float weightlessly under the straining block and tackle. The gunner and his mate grabbed the barrel where it hung and swiveled it around, positioning it above its carriage. The gunner gave the master a nod of his head.

'Slack away all! Slack away slow!' Dibdin ordered. The straining manila creaked and popped as it slipped through blocks and around the capstan drum, and the gun came easily to rest in its carriage.

'Slack away lively!' shouted Dibdin, and as the tackles went slack, seamen jumped to disengage them from the sling and pull the sling from the gun's barrel. The gunner clapped the caps over the trunnions, secured them, and another party of seamen stepped up to haul the gun to number-five gunport, starboard side.

'Very nicely done, Mr Dibdin,' said Pendexter in a conciliatory tone.

Dibdin spat over the side. 'Thank you, sir. We'd be closer to done if all the hands was aboard.'

'All the hands are not aboard?'

'No, sir. Thirteen of the liberty men didn't make it back this morning. Probably just waking up in some whorehouse now.'

This was hardly an appropriate observation to make to the captain, in Pendexter's opinion, and he was about to make that opinion known when Smeaton stepped onto the quarterdeck.

'Capital party last night, just capital!' he said with genuine enthusiasm.

'Capital indeed,' agreed Pendexter.

'And how did your advances upon the young Miss Williams end? All's well, I hope?'

'I dare say. I dine with her and the colonel this afternoon. In fact, it's high time that we go ashore, if we are to accomplish anything today. Bosun!' Pendexter shouted down to the waist.

McDuff turned and raced aft. 'Sir?'

'We shall need the longboat and crew—' he began, but Dibdin's powerful voice cut him off.

'Boat ahoy!' he shouted. All heads turned and looked over the starboard rail. A cable away a small boat was pulling for the *Icarus*, the four oars manned by smartly dressed seamen, a midshipman in the stern sheets.

'Dispatches!' came the voice of the midshipman. 'And orders from Admiral Graves!'

Pendexter took up the signal glass and trained it on the boat. 'Dear God, it's Thornbird.'

'You know him?' asked Smeaton.

'He's a midshipman on the *Preston*. A most ill-natured fellow. Well, we'll see how sharp his tongue is aboard my ship.'

Thornbird brought the boat easily alongside and scrambled up the boarding steps. He was followed by a seaman carrying a full canvas bag.

Pendexter remained aloof on the quarterdeck. Thornbird looked around before spotting him, then stepped aft.

'Ah, Lieutenant Pendexter, there you are,' he said, stepping up to the quarterdeck.

'I believe that courtesy dictates that you should address me as *captain*.'

'Indeed. Quite the to-do aboard last night, what?'

'Yes, it was a fine affair. Please forgive my not inviting you. It was really just for the quality of Boston; you may not have been at ease.'

'Oh, no offense taken. I wouldn't have come for anything. Not with the way the admiral was fuming and inquiring what the hell you were about. No thank you. Guilt by association, and all that.'

This sufficiently unnerved Pendexter that he was not able to reply, so Thornbird continued, 'I have dispatches here, sir, and letters to the West Indies.' He indicated the bag at his feet. Smeaton snatched up the bag and Thornbird pulled a sealed letter from his coat pocket. 'Orders from Admiral Graves to Lieu . . . Captain Pendexter, sir,' he said, handing the letter over.

115

'Thank you,' Pendexter said, taking the letter and plucking nervously at the hard wax seal. He tore the letter open and had begun to unfold it when he realized that Thornbird was still standing in front of him. 'Thank you, Mr Thornbird. That will be all.'

'I'm to wait in case there's a reply for the admiral.'

'Yes, fine, then wait in the waist, if you please.' Pendexter turned his back to the others as he unfolded the page, afraid that the note was some kind of censure. He was not disappointed.

To: Lt James Pendexter, commanding HM brig *Icarus*

From: Admiral Graves, commander in chief, North American Station

Sir:

Your orders, given you Thursday last, were quite clear regarding the need for haste in carrying dispatches and letters to the West Indies Station. Yet I find that three days later I must send the dispatches to you as you are still at anchor. Please take the mail, which the midshipman has delivered, and proceed to sea at once, in keeping with your written orders. If there is some reason that this is not possible, please send an explanation back with the midshipman.

Your obedient, humble servant,
Adm. S. Graves, R.N.

Pendexter folded the letter and tucked it in his coat. He could feel his face burning from the rebuke

116

and hoped that he was not blushing. He looked out to windward, feigning great interest in the weather. When he felt composed again, he turned to the master and Smeaton.

'Please prepare to get under way. It seems we are called on urgent business. Bosun! Prepare to weigh anchor!' Pendexter waited for the ship to burst into activity, but no one moved. Rather, they stared at him in disbelief.

'Weigh anchor? Now?' asked Dibdin.

'Yes, Mr Dibdin, damn it! It is traditional in the navy to go to sea on occasion!'

'Lieutenant?' Thornbird called from the waist.

'I have nothing to send to the admiral, so please go back to the flagship. We have enough to do here without tripping over you,' Pendexter said, trying to antagonize the midshipman, but Thornbird's expression had undertones of smug amusement. Pendexter wanted to strike him.

'Very good, Lieutenant. Good day,' he said with a quick salute. Thornbird was back in the *Preston*'s boat before Pendexter realized that the midshipman had twice addressed him as *Lieutenant*.

'But we've only a third of our water!' Dibdin continued once he again had Pendexter's attention. 'Thirteen of the liberty men are still ashore! So is the purser! Surely the admiral did not mean to weigh this instant? We should have a bit more notice than this!'

'I will not discuss the admiral's orders! They are for my eyes alone! Damn the liberty men, we shall have to leave them!'

'Sir,' called McDuff, 'shall we weigh or set the guns to rights first?'

'Weigh anchor, I said, now!'

117

'Sir, I can't give the admiral his proper salute with the guns we got on deck now!' whined the gunner, and Pendexter was about to answer when a voice hailed from the foretop.

'Water hoy putting off, sir!'

'We haven't time for that. We shall have to make do with the water we have,' said Pendexter.

'The purser will have to be reimbursed for his stores. Do you wish to act as purser in his absence, sir?' asked Dibdin.

'No, I do not! Hoist the recall and . . . Gunner! Fire a gun to leeward. If that don't get them, they will remain behind.'

'Purser's over in Charlestown, I believe, sir. I don't know how you'll work his reimbursement with the Admiralty.'

'Do you still want the longboat over the side, sir?' asked McDuff, and that, for Pendexter, was the end.

'Damn the longboat, damn the liberty men, damn the purser, just get the damned brig under way and do it now, you Billingsgate bastards, or I shall break you all!' and with that he stamped below, shouting, 'Call me when we're at short peak,' through the scuttle as he pulled open the door to the great cabin, ripping it from its hinges in his fury.

118

CHAPTER 8

Prisoners of the Crown

Biddlecomb and Rumstick stared at the lieutenant but did not move. A low murmur ran through the tavern, and men began to shift restlessly. The marines leveled their muskets, stiletto bayonets sweeping back and forth, and the cocks of twelve flintlocks clicked into the firing position.

'Sergeant, place these men in handcuffs,' said Norton.

The sergeant of marines, nearly as big as Rumstick and certainly as powerful, moved to the lieutenant's side. 'I only gots one pair, sir.'

'Very well. Place them on Rumstick there. If Captain Biddlecomb gives us any grief, then just shoot him.'

The sergeant grabbed Rumstick by the collar of his coat and pulled him to his feet. Biddlecomb hoped that Rumstick would not fight; it was easy to see the carnage that would result if a riot broke out. But Rumstick was still and sullen as the sergeant placed the handcuffs on his wrists.

'Right. Get up, you,' the sergeant said to Biddlecomb. Biddlecomb slid across the bench and stood beside Rumstick. He felt light-headed, like in a

119

dream, the kind from which you can usually force yourself awake. It was impossible that his luck could be so miserable. He struggled to maintain his superficial calm.

Lieutenant Norton stepped to one side, and behind him the file of marines stepped apart, six right and six left, leaving an aisle between them that stretched to the door.

'You seem to have a great deal of experience extracting citizens from taverns,' Biddlecomb observed.

'March,' said Norton, giving him a shove from behind. Biddlecomb walked down the corridor of soldiers, and he heard Rumstick's heavy tread behind him. The eyes of the young marines moved constantly, searching the crowd, while the points of their bayonets described little circles in the air.

The two men emerged onto the cold, black street and stood in the light cast from Sabine's windows. Biddlecomb heard the sergeant and Norton step behind them, and then the rasp of the marines' boots as they withdrew from the tavern.

'To the waterfront. You know the way,' came Norton's voice from the dark. Biddlecomb and Rumstick began walking, and the footfalls of the soldiers soon became the ordered clash of practiced march. Biddlecomb heard the sound of steel sliding on steel and knew that Norton and the sergeant had drawn their swords.

There were other sounds as well, other footsteps. The tavern had emptied onto the street, the drunk and excited mob following the procession to the waterfront. From the commotion, there seemed to be at least a hundred men. They had been moved to

120

violence already that day, before this outrage, before they had begun to drink. Biddlecomb half-turned again, trying to see how many Americans were following the cavalcade down to the harbor. Biddlecomb could hear their pace increase as they grew bolder. He half-turned once more, trying to judge the emotions of the crowd, and received a painful jab in the side.

'Eyes front, Brother Jonathan!' said Norton, prodding Biddlecomb again with his sword. Biddlecomb turned and faced forward.

The party was moving quickly down the hill. Biddlecomb could smell the water. The street was quiet save for the marching soldiers and the increasingly vocal crowd.

'Let them go!' shouted someone in the crowd, and other voices joined in.

'You've no right, you British bastard! It's agin the law!' another shouted. Biddlecomb heard a rock skip across the cobblestones, and another bounce off a storefront. Behind him a marine grunted and stumbled, and the dull thud of rocks striking the soldiers' heavy coats became more frequent.

He heard a rock strike just behind him, heard the sergeant stumble and curse.

'Marines, quick step!' the sergeant ordered, and together the marines began to advance at a jog. Biddlecomb felt himself pushed from behind and saw the sergeant shoving Rumstick ahead. The two men began to jog as the crowd behind them became more vocal still.

'You best run, you rascals!'

'Let them go, you bloody-backs! You sons of bitches!'

121

The party reached the bottom of the hill. Two cables away, across the wide street that bordered the waterfront, Biddlecomb could see the HMS *Rose*'s longboat bobbing next to the quay, the blue-jacketed crew resting easy at their oars. Beside the port stood a midshipman. The prisoners and their escorts jogged faster. Biddlecomb's breath was coming in gasps, and beside and behind him he heard the others breathing hard as well.

The longboat was only half a cable away now. Biddlecomb could see the midshipman clearly, tall and gangly like a boy who has grown quickly. He stood beckoning the approaching party with a wave of his arm, an absurd and useless gesture. They ran on in a hail of rocks and abuse, the crowd behind them keeping pace, their anger tangible.

Biddlecomb ran faster, urged on by Norton. He knew that the marines were on the verge of breaking into an open, panicked run for the boat.

'Marines! Form up!' shouted the sergeant, and the pounding of the marines' boots stopped, and Norton, Biddlecomb, and Rumstick ran on alone. Biddlecomb slowed his pace, and Norton, gasping, did the same. They turned to watch the rearguard action. The marines had formed into double lines, six of them dropping to one knee, all twelve muskets leveled at the Americans. The mob came to a ragged halt in the face of the weapons, some men caught with arms in the air, pausing in the act of hurling a stone. They fell silent, the marines and the colonials facing off on the dark road. Someone threw a stone, but it missed the motionless soldiers.

Then with a synchronization like a ballet, four of the marines peeled off from the line and retreated to

122

covering positions, then the others broke off as well, retreating beyond the pickets and in turn covering them. The colonials moved quickly over the ground yielded by the marines, gaining momentum as they charged.

Biddlecomb and Rumstick were shoved into the longboat. Biddlecomb made his way to the bow. Behind him he could hear Rumstick struggling and grunting. He turned to help. Rumstick fell hard against one of the seamen.

'Watch it, mate,' the sailor admonished.

'I'm in bloody handcuffs! What do you expect?' yelled Rumstick. Biddlecomb grabbed his friend under the arm and helped him forward.

The first group of marines had made it to the quay as well. 'Get in the boat! Get in the boat!' shouted Norton, who stood, sword in hand, on the cobbled street. The marines began to pile in as the pickets fell back.

The colonials flung themselves on the escaping British, who broke into a run under a hail of rocks and insane shouting. The Americans had closed the gap to ten feet when the sergeant gave the order.

'Fire!' he shouted, and four muskets went off as one. In the muzzle flash Biddlecomb could see a man's face explode as his body jerked backward. Two others fell and a fourth screamed and clutched his arm, which now hung like a broken branch. The colonials stopped, shocked by the flash and the noise, and in that instant the British turned and flung themselves into the longboat.

'Give way! Give way, all!' shouted Norton as he leapt into the stern sheets, the last of the party to board. The banks of oars came down and swept

123

the water, and the longboat moved forward. The Americans ran down to the water's edge, but twenty feet of water was already between them and the receding boat. One by one the Americans left off their shouting until all stood silently, and Biddlecomb, facing aft, saw them turn and walk back up the hill as the longboat disappeared downriver.

The night was quiet as they pulled away from the shore, the only sound the rhythmic grinding of the oars in the tholes and the splash of the blades in the river. Biddlecomb's eyes were quite adjusted to the dark, and with the full moon above he was able to see a great deal. The seamen at the oars lined the sides of the longboat, and the marines sat between them, erect, muskets held upright in a symmetrical line. In the stern sheets the sergeant sat erect as well, facing the marines. The midshipman held the tiller, and beside him Lieutenant Norton slouched on the gunwale.

Biddlecomb looked outboard of the longboat to the anchorage that was slipping past. Half a dozen merchantmen lay at anchor, and he was able to pick out the *William B. Adams* from the others. No lights were aboard her, only the anchor light hanging from the forestay, and there was no movement on her decks. He turned and looked at Rumstick, but Rumstick was staring at the bottom of the boat, his face expressionless.

Biddlecomb turned his attention back to the merchant fleet. The jibbooms of the ships all pointed due north now, like needles on a compass, and Biddlecomb saw that the tide had turned and was ebbing fast. He could see the water curling around the stems of the ships and streaming down their sides. An old piling came into view and the longboat rushed past it, and in a few seconds it was lost to Biddlecomb's view. The current was moving even faster than he had originally thought. The men at the oars would be grateful.

'You seem to have come without your frigate, Lieutenant,' Biddlecomb called out pleasantly, hoping to gauge Norton's mood and break the funereal silence.

'The *Rose* is at anchor off Prudence Island,' replied Norton, who then, in a harsh tone, added, 'The prisoners will remain silent!'

It was as fine a night as one could hope for in January in Rhode Island. It was cold, but not unbearably so, and there was little wind. Soon they had left the lights of Providence behind, and as they slipped down the river, their way was lit only by the moon. Occasionally they heard the rustle of an animal that had come to the river to drink and was startled by the boat. Near Fields' Point a deer suddenly thrashed its way to the shore, only ten yards from the bow, and a startled oarsman missed his stroke, fouling the man astern of him. Norton issued a terse and superfluous order, and the oars fell into rhythm again.

With each mile they made downriver Biddlecomb felt increasingly unwell. He had no delusions about the fate that awaited him, and he was staggered at how quickly his fortune had changed. He had always been lucky, things had always worked out for him. It was as if, in two days, he was being made to balance the account for the previous sixteen years of good fortune. He tried to ignore his growing nausea by making mental note of each spit of land, each

125

navigational hazard on the familiar Providence River. He had navigated this stretch of water by night as often as by day, and every turn, every bar, was familiar to him.

But landmarks could not distract him for long, and soon his thoughts were back on his legal predicament. The facts were undeniable. He had run the *Judea* aground with a full cargo of illegal molasses. He had participated in the cannoning of a British frigate. Norton knew it. Wallace knew it. He knew it. There would be no convincing a judge otherwise.

And that was not the end of the problem. Biddlecomb did not know where he would be put on trial, but he imagined that it would not be in Rhode Island. It could be Boston, or even England, where the possibility of angering the local population with a stern sentence would matter not a whit. His sentence would most likely be death. That at least was better than festering for years in some hellish prison, growing mad by degrees.

Biddlecomb turned and looked at Rumstick again, wanting desperately to see a sign of hope in his friend's face, but Rumstick was still staring impassively at the bottom of the boat. Biddlecomb turned his gaze outboard again, noting the familiar landmarks as the swift-moving longboat slid past. He ticked off Pomham Rocks, Sabin Point, and Bullock Neck as they were lost in the dark astern. He knew that Namquit Point now lay off the starboard beam, and on it the charred remains of the schooner *Gaspee*. He resisted his temptation to turn and look, instead watching Norton for some reaction, but Norton did not move from his slumped position in the stern sheets.

126

The longboat sailed past and the wreck came into Biddlecomb's view over the starboard quarter. The frames of the vessel were visible above the falling tide. They reached out of the sand, a giant black claw appealing to the heavens, the river boiling around them. The frames and the lower part of the foremast, which lay off the larboard side of the wreck, were all that remained of Lieutenant Dudingston's command. Biddlecomb glanced at Rumstick again, but even the sight of his previous action failed to arouse his interest.

Biddlecomb watched the land glide past and felt suddenly uneasy, and he knew that something was wrong, knew something more than his current situation made him feel that way. It was a feeling developed after years of inshore navigation, like an alarm bell ringing in the back of his head, but he could not tell what it was.

He looked to his right, toward the eastern bank, but it was too far to be seen, even in the generous moonlight. He looked over at Rumstick. Now his friend was looking up as well, a confused expression on his face.

The land that had been tending away from the longboat was tending back again, fifty yards off the starboard side.

Biddlecomb leaned against Rumstick, leaning his head a little toward Rumstick's ear. 'Conimicut Point,' he whispered, and even as he pronounced the words, the longboat staggered to a halt, hard aground on the sand lying two feet below the surface. The marines fell like bowling pins, landing in a red, cursing, thrashing heap. The sailors did not fare much better, and at least one man dropped his oar.

127

Biddlecomb watched it as it was swept downstream. The current was moving even faster than before.

'God damn it!' Norton exclaimed as he regained his seat. Biddlecomb scrambled upright as well, grabbing Rumstick under the arms and helping him up. The current had already caught the stern of the longboat and was swinging it around, pivoting the boat on its grounded bow.

'Over you go, you men!' ordered Norton, and the sailors leapt over the gunwale into the waist-deep water. Biddlecomb heard sharp intakes of breath as the men hit the frigid river. They grabbed the side of the boat and began to push in an uncoordinated manner.

'No, no! Belay that!' shouted Norton. 'Larboard side, push away; starboard side, pull toward you!' The men obeyed, pulling and pushing with audible effort, but the current held the boat fast on the sand.

'Get the bloody bullocks out of the boat,' suggested an anonymous voice from the dark.

'Watch your bloody gob!' screamed the sergeant, who then, in a gentler tone, added, 'Right, marines, out you go.'

There was a clash as the marines laid their muskets down on the thwarts, and then they followed the seamen over the side.

The longboat sat noticeably higher, relieved of the weight of over a ton of men and gear. The sailors and marines were now able to swing the boat back into the stream, and with hands still gripping the side they began to walk it over the shallows.

Biddlecomb turned, just barely, toward Rumstick

128

and looked up at his friend. Their eyes met, and Biddlecomb could see that they shared the same thought.

'Wait for it,' Rumstick said under his breath, and Biddlecomb nodded, so slightly that only Rumstick could see.

It seemed to take an inordinate time for the soldiers and sailors to walk the boat across the bar, and Biddlecomb feared that his feigned disinterest was wholly apparent. He looked at the men on the starboard side, just feet from where he sat. They were not pushing the boat any longer; rather they were holding it back in the curent. Biddlecomb felt the soles of his feet tingling like mad and he pressed them down hard to deaden the sensation. He saw Conimicut Point passing astern and knew that they were almost over the bar.

Just then the forwardmost man spoke. 'Water's getting right deep here, Lieutenant.'

'Very well—' said Norton, but he got no further.

Biddlecomb leapt to his feet, screaming like a banshee, and snatched up one of the heavy oars that lay across the thwarts. The sailor in the water beside him let go of the gunwale and yelled in surprise. Biddlecomb swung the oar in a great sweeping arc and smashed it into the men holding the starboard side of the boat. They let go, as much from surprise as pain, and the boat began to spin sideways. Rumstick fell on his back and lashed out with his feet, kicking the men within his reach on the larboard side. Biddlecomb swung the oar back, catching the other marines and sailors on the larboard side, knocking them away from the boat. A marine grabbed the blade of the oar and tried to pull him off-balance,

129

but Biddlecomb let go of the oar and the marine disappeared astern.

'Son of a bitch!' cried Norton, leaping to his feet. A few men in the stern still clung to the longboat beyond the reach of Biddlecomb's flailing oar, but now the current had a solid hold on the big boat and was sweeping it downstream. One by one the men lost their grip, flailing about in the water as they did.

Biddlecomb looked aft. Norton was standing now. He jerked his sword from his sheath and advanced forward between the seats as the sergeant struggled to his feet. Biddlecomb looked down for a weapon. There were muskets, but he doubted that they were loaded, and he did not care to counter an agile sword with a clumsy bayonet. A cutlass was on the thwart as well, left behind by one of the seamen. He snatched up the unfamiliar weapon and held it horizontally above his head as Norton slashed down on him. The heavy blade absorbed the shock of the blow.

He drew the blade back and swung at Norton, but the lieutenant had recovered and parried Biddlecomb's stroke. The sergeant blustered past Norton, anxious to join the fight. The clumsy marine sliced at Biddlecomb, but there was no room to swing and Biddlecomb easily deflected the blow, in the same move pivoting and slashing at Norton. Norton's sword caught the cutlass, but the strength of the blow threw him off-balance. Biddlecomb stepped forward and jammed his shoulder in Norton's chest, toppling the lieutenant back over the thwart, and turned to see the sergeant thrusting the point of his sword at his belly. Biddlecomb twisted and the blade pierced his jacket. He lashed out with his left hand, seizing the hilt of the sergeant's sword, preventing

130

him from drawing back, and smashed the hilt of his cutlass into the surprised man's face. He released the sergeant's sword as the marine toppled backward, then turned to face Norton as the lieutenant regained his feet.

The two men faced each other in a dueler's stance, each waiting for the other to make a move that could be exploited. Norton thrust, Biddlecomb parried and brought the cutlass around and slashed down, but Norton caught the blade with his hilt and twisted the cutlass aside. He thrust again, and again Biddlecomb parried using the weight of the cutlass to push the sword well away, providing himself with an opening. He slashed at Norton, his eyes fixed on Norton's throat, but the lieutenant was quick and his sword stopped the stroke that would have killed him. He took the full force of the blow on the thin blade of his sword, which broke like a toy six inches above the hilt. Biddlecomb drew back again and stopped, both men panting and looking at the broken weapon. Biddlecomb lowered the cutlass to his side.

'Congratulations, Biddlecomb,' said Norton. 'You will, of course, hang for this.'

'I had figured on hanging anyway.' Biddlecomb looked down at the sergeant, who still lay on the bottom of the boat, gripping his jaw. 'Get his keys and take the manacles off Rumstick.'

Norton bent down to obey, and suddenly the night exploded with noise and light and a blinding yellow flash from the stern of the boat. Biddlecomb felt his jacket jerk as if someone had tugged on it, hard, and he and Norton and Rumstick shouted out in surprise. Biddlecomb was blinded by the flash and stood motionless.

131

'The midshipman!' he heard Rumstick shout. Looking aft, his eyes beginning to see again, Biddlecomb could make out the shape of the midshipman standing in the stern sheets, his dirk in one hand, the smoking pistol in the other. Biddlecomb's vision grew stronger and he could see that the midshipman was trembling.

'Throw the pistol and the dirk over the side,' Biddlecomb ordered. 'Do it or by God I'll run the lieutenant and the sergeant there through.' He waved the cutlass at the officer kneeling before him.

The midshipman wavered, looking to his lieutenant for advice, but Norton remained silent. Then the midshipman turned and with a sob threw the weapons into the bay.

132

CHAPTER 9

Narragansett Bay

Ten minutes later the surrender of the longboat was complete. Norton and the midshipman sat in the bow, their hands bound behind their backs with lengths of cordage cut from the boat's painter. The sergeant sat beside them, still groggy, his face smeared with blood. Biddlecomb sat in the stern sheets holding a musket on the Englishmen while Rumstick kept the boat headed downriver with one of the long oars run out over the stern as the strong current continued to sweep them south.

'That was something, what you done with that cutlass,' said Rumstick. 'I didn't know you was a hand with a sword.'

'Did you not? Fencing is the only sport that I ever excelled in. Stanton taught me.'

'Damn handy sport, I reckon.'

They continued on in silence until at last Prudence Island was visible in the moonlight. Twenty minutes later the boat ground up on the rocks of Northwest Point. Rumstick went forward to untie the prisoners.

Biddlecomb turned to the two officers, who were rubbing their wrists where the rope had bound them.

133

The marine sergeant sat beside them, his head in his hands. 'Right you three, get out.'

Norton looked at him, confused, as if he had expected to be shot.

'Walk east and you'll find the *Rose*. Now get out of the boat,' said Biddlecomb, 'or I'll shoot you.'

Then Rumstick helped them, none too gently, to disembark.

The *William B. Adams* was a typical medium-sized merchant vessel, around three hundred tons by Biddlecomb's estimate. Her round bows and slab sides bespoke a vessel built to carry a great deal of cargo, if not necessarily to carry it fast. Her simple functional elegance reflected the attitudes of her North River builders and her Providence owners. She had none of the gaudy trim, gilded and painted, so in evidence on the ships of the British East India Company.

Biddlecomb considered these points as he watched the *William B. Adams* rounding Newport Neck under topsails and forecourse.

'Here she is,' said Biddlecomb, kicking Rumstick, who lay prone on the boat's wide bottom.

Rumstick stirred, cursed softly, and rising on one elbow, peered over the longboat's gunwale. 'Dog's a bit, ain't she the finest ship you ever seen?'

'Normally I would say no, but in these circumstances I have to agree.'

They had stepped the boat's mast after their prisoners had gone, and with the offshore breeze that came with the rising sun, they had run the length of Narragansett Bay, passing Castle Hill at ten o'clock that morning. For the rest of the day they had lain concealed in the marsh between Price and Cherry Creeks, exposing the stolen boat only enough to afford them a view of the shipping as it went in and out of the bay. They had no doubt that they were, by now, being pursued, but Narragansett Bay, with its many inlets, islands, and shallows, was ideally suited for eluding pursuit. They never saw one of the searchers.

Biddlecomb turned his face into the wind. The *Adams* was at least two miles off, and it would be a tricky business to intercept them.

'Let's get that lugsail set,' said Biddlecomb, and Rumstick moved to obey. They each grabbed a halyard, and in a moment the sail was hoisted and rippling in the breeze, and Biddlecomb took up the tiller.

'Sheet it home, and get the jib set as well,' Biddlecomb said. The longboat gathered way, emerging from its hiding place, suddenly lively as it met the Atlantic rollers head-on. With only two men in a boat built to carry fifty, the motion was quick and uncomfortable. The longboat bucked at every swell, showering the occupants with spray, and as they left the lee of the land, they could feel the breeze increase in force. 'Take a pull in that sheet, will you, Ezra?' said Biddlecomb, his eyes never leaving the ship, now a mile distant.

The *Adams* was picking up speed, her bluff bow rising and falling as it met the offshore swell and sending spray flying as high as the tip of her jibboom. 'We'll back the jib and heave to, let the *Adams* run down on us,' said Biddlecomb a moment later. Rumstick hauled the jib around and

135

the longboat's headway was checked. She rode up and down on the waves like a gull resting from flight.

The boat lay directly in the *Adams*'s path, but it still took a great deal of shouting and arm waving to attract the attention of those on deck, so occupied were they with final preparations for sea.

'There's Peabody, there!' exclaimed Rumstick, pointing at the portly figure on the quarterdeck who now held a telescope to his eye. Rumstick waved with renewed vigor, and the man turned and said something that sent the crew scurrying for bowlines and braces. The *Adams* turned slowly to larboard, as her mainsails swung around with a squeal of blocks. The way came off her and she lay still on the sea, rising and falling with the longboat.

'Get that jib set,' said Biddlecomb, taking his place at the tiller. Two minutes later the longboat swooped up to the leeward side of the *Adams*. Rumstick tossed what was left of the painter to the men, about twenty in all, who crowded the rail. He grabbed hold of the boarding steps and scrambled up the side with Biddlecomb right on his heels.

Captain Peabody came forward, hand extended. 'Rumstick, you dog!' he said, pumping Rumstick's hand with genuine delight. 'We quite despaired of ever seeing you again. Figured you to be rotting in some prison hulk somewhere. Welcome aboard!' The rest of the crew stood around, some grinning and slapping Rumstick's back.

'We managed to convince Wallace to let us go. He even give us the use of his longboat, gracious fellow!' said Rumstick.

'Oh, this is just great,' said one of the men in the

136

crowd. 'We got back our bosun who's a bloody traitor!'

'Pleased to see you too, Haliburton,' Rumstick said.

'You can keep them opinions to yourself, Mr Haliburton,' Peabody said, his voice angry.

'So Wallace allowed you the use of his boat?' said another voice from the fringe of the crowd. Biddlecomb turned to see the speaker. He wore a black coat and stained breeches, and his long neck and hooked nose made him look more like a bird than any man that Biddlecomb had ever seen.

'And when it is discovered,' the man continued, 'I have no doubt that we shall all end up in a prison hulk. The British will not thank us for harboring escaped prisoners.'

'Mr Fry!' said Peabody with ill-disguised exasperation. 'I do at times wonder where your loyalty lies.'

'My loyalty,' said the sour-looking Fry, 'lies with the ship and her owner, and I do not wish to see the *Adams* seized by the British.'

'You traitorous, blackheart bastard,' Rumstick began, then Haliburton cut him off.

'He ain't the traitor, mate. He may be a piss-poor seaman, but he ain't no traitor. You're . . .'

Biddlecomb stood back, amused by the display and impressed with the way Haliburton had in one sentence insulted both the first mate and the bosun. He wondered how long Captain Peabody would tolerate it.

'Stop this! Stop this at once, do you hear? Haliburton, shut your gob,' Peabody commanded, and all fell silent. 'Mr Rumstick is welcome aboard this ship and always will be. Mr Fry, this is my responsibility

137

and you will follow orders. And you, sir,' he said, turning to Rumstick, 'will show the mate the proper respect or I'll set you ashore, damn me if I won't. Is that understood?'

'Aye, sir,' said Rumstick.

'Indeed,' said Fry.

'Very good,' said Peabody. 'Now remember, we're all of us Americans here, there ain't no need for politicking. This time of year the sea is like to give us all the problems we need. I think we best sink that longboat and get under way.'

'One more thing, Captain,' said Rumstick. 'This here's my good friend, ah . . .'

'Jack Woodhead,' said Biddlecomb brightly.

'Jack Woodhead, exactly,' said Rumstick. 'Now, Jack here is a seaman, able-bodied, can hand, reef, and steer. I had hoped as you might be inclined to offer him a berth.'

Peabody looked Biddlecomb over. 'Can hand, reef, and steer, can you?'

'Aye, sir. I've been going to sea these sixteen years past.'

'Well, if Rumstick says you're able, that's all I need to hear. Mr Fry, put this man on the books, rated able-bodied. Mr Fry here is first mate. Mr Fry, this here's . . . what's your name again, son?'

'Jack Woodhead.'

'Why, damn my eyes, that there's young Captain Biddlecomb!' shouted a voice from the crowd. The watching seamen were pushed aside, and to his great dismay Biddlecomb saw Hezekiah Harted limping toward him and wiping his filthy hands on a more filthy apron, a week's growth of beard on his face, his blue eyes wild.

138

'You recall me, don't you, Captain? Hezekiah Harted! I sailed with you back in '71, on the old *Judea*.'

Biddlecomb did indeed remember him. He had shipped him for that one trip and had then deemed him too insane even to sail before the mast. Peabody evidently did not share that opinion, or he did not yet know Harted.

'Hello, Hezekiah. How have you been?' asked Biddlecomb, wishing that the man would go away and knowing that he would not.

'Fair to middling, Captain, fair to middling. Too old to be a foremast jack, so I'm shipping out as cook. Damned disgrace.'

'Biddlecomb?' asked Fry, pushing his way through the assembled men. 'You say you're Jack Woodhead, a seaman, and Harted here calls you "Biddlecomb," and "Captain Biddlecomb" no less.'

'Hezekiah is right. My name is Biddlecomb. I apologize for the deception but—'

'Ain't never been a driver like young Captain Biddlecomb here!' interjected Harted. 'I recall when we was ten days out of Rio, one of them there pampero squalls comes up and—'

'That's quite enough, thank you, Hezekiah,' Biddlecomb interrupted. 'I'm a foremast hand now, so let's leave it at that.'

But Fry would not leave it. He considered Biddlecomb through squinting eyes. 'You come aboard this ship, and the first thing out of your mouth is a lie. And now, sir, you claim to be a ship's captain? We have a captain aboard this ship and we do not need another.'

'I wish to sail before the mast, nothing more,'

139

replied Biddlecomb in as meek a tone as he could manage.

'Aye,' interjected Harted with a laugh, 'until he has a mind to be first mate, Mr Fry, and sends you packing forward!'

Biddlecomb and Fry glared at the cook.

'Sir,' said Rumstick, addressing Captain Peabody. 'I'm sorry for this here mess. I figured it would be best if Isaac didn't give his real name, or tell what he's done. But he'll do just fine as a foremast hand. He'll do his duty and keep his mouth shut, ain't that right, Isaac?'

'That's right.'

'Oh, hell, yes!' Harted interjected. 'Captain Biddlecomb can do anything he sets his mind to!'

'Will you stop calling me that, God damn your eyes!' shouted Biddlecomb. Harted assumed a wounded expression, then turned and shuffled away.

'All right. We've wasted far and away enough time on this already. Biddlecomb, I expect you to obey orders like the others or I'll set you on the beach. Mr Fry, put Biddlecomb on the books.' Peabody turned to the crowd of men, who were watching the altercation like spectators at a cockfight. 'I'd like to get under way again, if it don't disturb you gentlemen's leisure.' The crew was already scattering by the time he could follow that up with a cry of 'Hands to the braces!'

The men were still casting off the main braces when Peabody roared, 'Let go and haul!' The order was nearly lost in the fire of a swivel gun mounted ten feet from where Biddlecomb stood. He wheeled in surprise. Three men stood behind the smoking gun, grinning and peering over the side. The swivel had

140

blown ten feet of garboard out of the longboat, and already the boat was half-full of water and sinking fast.

Biddlecomb felt a sensation of relief, like reclining in a warm bathtub, a sensation of having escaped. He looked north toward the land they were leaving in their wake. Then he remembered that he had felt that same way after passing Castle Hill in the *Judea*, and again after leaving Bristol aboard the *Nancy*, and the sensation was gone.

Overhead the main yards swung round again and the mainsails filled out with a snap. The *William B. Adams* settled down on her course again, to follow the trade winds due east for nearly two thousand miles before turning south. She was bound away for Jamaica, bound away across the stormy Gulf Stream.

CHAPTER 10

'Then to Proceed with All Diligence'

The *Icarus* had not been under way for twenty-four hours before the men left behind in Boston were gravely missed. It had not occurred to Smeaton that their absence would require him to rework the sail-handling stations, and it had not occurred to Dibdin that a first officer might have to be reminded of that fact. The result of this combination of omission and assumption was that when the men were called to station for tacking ship at the change of watch at four o'clock in the morning, there was not a man to attend to every duty that required attention, and in the darkness their absence was not noted on the quarterdeck.

Bloody Wilson stood at the forward pinrail, starboard side, his hands resting on the main topsail brace. Behind him stood the two waisters who backed him up in bracing the main topsail yard when tacking. The waisters were not seamen per se, they certainly did not rate as able-bodied, but they were big men and what they lacked in intellectual power they made up for in strength of arm. Wilson would provide any seamanship that was necessary.

'Ease down your helm!' shouted Pendexter from

142

the quarterdeck. It was the new captain's first time tacking the brig. His voice sounded louder than necessary.

Forward in the darkness the fore topmast staysail and jib began to flog. The noise was intrusive and distracting on the hushed deck, but to Wilson it was the familiar prelude to this maneuver.

'Helm's alee!' shouted Pendexter, and the flogging grew louder as the foresheets were cast off and the sails streamed aft in the wind. The stars began to sweep past as the brig turned. The fore topsail wavered and flogged, then came hard back, followed by the main.

'Mainsail, haul,' muttered Wilson to himself, anticipating the next order. The main topsail was coming hard aback as the brig continued to turn. 'Mainsail, haul, now,' muttered Wilson, 'or we'll have the devil to pay bracing this bugger around.'

'Mainsail, haul!' shouted Pendexter, and Wilson grabbed the main topsail brace and jerked it out and down, out and down, as the waisters took up the strain. The yard creaked slowly around, three feet, six feet, and then it stopped. Wilson could feel in the brace that something was not right aloft, something was holding the yard back. It was not just the wind. Wilson had been enough years at sea to know every nuance of a line under strain. He could read the message in the rope. And then he remembered Wright.

Wright was the maintopman whose job it was to cast off the main topsail bowline when coming about. If the bowline was not cast off, it would hold the edge of the sail in place and prevent the yard from bracing around. And Wright was, at that moment,

143

somewhere in Boston, which was now over two hundred miles astern.

'Mainsail, haul, God damn your eyes!' shouted Pendexter. Wilson wanted to call out for the bowline to be cast off, but calling out was frowned upon in the Royal Navy and would no doubt earn him a stripe from McDuff's starter.

He turned to the waisters behind him. 'Cast off the main topsail weather bowline!' he hissed, but the waisters just stared at him with looks of bewilderment.

'Cast off the buggering bowline!' he hissed again.

'God damn you!' shouted Pendexter. 'That man there!' He pointed at Wilson. 'Mind your business and haul or I'll know why! You have got us in irons! Get some more men on that brace!'

Before Wilson could object, he was surrounded by four more men, each reaching for a grip on the topsail brace. It was too late to save the evolution, Wilson could see that much. The brig was indeed 'in irons,' pointing straight into the wind with her sails all aback.

'Mainsail, haul!' Pendexter shouted again, and the waisters hauled with a will, pulling Wilson with them. By now it was pointless, of course. Even if they could brace the main topsail yard around, it would not get them out of irons. Wilson wondered where Dibdin was. The lieutenant could benefit from his advice.

The waisters flung themselves back against the resisting brace, hauling a few inches of slack. They straightened and jerked again, and this time the yard gave way and the men fell to the deck in a flailing heap. Overhead they could hear the tearing and

144

thrashing canvas. Wilson knew that the weather leech had torn clean out of the main topsail.

'God damn it to hell!' cried Pendexter, fairly leaping off the quarterdeck and racing forward. 'Why wasn't the bowline cast off?' he demanded of the deck in general. 'Who is stationed at the weather bowline?'

Wilson wondered why Smeaton did not know the answer to that question, such things being the responsibility of the first officer. But Pendexter was not asking Smeaton and Wilson remained silent as befitted a man-of-war's man.

'Who is responsible for this weather bowline?' Pendexter demanded again. Forward the jibs pounded in confusion, flogging in the wind. The square sails were firmly aback and the brig was wallowing in irons, slowly making sternway. Wilson was glad that they had plenty of sea room, and that the wind was not blowing hard.

'I want the man responsible or, God help me, I'll flog you all!' Pendexter shouted. His voice was starting to sound unnatural.

'Wright,' said a voice in the dark. Wilson recognized the voice. It was Israel Barrett.

' "Right"? "Right" what? What does that mean?' said Pendexter, menacing and calm.

'David Wright, maintopman, sir,' Wilson said, breaking his silence.

Pendexter turned on him. 'And where is this "Wright"? Why is he not attending his duties?'

'He was left on the beach, sir. In Boston.'

There was silence, save for the flogging headsails, and then Pendexter turned on his heel and marched back to the quarterdeck.

145

'Sheet home those headsails!' he ordered. 'Main-mast, let go and haul!'

When Pendexter announced the next morning that punishment was to be meted out for the fiasco of missing stays, Wilson was not surprised. He expected an announcement of sail maneuvers. He expected to see the crew tack and wear ship, tack and wear ship, set the douse sail, strike yards and masts to the deck. He expected a day of constant, exhausting drills, where the men were run until they dropped. That, in his experience, was the way punishment was handed out in the navy. It was disagreeable and it made for a crack crew all at the same time.

The fact that the men did not necessarily deserve punishment for the affair was irrelevant. A certain amount of injustice was to be expected by the lower deck, a certain amount, and no more. Punishment for something that was clearly the first officer's fault was nearing the edge.

But the sail drills did not materialize. Instead Pendexter turned the men over to the boatswain, assuming, apparently, that allowing McDuff to do with the men what he wished was severe enough punishment. In this Pendexter was right.

And there was nothing that McDuff loved more than to see the *Icarus* scrubbed, scraped, blackened, and painted. He first ordered the decks holystoned with far more than the usual care. The operation took four hours, with all hands working, and when at last McDuff was satisfied, the men were set up with paint and tar and brick dust to polish the brass. The masts were painted again, the anchors chipped and blacked again, the standing rigging and woolding received fresh tar. This was certainly punishment, Wilson

146

considered, though he did not see how it would help them to better put the brig about the next time.

McDuff and Longbottom were everywhere, up and down the decks and aloft, seeing everything, coming down on any perceived sloth like the wrath of God, their starters in constant motion. Pendexter had given them free rein to enforce discipline and punish as they saw fit, that much was clear to Wilson. He hoped that Pendexter would soon realize what kind of men they were and bring them under control. He reminded himself that it had taken Bleakney a week to comprehend McDuff's and Longbottom's sadistic inclinations and to reign them in again.

Wilson looked down the shank of the best bower, which he was chipping and blacking, at the young man who was assisting him. Boy, really; Wilson doubted he was above sixteen years of age. There was a nasty welt on his left hand, and dried blood on his cheek where Longbottom's starter had slashed him. He had been in the navy only five months, and he was not very bright in any case, on shipboard or otherwise. As he scraped at the anchor stock Wilson could see that he was on the verge of crying.

'You keep at it, Wilson, and no daydreaming,' Longbottom spoke from the bow. Wilson turned and looked at him.

'Don't you worry about me, Edward Longbottom,' Wilson said slowly.

'You just watch your gob, Bloody Wilson. You may think you're the crack foretopman here, but I know different, and so does the bosun.'

Wilson stared into Longbottom's eyes, noticing for the first time how unusually far apart they were. He

147

waited for a moment, knowing that he could unnerve Longbottom with his silence. 'What is it you're saying, Longbottom?' he asked at last.

'I'm just saying that this here captain ain't like Old Lady Bleakney with his bleeding "Don't be so hard on the men!" This here captain, he appreciates me and Mr McDuff, and he told Mr McDuff that him and me, we're to keep discipline how we sees fit. So don't you be mouthing off to me, Bloody Wilson, because it don't matter now how much the foremast hands like you, or the master likes you, 'cause me and Mr McDuff are running this show, like we should be.'

Wilson stared into Longbottom's reptilian eyes, considering the threats, real and implied, in his words. Pendexter did not seem overly concerned with running the ship, Smeaton even less so. There was little that Dibdin could do in that circumstance, particularly if Pendexter had given McDuff explicit orders to maintain discipline in his own way. The bosun and his mate could make the *Icarus* into a perfect hell ship.

Longbottom shifted uncomfortably and Wilson realized that he had been staring into his eyes this whole time. He turned without a word and continued to chip away at the anchor.

'And don't let me catch you slacking off again, there,' Longbottom yelled the threat at Wilson's helper over the ring of the chipping hammers, 'or you'll feel my starter again, I promise.' With that he turned and walked aft.

The four men that sat at mess table six were generally a happy group. They had managed, through the naval custom of allowing men to switch messes every month, to assemble a companionable and professional clan. With Wilson as part of the mess they rarely lacked for conversation, and with Barrett there as well they rarely lacked for stories. Paul Harland, foretopman, was, after Wilson, the best seaman on board. The fourth member, David Wright, had been left ashore. Even having one-quarter of the mess gone would not, under normal circumstances, greatly reduce the lively chatter usually associated with that mess.

But today they ate their dinner in silence, as did the rest of the lower deck, and the only human sounds heard above the groaning of the brig were the occasional grunts or curses of a ship's company at mealtime. Even the infinitely amusing speculation on the doings of David Wright, still somewhere in Boston, could not shake the introspective silence of the troubled men. Wilson ripped the last bite of salt pork apart with his teeth and began to gnaw on it.

'Bleeding Longbottom ain't let up, has he?' he said. Silence on the lower deck bothered him. It was a sign of trouble on shipboard.

Barrett grunted. 'It's like living his dream, him and McDuff. Bleeding captain letting them do as they please.'

They continued to eat in silence, hunched over the wooden table under the low deck beams and eating dried peas with their sheath knives.

'I'm gonna get that bastard, I tell you, next time we get a run ashore. Find him alone . . .' Harland said, but Israel Barrett kicked him hard in the shins and gestured with a nod of the chin toward the brick

149

oven that occupied a large portion of the forward end of the lower deck.

Bolton stood by the oven, his stooped back stooped even farther under the low deck beams, clasping his bony hands together and waiting for a pot of water to boil. He was trying hard to appear uninterested in the conversation, and Wilson had no doubt that he hoped to carry gossip as well as boiling water back to Pendexter. Wilson had never known a captain's steward who did not keep his position secure by keeping the captain informed of what was said on the lower deck.

At eight bells the following morning, after the *Icarus* had spent a frustrating night slatting in the light airs, Bloody Wilson was quite content to lay aft and take the helm. He enjoyed his trick as helmsman, enjoyed the feel of the thick tiller against his thigh, the subtle nudges that he would give to keep the brig on its true course, the way the lively vessel responded to the rudder.

And this morning he had more reason to relish his hour trick, for it was an hour that he was safe from the ministrations of the bosun and his mate. They had started in early that morning, rousing the watch below for duty, cutting down hammocks and striking the last men to appear on deck. They had inspected each hammock before it was stowed in the netting, cursing any man whose hammock was not perfectly rolled and forcing him to roll it again. The men had muttered, looking aft to the quarterdeck for relief, but the first officer had the deck and he was staring off to windward and seemed unconcerned with the routine in the waist.

Wilson stepped aft to the tiller and nodded to

150

Dibdin, who stood, as he always did during his watch, just foward and to the weather side of the helmsman.

'East by southeast,' said the man at the tiller as he relinquished his charge to Wilson.

'East by southeast, aye.'

'Looks like we're finding our wind again,' commented Dibdin, nodding toward the sails, now billowed and firm. 'How's your weather helm, Wilson?'

Wilson bounced the tiller off his thigh, feeling the weight on the bar. 'She seems right, sir,' he said, testing the helm again. 'She's fine, sir, fine as you please.'

'Good. Let me know if she gets too much with the wind building. We can take in that main topmast staysail.'

'Aye, sir,' said Wilson, and the two men returned to their thoughts as the brig pushed on, east and south.

The holystoning was still under way, a majority of the ship's company crawling on hands and knees to the most inaccessible corners of the deck, when Pendexter and Smeaton appeared on deck. A ship's boy struck one bell and the officers stepped up onto the quarterdeck. Three paces behind came Bolton, carrying Smeaton's pistol case, a horn of powder around his neck.

Pendexter took up the slate on which were written the hourly log entries and glanced over it, then replaced it in the binnacle box without comment. He looked down the length of the deck, then up at the set of the sails.

'All's well, I trust, Mr Dibdin?' he asked cheerfully.

151

'Right well, sir.'

'I see Mr McDuff is hard at it, keeping the *Icarus* as smart as she can be.'

'He's still a bit free with his starter, sir. Drives the men harder than what he needs to. You might have a word with him about that, sir,' said Dibdin, turning to the lieutenant.

'Well, now, Mr Dibdin,' said Pendexter, a bit flustered. 'I don't see Mr McDuff complaining about your navigation, so perhaps you should not concern yourself with how he does his job.'

But Dibdin would not be put off. 'Beg your pardon, sir. I mean no disrespect, but I've been in a great many ships, and I can tell you, it may seem that McDuff is keeping discipline, but he ain't. The way he treats the men is the very worst thing for discipline. Go down on the lower deck sometime, during dinner, and see how quiet it is. That's foul weather on the horizon, sir.'

Pendexter cleared his throat and glanced out to windward before turning back to the master. 'Now see here, Mr Dibdin. Mr McDuff believes in a taut ship and so do I. I tolerate no slackness aboard the *Icarus* and I expect my officers and warrant officers to do likewise. To tolerate no slackness, I mean. If the men attend to their duties, they have nothing to fear. Mr McDuff may be harsh, but he's just in his discipline.'

Wilson knew that Pendexter had made that speech as much for his benefit as for Dibdin's, hoping that Wilson would carry the word to the lower deck, hoping that he would regale the crew with the story of the firm but fair captain. Not bloody likely.

152

'Aye, sir,' said Dibdin, stepping forward off the quarterdeck and disappearing below.

Smeaton stepped up to the break of the quarterdeck and hailed the bosun. 'I say, Mr McDuff, I shall need a hand, if you can spare one.'

McDuff nodded and looked around. He poked a nearby seaman with his starter. 'Here, Barrett, lay aft and report to Mr Smeaton, and shake a leg.'

Barrett stood and walked aft, stopping at the break of the quarterdeck and saluting. Wilson could see from the neutral expression on the old sailor's face that he was expecting Smeaton's order to be stupid.

'Very good, ah, what's your name?'

'Barrett, sir. Israel Barrett, foredeck man.'

'Yes, very good, Barrett. Now look here. I want you to run down to the gunroom where you'll find a case of empty wine bottles. Take them up to the larboard cathead there. I'll give you a signal, and each time I do, I want you to toss one of the bottles over the side, toss it about four fathoms from the ship. Do you understand?' Barrett nodded. 'Very good. Run along then.'

Barrett looked at Wilson and raised his eyebrow in a manner so subtle that only Wilson was aware of the gesture of disgust, then he disappeared below.

'Bolton!' called Smeaton, turning aft. 'I say, load those pistols, and I'll thank you not to spill powder all over the deck this time.'

The two officers stood on the leeward side of the quarterdeck for half an hour peppering the waves with pistol balls. From what Wilson could divine from their conversation, and from the occasional stolen glance over the side, there was a great disparity

153

in the men's skills, Smeaton being the superior marksman. As slow as the brig was moving, there was time for only one shot apiece. Pendexter always took the first shot, and generally he left the bottle intact for Smeaton to finish off.

'It's really a matter of knowing the weapon, James,' said Smeaton after Barrett had thrown the last of the bottles over the side. 'And I've had these pistols ten years now, since I was a lad, and I practice with them constantly.'

'Yes, no doubt you're right, John. No doubt practice makes the difference,' said Pendexter, though he did not sound mollified. Wilson had never heard two officers on duty addressing one another by their first names. That this was the captain and first officer made it odder still.

'The practice is essential,' Smeaton continued. 'You know that I've been called out, or been forced to call others out, over half a dozen times in the past five years. Were I not a practiced shot, I should be dead long ago.'

'Quite so. Still . . .' began Pendexter, but Dibdin was back on the quarterdeck. He approached the officers and saluted.

'Beg your pardon, sir, but I imagine you've noticed the glass this past hour?'

'Uh, yes, certainly, Mr Dibdin,' Pendexter said. 'And, uh, what do you make of it?'

'Well, it's fallen fast, sir, and still falling,' Dibdin replied, as if no more needed saying.

'Yes, well . . .' Pendexter said, glancing around. It appeared to Wilson that Pendexter was not quite certain what to make of Dibdin's report, but he did not see how that could be possible.

'It's going to blow like a bastard, sir,' Dibdin supplied.

'Oh. Well, we had best get the topgallant gear off her, what?' Pendexter said brightly.

'I think,' said Dibdin, 'that would be a fine idea.'

CHAPTER 11

William B. Adams

It was much colder now, and the sun had not made more than a token appearance in several days. This was a notable change from the weather that the *William B. Adams* had seen in the three days since they had left Block Island over the horizon. During that time the skies had been crystalline blue, the wind cold out of the northwest, a steady fifteen knots of wind that pushed the *Adams* 130 miles during each twenty-four hours. The sea came in long rollers, but only on those occasions when the *Adams*'s blunt bow slammed headlong into a wave, and a veil of spray was flung aft along the deck, did it intrude upon the ship.

But that was past, and Isaac Biddlecomb did not need to look at the barometer to know that it was steadily falling. The sky was a uniform dark gray and the sea reflected and mimicked that color. The long rollers were topped with a short, steep chop, and the ship regularly butted these waves, resulting in an almost constant spray raining down on the deck and soaking men and gear. The wind had hauled around to the southeast and built steadily, and Biddlecomb knew that it would continue to do so.

156

Rumstick and Biddlecomb paused in the main top and ran their eyes over the topsail that they and the combined watches had just reefed. 'I fail to see why Fry waited until now to tuck the deep reef,' Biddlecomb said. 'If we'd done it two hours ago, it would have taken fifteen minutes, not an hour and a half.'

'Fry's afraid to crack on sail, but once it's set, he's afraid to take it in. He ain't any kind of seaman.'

'So why does Peabody ship him as mate?'

'He's family, I understand. Nephew or something. But I'll warrant Peabody's about had it with him.'

'I would imagine.'

'Come,' said Rumstick, grabbing a topmast shroud and swinging outboard of the main top, his foot searching for the futtock shrouds, 'let's lay to deck and see what's in store for us. Striking topgallant gear, if I don't miss my guess.'

Rumstick did not miss his guess, and no sooner had the two men set foot on deck than Peabody called Rumstick aft and ordered him to roust out all hands and get the topgallant masts and yards down. Biddlecomb was not surprised, as the wind was still building, and there was no telling how hard it would blow. He personally would have waited another watch at least, but of course Peabody knew his ship best.

Twenty minutes later, John Haliburton, the acerbic ship's carpenter, stood in the waist, his arms folded, his face twisted in a triumphant gloat. 'You won't find the damn top rope neither, on account of that thieving Rumstick went and sold it!' he announced to the men rummaging around the bosun's stores and the

157

forepeak for the three-hundred-foot coil of rope used to send the topgallant masts down to the deck.

Haliburton was not a man who kept his opinions bottled up, whether they concerned Fry's utter lack of seamanship or Rumstick's treason against the king, to whom Haliburton remained obstinately loyal. He seemed to have no regard for what he said or whom he offended. Biddlecomb was not surprised to see that a feud between the bosun and the carpenter led to a certain amount of inefficiency in the ship's operations.

The topgallant yards had been struck without the top rope, thanks to Rumstick's system of using the halyards for striking the light spars. Biddlecomb had attended to the main topgallant yard, tossing around one hundred feet above the deck, his hands numbed to the point of being useless, while below him, and just audible over the wind, he could hear Rumstick and Haliburton argue over the length of the handspikes, the greasing of the windlass, the right of the British to tax Americans, and the lead of the yard rope.

An hour later Biddlecomb returned to the deck, chilled throughout, to be greeted by the carpenter's triumphant accusation.

'I didn't steal the top rope, you infernal, whoreson British tool, so shut yer bloody gob,' said Rumstick, who was becoming increasingly irritated. 'I'm going to stick—'

'The top rope is still in the tiller flat,' Biddlecomb said, sick of the bickering and clasping his hands under his arms as he waited for the feeling to return. 'It was never shifted back to the forepeak. Did either of you idiots look in the tiller flat before you began to hurl accusations?'

158

Forty-five minutes later, the top rope was roused up and sent aloft, the snatch blocks located and moused in place, the windlass greased to Rumstick's satisfaction, and the virtue of the mother of every man who had joined the fray called into question.

'Sweet Jesus, Rumstick, are you still working on that fore topgallant mast?' asked Peabody, arriving on deck from the chart room.

'Aye, sir. And it's a crime. It's the carpenter, sir.' Rumstick kept his voice low so that it was just barely audible to every man on deck. 'I try to see he does his duty, I help him when I can, sir, but he, well . . .' Rumstick made a gesture that suggested drinking.

'Why you lying whore's son,' protested Haliburton, but Rumstick raised his hand to silence him.

'Mr Haliburton, please. We are ready to send this topgallant mast down and your constant arguing is holding us up.'

Haliburton spluttered and turned red, the waiting seamen grinned, and Peabody stamped his foot in frustration.

'Damn you, Rumstick, you don't fool me!' Peabody yelled. 'I see what's going on here! The two of you work together, and damn your politics, and get that mast on deck now, or I'll send you both packing forward! Do you understand?'

Rumstick and Haliburton nodded and Peabody stamped aft to the quarterdeck, leaving the seamen grinning at each other.

'Fine, let's get to it,' said Rumstick, casting around for friends of Haliburton's to send aloft in the frigid, howling wind. 'Coggins, Pope, lay aloft!' he shouted, and the two crestfallen men climbed onto the shrouds and struggled upward.

159

It was another hour before the fore and main topgallant masts lay on the deck, securely lashed to fore and main fife rails. The rain had started even as Coggins and Pope were climbing aloft, a freezing, blinding rain, driven horizontal by the wind and mixing with the spray to form a continuous shower of icy, brackish water that soaked the men. As Biddlecomb toiled with the others in the growing gloom, he tried not to think of his oilskins, hanging dry and warm in the forecastle, which he did not have a moment to fetch.

It was six bells in the afternoon watch before Biddlecomb and the rest were allowed below to eat supper and fetch their oilskins. Peabody was still standing the watches down, allowing the men their four hours below as was the routine, but Biddlecomb guessed that this would end with the worsening weather. He would be surprised if all hands were not required on deck for the entire night.

'My apologies for the grub, Captain Biddlecomb,' said Hezekiah Harted as he ladled out a cold stew, the fat lying in a congealed solid on the surface. 'Captain Peabody says no galley fires, on account of the weather.'

Biddlecomb looked into the man's wild eyes, and then down at the filthy apron and equally filthy trousers, neither of which, he knew for a fact, had been removed since the onset of the voyage or, he imagined, for some time before that. He had given up on asking Harted to please not address him as *Captain* Biddlecomb.

'That's all right, Hezekiah,' Biddlecomb said, trying to escape before the man engaged him in conversation. Biddlecomb preferred a cook who did not physically revolt him, though he had rarely encountered one.

'You got your secret place yet, Captain?'

'Not yet, Hezekiah,' said Biddlecomb, backing away and fighting to maintain balance on the heaving deck. The ship groaned in her twisting agony, and the swinging lanterns threw wild, dancing shadows that made the cook appear even more macabre.

'Well, you best hurry. We could meet them any day.'

Biddlecomb nodded and smiled and hurried into the forecastle and away from Harted. He elbowed a seat at the long table and began to shovel the noxious stew into his mouth.

'He's right, you know, Isaac,' said Haliburton, whose behavior often approached sociable when Rumstick was not around. The carpenter stepped into the forecastle and settled down with his own cold stew. 'You better find your place, and soon.'

'What place?' asked Biddlecomb through a mouthful of stew. 'I thought he was just loony.'

'He means a place to hide. Some good place in case we get boarded by an English press gang.'

'A press gang! On the high seas? Why in the hell would we be boarded by a press gang?'

'English man-of-war needs men, they board any merchantman they come across and take who they need. English, American, it don't matter to them.'

'It's illegal to press Americans!'

'They still do it.'

Biddlecomb was stunned. He had heard rumors of British impressment on the high seas, but he had never given them any credence, and he had never

161

taken any kind of preparations aboard his own ships. Had he just been lucky all this time?

'Do you yourself know anyone, personally, who has been pressed that way?' Biddlecomb probed.

Haliburton was silent as he chewed and swallowed a stubborn piece of meat. 'Sure,' he said at last. 'My last ship, the *Salem* out of New York. They stopped us and took three men.'

'Why didn't they take you?'

'Couldn't find me. I was the ship's carpenter. I had a good place.'

Haliburton turned his attention back to his stew while Biddlecomb pushed a piece of meat around his plate with the point of his sheath knife. He turned this new information over in his mind. A new line of questioning occurred to him.

'But, John, you're a loyalist, and a vocal one at that. Why did you hide from the English?'

Haliburton snorted and shook his head. 'You stupid? You think just 'cause I believe Americans is British subjects I want to serve in the damn navy? You think in London they don't hide from the rutting press? Lousy rations, bloody hard work, and floggings all the time, little pay, and you're lucky if you gets that, and never let off the ship 'cause a pressed man will run every chance he gets. That life ain't for me. I got a wife and four kids in Providence.'

Haliburton waved his sheath knife at Biddlecomb for emphasis and continued, 'And unless it sounds good to you, you best see me after this blow about setting you up with some place.' He scooped up a knifeful of stew and shoveled it in his mouth. At last, with a reluctant tone he added, 'I'll set Rumstick up with a place too, but don't you go telling him I

162

said that. That son of a bitch has been fighting against the British for five years and more, now. Fighting for American independence. You can forget independence if you're pressed; you're no better than a slave. Rumstick'd lose what little mind he's got if he were pressed. Reckon I would too.'

The sound of the storm, muffled in the warm forecastle, suddenly came shrieking down into the tween decks with the opening of the scuttle, and with it came a frigid blast of air. Biddlecomb heard Rumstick shouting over the wind.

'All hands on deck! Tumble out! Tumble out! All hands on deck!' The men in the forecastle shoveled the last of their dinner into their mouths and reached for their oilskins and southwesters.

Biddlecomb had anticipated the weather worsening, but he was surprised, as he emerged from the shelter of the lower deck, at just how far the weather had deteriorated in the past hour.

It was black night now, though the sun was an hour from setting. The wind was like a solid thing that struck Biddlecomb and sent him reeling from the unexpected blow. He grabbed the main fife rail to steady himself and hung on as he regained his bearings.

Under close-reefed topsails, fore and main staysails, and a deep-reefed mizzen, the *William B. Adams* was plunging through the night. The seas had built to well over thirty feet, towering over the *Adams*'s bow, flashing white from their crests as they rolled down on the little ship. The *Adams* came down, down, into the troughs as the black sea reared up ahead, then lifted and rose to the wave, up until it seemed that the sea would hurl the ship into space. Then the

163

water passed under the keel and the ship sank, sickeningly, into the trough again. The scene was illuminated, frozen like a painting, in the many flashes of lightning, and the roar of the wind was joined by an almost continuous rolling thunder. The wind drove the rain and spray horizontally over the deck, and every breath brought with it equal parts air and water.

Biddlecomb saw that the watch had rigged lifelines down the length of the deck to which one could cling when moving fore or aft. We'll need those, he thought, and as if to prove the point a boarding sea crashed over the bow and the water ran waist deep down the length of the deck. Biddlecomb felt something slam against his legs. He plunged his hand down and grabbed a fistful of cloth and hung tight as the water receded and revealed the *Adams*'s apprentice, Eliphalet Fox, spitting and sputtering on the wet deck. Biddlecomb dragged him to his feet and placed his hand on a secure handhold.

'Watch out for green water coming aboard!' Biddlecomb shouted his advice over the wind. 'When you see it, clap hold of something or you'll be swept away! Wrap your arms around the standing rigging if you can!' The boy nodded, but he appeared half-dazed and Biddlecomb wondered if he really understood.

'Come with me! We'll lay aft and see what the mate needs done!' he shouted again, and half-dragged the boy across the deck to the lifeline. He placed Fox's hand on the stout line, and Fox, understanding its function, nodded and entwined his arm around the rope. Biddlecomb nodded back and they began to work their way aft.

164

Rumstick was two yards in front of them, staggering forward, before Biddlecomb saw him. Rumstick put his face to Biddlecomb's ear and shouted.

'Peabody wants you aft on the wheel! But I need your help first! Best bower's about to carry away!'

The loss of the best bower, the ship's primary anchor, would be unfortunate, but the greater threat was of the anchor's doing extraordinary damage as it flailed about prior to carrying away. Biddlecomb nodded. 'We best bring him with us!' he shouted, jerking his thumb toward Fox.

'Right! Fox, you stick with us, hear?' shouted Rumstick. The boy nodded and Rumstick stepped around them and led the way forward.

The best bower, nearly two tons of forged iron, was held to the side with one remaining lashing, and it slammed fore and aft five feet with each plunge of the bow, the inboard fluke tearing soggy hunks of wood from the bulwark, the shank slamming against the cathead and threatening to dislodge it. Haliburton was already there, coils of rope over his shoulders, and without a word the three men fell to securing the anchor. There was no argument now; for all of Haliburton and Rumstick's animosity each respected the other's abilities in matters of seamanship, and now there was no thought for anything beyond the ship.

For forty-five minutes Biddlecomb, Rumstick, and Haliburton wrestled with the anchor, passing lashings and hauling taut as the anchor slid into position. Their throats burned from the salt water they swallowed and from screaming just to be heard. Biddlecomb drew the final frapping turn tight as the

165

bowsprit buried itself in an oncoming wave and the sea boiled over them.

'Lay ahold!' Biddlecomb shouted at Fox, dragging the boy to the deck and clapping hold of the lifeline as Rumstick and Haliburton did the same. The sea crashed down on them, the open ocean pounding over their arched backs, the pressure tearing at their grips as the water swirled aft along the decks. And then the bow rose again and the ship shook off the tons of seawater and lifted to the next wave. The spritsail yard had carried away in the onslaught and disappeared astern, leaving a tangle of shredded cordage hanging from the bowsprit.

'Won't do any harm, not with the jibboom run in!' shouted Biddlecomb as the men looked at the damage.

'Ain't a damn thing we can do now, anyway!' replied Rumstick. He turned and worked his way aft, with Biddlecomb, Haliburton, and Fox following in his wake.

They made their way from the bow to the quarterdeck, pulling themselves hand over hand along the lifeline and twice pausing to hold tight as the decks went awash. At last they reached the quarterdeck where Peabody and Fry and two miserable helmsmen were riding out the night. The helmsmen had lashings around their waists that were tied in turn to a ringbolt in the deck. The lashings would keep the men from being flung overboard if the wheel suddenly spun out of control.

Peabody stood aft by the wheel and Fry huddled beneath a leecloth triced up in the mizzen rigging, seeking what pathetic shelter it offered.

'Where in the hell have you been, God damn your

166

eyes!' Fry shrieked when Biddlecomb was a few feet from him. 'You were to relieve the helm over a glass ago! Damn you, we have no time for your slacking in this weather, God damn your eyes!' Fry readjusted his grip on the mizzen shroud. He sounded, to Biddlecomb, as if he had gone completely insane.

Biddlecomb stepped around the mate and struggled aft to the helm, young Fox following behind.

'Best bower's secure, and the spritsail yard's gone! Nothing we can do about it!' Rumstick was shouting this at Peabody, though the two men were almost face-to-face. Peabody nodded, then pointed down the after scuttle, indicating that he was going below. Rumstick nodded as well, pointing forward to indicate the direction that he was headed.

Biddlecomb stepped up behind the helmsman on the weather side of the wheel and grabbed the spokes, freeing the man's hands and allowing him to untie his waist lashings. He turned to see Larson, the big Swede who occupied the bunk just above Biddlecomb in the forecastle, doing the same on the leeward side. Five minutes later Biddlecomb and Larson were lashed to the ringbolt and the weary men who had stood at the wheel for the past five hours struggled forward. Biddlecomb looked around for Fox. The boy was standing at his side and a little behind, and Biddlecomb imagined he was as safe there as anywhere.

The wheel fought with all the cunning of its ilk, sometimes going limp in the hand as the ship rode over a wave, sometimes giving a savage kick as the stern buried itself. But Biddlecomb fought back with the experience gained through hundreds of hours at

167

ships' wheels, and Larson lent his own experience and strong arms to the effort. Nonetheless they were exhausted after fifteen minutes, and Biddlecomb thought grimly of the three and a half hours that they had yet to go.

Peabody stepped through the scuttle and onto the quarterdeck, his body momentarily framed in the dim light from the chart room. He shut the doors quickly and was lost to Bidddlecomb's sight. And then he appeared again at Biddlecomb's side, peering first at the compass, then out to sea, then up at the sails.

'Mr Fry!' Peabody shouted, and his voice was just audible on the quarterdeck. 'Mr Fry!'

The mate jumped and turned quickly, stepping across the deck to the captain.

'We are getting set too far north!' Peabody continued. 'I am afraid we shall find Nova Scotia under our lee! We must wear ship! We must do it now!'

Fry said nothing, just stared at Peabody and shook his head in small movements from side to side. It was a dilemma, Biddlecomb could see that. They had to turn the ship, somehow. It was obvious to anyone that they could not tack, could not put the bow of the ship through the wind and let even the little canvas still aloft come aback. That would tear the sticks clean out of her. But even the longer and safer maneuver of wearing ship, turning her stern through the wind, would be no mean feat in those winds and seas. But it had to be done. It was better than piling up on a lee shore.

Biddlecomb had been wondering about Nova Scotia. They had been driving along on a starboard tack for some time now, and with the set of the Gulf Stream . . . Of course Biddlecomb had not been able

168

to see a chart, but his mental dead reckoning seemed to be in agreement with Peabody's navigation. But how to wear ship? The fore staysail would have to go once the stern was through the wind, of course, or they could never hope to get the bow back up into the wind. Yes, first tend to the fore staysail, then ease the helm over as the *Adams* mounted a swell . . .

Biddlecomb worked his calculations from force of habit, and in his mind he had the ship halfway around on the other tack when an uneasiness intruded on his thoughts. He looked up, unsure of what was wrong. And then he knew. The *Adams* was not rising to the swell.

There was a rhythm to the waves, and Biddlecomb's body was used to that rhythm, and it told him that now the ship should be rising, cresting the next wave. But it was still sinking, farther and farther down into a valley of water. And that could mean only one thing: the wave that was rolling down on them now was bigger than the rest, vastly bigger, a freak of wind and sea. A rogue wave.

Biddlecomb peered forward, and in the flashes of lightning he could see it, a mountain of water, twice as big as the huge seas over which they rode, and hurtling down on them as they in turn were sucked into the hole it pushed before it. He could see the boiling crest of the wave's top high above the deck.

He had no illusions about what would come next, when the water came down on the ship like the wrath of an angry God, and he hoped the *Adams* could take it. He felt his stomach convulse and he grabbed tighter to the spokes of the wheel. He glanced quickly at Larson, could see the same thoughts reflected in his face. If the *Adams* could not withstand the pounding, then in the next five minutes every man aboard her would die.

He looked quickly around the quarterdeck. Peabody and Fry had flung themselves into the mizzen shrouds, threading their arms and legs through the rigging. And Fox stood at the weather rail, one hand resting on the lifeline, oblivious to the danger.

'Get in the shrouds! Grab the shrouds, God damn it!' Biddlecomb shouted, but the boy just looked at him and shook his head to indicate that he could not hear.

'Get in the shrouds!' Biddlecomb shouted again, gesturing with one arm. He could not let go of the wheel, and even if he did, he was lashed in place by the line around his waist. In a second the water would be on them.

And then Peabody saw the boy. He leapt from the shrouds and grabbed Fox by the collar, yanked him around, and shoved him into the shrouds. Then the boy understood. He scrambled into the rigging, weaving his limbs between the lines.

And then the wave was on them.

The *Adams*'s bowsprit drove into the side of the sea as the breaking wave, seventy feet high, dropped its tons of water on the ship's frail decks. The water crashed down on the bow, submerging the entire ship to the foremast, and rushed aft sweeping away men and gear.

'Captain!' shouted Biddlecomb. Peabody did not have time to regain the safety of the shrouds. Biddlecomb abandoned his grip on the wheel and lunged at the captain, grabbing him in a bear hug and dragging him to the deck. He wondered if the waist lashing would hold them both.

170

The water struck with such force that Biddlecomb's breath was knocked away. It smashed the two men into the taffrail, rolling them over like paper blown in the wind. Biddlecomb strained to hold Peabody as the two men were lifted off the deck. The waist lashing came tight around Biddlecomb's body, as if straining to cut him in two.

They hung there, supported by the rushing water and pounding against the taffrail. Biddlecomb's hands came down on the wood with the force of Peabody's two hundred pounds. He felt his grip slipping.

'Hold on to me!' he screamed, and received a mouthful of water. He choked and gagged and tried to breath but only swallowed more water. It occurred to him that Peabody might be dead, killed in that first concussion of water.

A second rush of water came aft and Biddlecomb's feet were lifted over his head and he felt his waist come down on the taffrail, his breath knocked out again, his feet dangling in air over the stern. He grabbed the rail and dragged himself inboard. Then the seas fell away and the deck heaved and gleamed where Biddlecomb lay, and Captain Peabody was gone.

CHAPTER 12

Trough of the Seas

Biddlecomb pulled himself to his feet, clutching at the spokes of the wheel. He allowed himself a second, less than a second, to reflect on Captain Peabody's fate, then pushed the thoughts aside as more immediate concerns overwhelmed him.

The *Adams* was lying down on her larboard side, or nearly so, and the deck sloped away at a crazy angle. Biddlecomb held the wheel as much to keep himself from sliding away to leeward as to keep the ship under control. Slowly, painfully, the *Adams* shook off the tons of water from her deck and came upright, her sails slatting in the diminished wind between the two waves.

The ship had slewed around as the wave passed over, and now she was lying in the trough, broadside to the sea. Rather than meeting the huge waves bow-on, the *Adams* was now presenting her high, flat side to the sea, and the next wave would roll her completely over. Biddlecomb saw a figure moving down the starboard side of the quarterdeck, moving fast despite the ship's severe angle. It was Rumstick, laying aft for orders. Thank God he's all right, thought Biddlecomb. I need him now.

172

Rumstick came aft to the helm, squinting through the driving rain as he searched for the captain. Haliburton was just behind him.

'Ezra!' Biddlecomb shouted. 'Peabody's gone, over the side!' Rumstick nodded, and in that instance Biddlecomb made a decision.

'I'm going to wear ship, keep her coming around to larboard!' he shouted, and Rumstick nodded again. Behind him Haliburton was nodding as well.

Biddlecomb felt the ship rise and knew that the next terrific wave was upon them. If they remained sideways to the sea, as they now were, for even a minute longer, they would be rolled completely over. He heaved up on the wheel, putting the helm over to larboard, and Larson followed his lead. The *Adams* turned as she rose on the wave, turning her stern into the seas.

Haliburton clung to the cabin top for balance as Rumstick stumbled across the deck and grabbed the wheel from Biddlecomb. 'I'll take the helm! You see to putting us about!' he shouted, and Biddlecomb nodded, surrendering the wheel. He glanced over at Larson. The Swede was planted like a tree to the deck.

Biddlecomb jerked his knife out of the leather sheath strapped to the small of his back and cut the waist lashings away. The *Adams* was falling off now, turning her stern to the wind. That was good, for a few moments at least.

'Keep her coming around!' he ordered, staring aft at the oncoming sea. 'Meet her! Keep her stern to this next wave!'

A black shape materialized at his side. Biddlecomb tore his eyes from the water and looked. It was Mr Fry.

173

'I am wearing ship, Fry! Jump forward and see to the braces!' Biddlecomb shouted, but Fry did not move.

'You will do nothing of the sort! You are not in command here! I am!' Fry screamed, and Biddlecomb realized, to his surprise, that indeed he was not in command. Nonetheless, he knew that his actions were the only ones that would keep the *Adams* from foundering.

'We shall maintain this heading! Run before it!' Fry was screaming.

Perfect. Instead of being set down on Nova Scotia, they would sail straight into it. 'God damn it! Peabody said we had to wear ship! We're halfway around already! If we don't wear ship, we'll pile up on Nova Scotia!'

'I am in command! I shall not say that again!'

This was absurd, and worse, it was putting the ship in great danger. Biddlecomb felt the deck swoop up beneath him as the stern rose to the following sea.

'Fry, you stupid, no-sailor son of a bitch!' Haliburton was shouting across the deck. 'You want to kill us all?'

The *Adams* was running with the wind and the sea directly astern, and despite her much reduced canvas she was moving extremely fast. Biddlecomb braced himself as the sea lifted the ship. She surfed down the front of the giant wave, like a huge cart out of control and careening downhill, and Biddlecomb could not tell if the wave would pass beneath them or if they would bury their bow in the sea. If they buried the bow, then they would pitchpole. The bow would stop, like the front wheels of the cart suddenly locking up, and the wave would lift the stern and

174

tumble the ship end over end and she would be torn apart.

Biddlecomb squeezed the taffrail until his hand ached. He felt the ship move under him, saw the trough of the wave as they hurtled toward it. And then, suddenly, the deck sank beneath him and the bow rose high in the air, obscuring the sea. The wave had passed beneath them.

'We'll pitchpole for certain next time!' shouted Rumstick.

'Start coming around now!' shouted Biddlecomb. 'We'll wear ship now!' They were safest in the valley between the waves.

'No!' shouted Fry. 'You shall do nothing without my orders!'

Biddlecomb swung around to confront the mate and was nearly knocked to the deck as Rumstick's arm shot out and grabbed Fry by the collar. He jerked the mate like a rag doll across the deck until their faces were inches apart. His left hand never lost its grip on the wheel.

'Isaac is wearing ship! You tend to the braces!' That was all he said. He released Fry, pushing him away, and with a dexterity surprising for a big man he brought a leather seaboot up to Fry's back and propelled him forward. Fry fell to the deck, scrambling on his hands and knees until he regained his footing and disappeared forward.

Rumstick and Larson spun the wheel and the *Adams* responded, turning to larboard. Biddlecomb looked up at the deep-reefed topsails. They would have to be braced quickly or the sails would come aback and tear the rig apart.

The next wave was visible now, an avalanche of

175

water rolling down on them in the dark. They had turned half a circle and were broadside to the sea again, starboard side now, and again they were in danger of being rolled over.

'Turn, you motherless whore, turn,' Biddlecomb muttered to the ship beneath his feet.

A motion caught his eye. He looked aloft and saw the topsail yards swinging around, bracing up on the larboard tack. The canvas shook and then boomed out as the wind caught its after side. Biddlecomb felt the ship leap forward, turning faster into the wind. 'Mr Fry, all of your sins are forgiven,' Biddlecomb shouted, though he could barely hear himself.

And then the *Adams* stopped turning. Her broad, flat side lay exposed to the oncoming sea and she hung motionless, despite the drive from her topsails. Why? Biddlecomb had perhaps thirty seconds to think before the wave would roll them over. He turned to Rumstick.

'Is your helm still hard a-larboard?'

'Aye, hard over! She won't come round!'

And then Biddlecomb remembered the fore staysail. As the *Adams* wore around that sail must have come aback. Set on the bowsprit as it was, it would exert enough leverage to hold the bow down, to prevent the ship from turning. He had not remembered it.

He felt the deck rising again below his feet, felt the *Adams* heeling farther, now to starboard, and knew that the wave was on them and starting to push them down. He turned and raced forward, passing himself hand over hand along the lifeline to keep from falling on the steeply angled deck. He reached the break of the quarterdeck and leapt down, but his leather shoes

176

would not grip the wet and slanting deck. He landed in a heap, slid down to the leeward side, and came to a rough stop against the bulwark. His head slammed the planking and his eyes lost focus, but he shook it off and pulled himself to his feet.

Through the dark and the spray and the flashes of lightning he could see men at the pinrails, standing with braces in hand and clinging to rigging and lifelines. Biddlecomb grabbed the lifeline himself and hurried forward.

The *Adams* rolled farther as the huge sea overwhelmed her. Biddlecomb could see the water boiling over the starboard bulwark, boiling around his feet, as the ship rolled her rail under. They had already rolled past forty-five degrees and were still going over, heading for a knockdown. Biddlecomb wondered when the cargo would shift and end it all.

He pushed past the frightened men at the forward pinrail. Why didn't they see the staysail? Biddlecomb wondered. How could the staysail have held together this long?

And finally he was at the bow. The staysail sheet ran diagonally across the deck, straight and hard as an iron bar. The staysail was aback, a solid and unyielding thing holding the bow down, holding the *William B. Adams* broadside to the sea. Biddlecomb felt the ship roll again. Water poured over the bulwark and the starboard side of the deck was lost from view. They had seconds now before they rolled completely over.

Biddlecomb clawed his way up to the fife rail, more like climbing a ladder than walking a deck, grabbing fistfuls of rigging and hauling himself up until he could reach the staysail sheet.

177

He jerked the knife from his sheath and slashed down at the line. The blade touched it and the straining rope dissolved into its component yarns and parted with a sound like a musket, loud even over the howling wind. The staysail flew off to leeward, flogged twice, and was gone, torn into ribbons of cloth and blown off into the night.

Biddlecomb felt the *Adams* slew violently around as the bow, released from the pressure of the staysail, flew up into the wind, the ship coming upright as she turned. He prayed that Rumstick and Larson would meet her, check the swing, and not let her fly up into the wind. If the topsails came aback, the *Adams* would be a mastless hulk in seconds.

Biddlecomb hung on to the rigging, suddenly aware of the awful cramps in his hands. He loosened his grip as the ship came more upright. Up and up into the wind she came, the bow pointing higher and higher as the wave rolled under them. He felt the gale on his face, felt the changing angle of the wind as the ship turned.

Too far! They had turned too far! They were going aback! Biddlecomb thought, and there was nothing he could do.

And then the bow plunged down as the crest of the wave moved under the ship and the *Adams* paid off, turning away from the wind once again. Rumstick had not let her come aback.

Biddlecomb released his breath. They were safe, he thought. At least as safe as they could be.

Though the ship still heaved and bucked like an insane thing, she was no longer pressed down at that sickening angle, and it was not difficult for Biddlecomb to fight his way to the weather side and

178

grab hold of the lifeline. He wrapped his arm around the reassuring rope and staggered aft again.

He made his way up to the quarterdeck and aft toward the wheel. Fry was back, standing on the leeward side, well out of Rumstick's reach, seeming to be greatly absorbed in the workings of the ship.

'Biddlecomb! Come here at once!' he shouted, never taking his eyes off the rig. Biddlecomb stepped over to the leeward side.

'Biddlecomb, I am prepared to forgive your . . . act . . . and not bring you up on charges of mutiny, or Rumstick or Haliburton, if you will recognize that I am the captain of this vessel. I am the captain! And so help me, if you turn the men against me, I'll have you arrested and . . .'

Fry was working himself into a frenzy. He stamped his foot and stared into Biddlecomb's eyes with a pouting look so like a spoiled and petulant child's that Biddlecomb could not help but laugh. Fry stopped yelling and frowned.

'Aye, you're in command. Godspeed, Captain Fry.'

Fry's expression brightened. 'Good. Good. You go forward and see to any repairs that must be made.' He turned his eyes aloft once more, a signal to Biddlecomb that he was dismissed.

For two days the *William B. Adams* struggled along under the merest scraps of canvas, bashing her bows into the Gulf Stream rollers and tossing so violently that it was a great effort just to move about the ship. Every man aboard was exhausted from the effort, exhausted from the prolonged watches when all hands were needed to fend off one disaster or another, and exhausted from the fitful sleep they

179

found in sodden clothes and bedding and the fore-castle flying up and down with the seas.

During that forty-eight hours the ship drove east by south while the wind pushed her north by west and the Gulf Stream carried her north and east. The end result of these conflicting forces was that the *Adams* did not move significantly beyond the point where Biddlecomb had won her around.

Biddlecomb guessed that this was the case, based solely on his deduced reckoning, but he did not offer his opinions to Fry, and Fry most certainly did not ask for them. Indeed, Fry was hardly to be seen during the two days that the *Adams* fought with the storm, being wholly occupied with moving Captain Peabody's effects out of the master's cabin and moving his own property in.

On the morning of the third day, the larboard watch, of which Biddlecomb was a member, tumbled out on deck to find a clear blue sky, dotted here and there with budding white clouds, and a steady fifteen knots of wind from the northeast. It was the high pressure system that often rewarded those who lived through a storm, and the watch on deck was already shaking the reefs out of the fore topsail. All that was left to remind the men of the storm was the lumpy, big sea, the tangled wreckage on the bowsprit, and the absence of Captain Peabody's steadying presence aft.

Captain Fry stood on the weather side of the quarterdeck of the *William B. Adams* and stared absently out to sea. In the waist Rumstick was telling off the work parties, giving jobs to the off watch that would set the ship back to her original state.

In less than an hour the foredeck was transformed

into a makeshift rigging loft and sparmaker's shop and the larbowlines set to reconstructing the ruined gear of the spritsail yard. Cordage was heaved out on the stretch, wormed, parceled and served, and liberally coated with warm Stockholm tar. The men worked steadily at their stations, and Rumstick took full advantage of his captive audience to expound on his political doctrine. The end of the storm marked as well an end to the truce between the ship's political factions, and Haliburton and his crew set the spar stock from which they were fashioning the new spritsail yard directly to windward in order to rain wood shavings down on the bosun and his freshly tarred rigging.

In the great tracks of the North Atlantic, in a world generally at peace, there was little to threaten a merchant ship at sea beyond the sea itself. For this reason most merchantmen, including the *Adams*, kept, at best, an indifferent lookout when sailing on the deep water. The brig was almost hull up from the deck before she was sighted.

'Sail, ho!' cried Eliphalet Fox from the bow as he squinted over the water.

'I am pleased, Fox, that you managed to spot the vessel before it ran into us,' Captain Fry replied in the ironic tone in which he couched a majority of his remarks. He stood on the weather side of the quarterdeck, a telescope pressed to his eye.

The tasks of the rigging and sparmaking gangs were quite forgotten as the men crowded the rail, staring at the strange sail. It was the first that they had seen in a week. Rumstick, whose duty it was to drive the hands back to work, skipped up into the shrouds to get a better look.

181

The brig, which had been on an opposite tack from that of the *Adams*, was coming about. The *Adams*'s men watched the sails flog as the yards were braced around, and then the brig settled on the new tack, on a course to intercept the *Adams*. Biddlecomb swung himself into the shrouds and climbed up beside Rumstick.

'What do you make of her, Isaac?' asked Rumstick in a low voice.

Biddlecomb squinted over the bright water, running his eye over the rig, noting the loftiness, the cut of the sails, the length of the spars, the rake of the masts. It was the sails that troubled him.

'Look at those topsails, Ezra. And the topgallant. No roach at all, cut real flat.'

'What are you thinking?'

'They're man-of-war sails.'

'Could be Dutch, or a Frenchman.'

'Or a Don,' said Biddlecomb.

'Or a Don.'

The two men continued to stare at the brig as it charged down on them. A fluke in the wind heeled her over, and from around the big gaff-headed mainsail the ensign snapped straight out, broadside to the *Adams*, and then streamed forward again. There was no mistaking it. It was the ensign of the Royal Navy.

'Oh, sweet son of a bitch,' Rumstick muttered, and there was an edge of panic in his voice.

'Deck, there!' cried Appleby from the main crosstrees as the *Icarus* settled onto the new tack. 'She's a Yankee, sir, Yankee colors. On starboard tack, running to the northward!'

Pendexter stared out over the starboard rail, out at

the ship with which they were rapidly closing. Finally he turned and addressed the master. 'Mr Dibdin, we shall run down on the Yankee and order her to heave to. Mr Smeaton, you shall organize a boarding party. I want at least three prime seamen from that ship to make up for the loss that we suffered in Boston.'

Dibdin's mouth hung open. 'You don't mean to press men out of the Yankee, do you?'

'I most certainly do . . . Mr Hickman!' Pendexter called out to the gunner. 'A shot across her bow, please. Pray try not to hit her.'

Pendexter turned back to Dibdin and continued, 'Brother Jonathan is a subject of the Crown whether he believes it or not. I never hear these Yankees complain when the Royal Navy protects them from the French, or from pirates. Now they can bloody well serve in His Majesty's navy.'

'But the courts have ruled that Americans are not liable to impressment.'

'I do not see any courts out here, Mr Dibdin. Out here I am the law, and I will not kowtow like some weak-kneed magistrate who is afraid of the rabble. I intend to replace those men that deserted in Boston, whom, I might add, you were partially responsible for. If you are afraid, sir, you may go below.'

Pendexter could see Dibdin's hands twisting behind his back. The muscles in his jaw stood out. Then he spun on his heel and stamped up to the break of the quarterdeck.

'Clear away the longboat!' There was nothing else that he could say.

183

CHAPTER 13

A Place to Hide

If any question remained in the minds of the *Adams*'s men concerning the brig's intentions, the round shot fired from her bow chaser answered it. The *Adams*'s forestay parted and the outer jib collapsed and fell into the sea, wrapping itself around the ship's cutwater. The crew of the *William B. Adams* paused, just for a second, then turned as one and bolted for the scuttle, streaming around Biddlecomb and Rumstick.

' 'Vast! 'Vast running!' shouted Fry. 'Hands to the braces! Stand by to heave to, mainsails aback! Rise tacks and sheets!' The men reluctantly abandoned their retreat and moved to the pinrails, and five minutes later the *Adams* lay hove to on the confused sea.

Biddlecomb turned and looked over the windward rail, across the water to the brig. It was a hull up now, and even without a glass Biddlecomb could discern the long man-of-war's pennant snapping out from her masthead like a serpent's tongue. Her buff hull was set off by black stripes at the gunwale and waterline that ran from the stem aft to the small quarter galleries. The bulwark was pierced by

184

gunports, the guns run out. The brig turned and rounded up into the wind, her mainsails swinging around as she hove to.

There was no more time to watch.

Biddlecomb turned to ask the help of his shipmates and to his surprise found that the deck was practically deserted. The running rigging, usually coiled and hung neatly on the pins, was left in heaps on the deck. The leeward braces had not even belayed, and the lines swayed and undulated with the roll of the ship. Larson remained on deck, as did Hezekiah Harted and Eliphalet Fox. The rest were gone.

'You better hide yourself, Isaac. You too, Ezra,' said Larson.

'We will,' said Biddlecomb. 'But what about you, and those two?'

'I'm safe if I just jabber away in Swedish when them bastards come aboard, make like I don't speak English. They won't take me. They won't take Eliphalet, they're looking for prime seamen. And Hezekiah's too loony, even for the Royal Navy.'

'Where should we hide ourselves?' asked Rumstick. His usual calm was deserting him with the prospect of years of involuntary servitude to King George.

'The hold would be best,' Larson supplied. 'Right forward, where the casks go from four deep to three, I bet you could squeeze in, right agin the ceiling.'

Biddlecomb considered this. It was a good hiding place. Only a very determined search would find them there.

'You had best hurry.' This time it was Fry supplying the advice. Biddlecomb and Rumstick turned. The new captain was standing above them on the raised quarterdeck.

185

Fry nodded his head toward the brig. The British longboat was in the water and manned and the boat crew was casting off the yard tackles.

'Come, Ezra, let's get the hell out of here,' said Biddlecomb, hurrying, nearly running, toward the scuttle.

There was little air, and no light at all, in the *Adams*'s hold. Tier after tier of barrels had been stowed in even rows fore and aft, and when the hatches had at last been battened down, it was presumed that they would remain there, undisturbed, until the ship was alongside in Jamaica. Biddlecomb and Rumstick moved cautiously, their arms flung out before them, running their hands over any solid objects with which they came in contact, in an attempt to get their bearings.

'I'll hide on the larboard side, here. You take the starboard. It's better if we don't hide together,' said Rumstick in a low voice.

'Aye,' agreed Biddlecomb in a whisper.

'I don't mind telling you, Isaac,' Rumstick began in a halting voice, 'I'm damn scared. I don't know when I've been this scared. I don't think I could take being a slave aboard a British man-of-war.'

Biddlecomb could not see his friend's face, but he could hear the fear in his voice. It was something he had never heard before. 'I'm scared as well,' he said, and he was.

The two men moved to opposite sides of the hold. Biddlecomb reached out and felt the rough wood and the rounded top of a hogshead. Keeping his hand on the tier of casks, he made his way forward down the narrow opening between the stacks. His foot came down on a rat, which screeched and darted

186

away, the noise like a lion's roar in the silent hold. From somewhere behind him Biddlecomb heard Rumstick curse.

Biddlecomb continued forward, stepping carefully, until he guessed that he was at the spot near the bows where the curve of the vessel's side required that the casks be stacked three deep rather than four, and a small gap was left between the outboard barrel and the side of the ship. He reached over the top of a barrel and gripped the barrel's hoops as best he could, at the same time finding a foothold among the casks. Then with a lunge he leapt for the top of the tier, pulling himself up and crashing his head with all his force into the deck beam above. He rolled onto the upper tier, clutching his head and groaning and cursing.

'Are you all right, Isaac?' whispered Rumstick.

'Yes,' said Biddlecomb through clenched teeth.

When the pain had subsided, Biddlecomb rolled onto his hands and knees and crawled over the casks toward the ship's side. One, two, three, four, he counted the barrels beneath his hands. He was still too far aft. He turned forward and crawled along low to avoid the deck beams, his shoulder rubbing on the ceiling planking.

When his left hand came down not on a hogshead but in thin air, he knew that he was at the curve of the bow. He swung around, sitting on the casks, his feet dangling in the void, and kicked the shoring away, giving himself room in which to hide.

'How are you, Isaac?' Rumstick's voice was loud in the silent hold though he was still speaking softly.

'I'm fine, Ezra. Have you found the opening?'

'Aye, and it's damned tight. I can just fit.'

187

Biddlecomb tried to imagine his large friend squeezing into a space that he himself found confining. He was about to comment on that fact when the hold was shaken with a dull thud and the strange reverberating sound of something striking the ship below the waterline.

'Brig's boat is alongside,' said Rumstick, and the two men fell silent.

Biddlecomb was certain that twenty minutes had passed since they had heard the boat come alongside, but on reflection he decided that they had been there only ten minutes. Actually, he admitted to himself, he had no idea of how long they had been hiding.

It was the complete absence of everything, light, sound, save for the gurgle and thump of the water hitting the ship, that was so maddening. Their lives were threatened, they were being hunted, and all they could do was sit in complete silence. And wait.

At last the light and the voices came. They were foreshadowed by footsteps, at first so faint that Biddlecomb could not be certain that they were footsteps at all, and then growing louder, and with them a yellow light, cut here and there by shadows, that illuminated the overhead so that Biddlecomb could see each beam. The steps moved down the hold, booted feet that moved with determination. The shadows on the overhead swam and shifted as the light moved down the row of casks, then stopped when the footsteps stopped. There was silence again, and Biddlecomb was suddenly aware that he was holding his breath.

'Right, come on out, you two. No sense in hiding.' The voice was clipped, aristocratic, and British.

Biddlecomb almost leapt with surprise. He had to force himself to remain silent, to not move.

'Come now, I shan't warn you again.'

Silence. Biddlecomb felt a thousand needles pricking the bottom of his feet. He thought he might be sick.

'Harland, start with the pike. Start there,' said the voice. Biddlecomb could hear the sound of metal on wood from somewhere in the row of casks. He turned his head slowly and sighted down the side of the ship. Square patches of light danced on the side of the ship where the lantern shone between the barrels. From one of those squares of light the iron point of a pike emerged and pricked the hull planking.

'Move it forward, here, and try again,' commanded the voice. 'And use a bit of muscle this go-round.'

The pike clattered on the hogshead again, thrusting between them and embedding itself deeper into the wood, closer now to Biddlecomb. They were working their way closer, probing with a pike. Biddlecomb squeezed against the hull, drawing himself away from the patch of light that shone on his sleeve, the patch where the pike would enter. He shrunk away as if the light were red-hot metal.

The pike thrust in again, and the man who wielded it had to twist the pole to extract it from the wood in which it was embedded.

How the hell did they know? How did they find us here? Biddlecomb thought through his fear.

The next thrust would enter his hiding place. Biddlecomb withdrew farther, keeping his arm clear of the patch of light.

He heard the rasp of the steel on wood and the

189

pike shot in, the stiletto point catching Biddlecomb's left arm and opening the flesh half an inch deep.

Biddlecomb gasped with pain and surprise, then bit down hard on his lip and was silent.

The steps did not come. The press gang did not move on. They had heard him.

'Right, then. Come on out, you,' said the voice.

Biddlecomb remained silent, drawn up in himself. He clutched his wounded arm and felt the blood squeezing between his fingers. He imagined the blood dripping from the point of the pike.

'Mebbe Harland killed him,' ventured another voice with the accent of the lower deck.

'I didn't kill him, Wilson, you whoremonger—'

'Silence! Remove those hogsheads! Roll them out of the way!' said the first voice. This was absurd and unnecessary. Capture was now inevitable.

'All right, God damn you to hell!' shouted Biddlecomb. 'I'll come!'

He reached up and grabbed hold of the uppermost barrel, noticing, as his arm came into the light, that the blood had completely soaked his sleeve. He pulled himself onto the top of the tiers, gasping from the pain in his arm, and crawled inboard, swinging himself off and dropping to the deck with the help of the British seamen. He straightened and looked at his captors.

There was an officer, wearing a blue coat with white facing, white waistcoat and breeches. The buckles on his shoes glinted in the lantern light, as did the gold trim on his cocked hat, and from under the hat blond hair was tied back in a queue. A midshipman. Or a lieutenant. Or some damned thing. Biddlecomb neither knew nor cared.

190

Behind the officer stood the press gang with cutlasses and pistols and Harland with his boarding pike. Biddlecomb could see his own blood, wet on the point.

And behind the well-armed men, half-lost in the shadows, stood Fry. He stared impassively at Biddlecomb, and if he was delighted or revolted by his treachery, Biddlecomb could not tell.

'Bind up that arm, Wilson,' the officer ordered, and one of the boarding party stepped forward and whipped out his sheath knife. He cut Biddlecomb's torn sleeve away and used it to bind the wound.

'You said there were two,' intoned the officer, his words directed at Fry though he did not take his eyes off Biddlecomb.

'Where is Rumstick?' Fry spat out the question.

Biddlecomb paused, allowing his anger to subside before trusting himself to answer, assuming his dispassionate quarterdeck countenance. 'I don't know. He chose not to hide in the hold. Damned good choice, I'd say.'

Fry peered with his vulture's stare. 'You're a liar. He's down here.'

'Thrust the pike in there again,' said the officer.

'No, no! There's no room in there for two men!' said Fry peevishly. 'He must be on the larboard side.'

The boarding party turned to the larboard side, and as they did, the quiet of the hold was torn apart by an unearthly shriek and Rumstick launched his 250 pounds off the uppermost tier, arms spread, into the knot of astonished men. The officer and the seamen went down in a flailing heap, save for Wilson, who held his sheath knife to Biddlecomb's neck, and Fry, who stepped neatly aside.

191

The heap of men on the deck writhed and kicked, and in the light from the overturned lantern they looked like some weird creature in its death throes. It looked for a moment as if Rumstick would get the better of the press gang, until the officer managed to stand and draw his sword.

'Stop it!' shouted Biddlecomb. 'Rumstick, I order you to stop this this instant!'

Much to Biddlecomb's surprise Rumstick obeyed, releasing Harland's head, which he had locked in the crook of his arm, and another man's foot, which he was twisting painfully. His face was streaked with blood and he had an angry welt over his right eye, though he appeared less injured than the men he had attacked.

'There is no need for this, Rumstick,' Biddlecomb continued, his mind flailing around for something, anything. 'They can't press us anyway. Not with the Royal Decree.'

Rumstick looked dubious. 'What is the "Royal Decree"?'

'Yes, do tell,' said the officer, leaning on his sword as if it were a cane and regarding Biddlecomb.

'You, sir, must be aware of the Royal Decree. You, an officer in His Majesty's Navy.'

'Educate me, I beg.'

'Why, King George issued it, just after the *Pitt Packet* affair. You do recall the *Pitt Packet* affair?'

'I do. A bloody shameful business.'

'Shameful indeed,' continued Biddlecomb. 'And quite an embarrassment to the Crown. The king decreed then that no Americans shall be pressed. None at all. And frankly I believe that the Crown

192

would look most unfavorably on an officer who brought them further embarrassment.'

This was the key, instilling the idea of a career ruined. Biddlecomb hoped that he had not overplayed it. He looked into the officer's eyes, and the officer returned his stare. Biddlecomb knew from countless business dealings, many of them based on similar or wilder fabrications, that this man was hanging between believing him and not.

'You have heard, no doubt, of Lieutenant Stanton, late of His Majesty's schooner *Providence*?' Biddlecomb continued.

'I have not.'

Biddlecomb looked surprised. 'You must not be stationed in Rhode Island,' Biddlecomb guessed. The officer's expression did not waver and Biddlecomb knew that he had guessed right. 'He pressed Americans out of a homeward-bound merchantman. He was broken, discharged from the service. The court-martial was held in Newport. It was quite big news.'

The officer considered this. At length he said, 'I have never heard of this "Royal Decree." '

'I find that most hard to believe. How long have you been on the North American Station?'

The officer ignored the question. 'If this Royal Decree exists, as you so adamantly claim that it does, then why were you hiding?'

It was a good question, and Biddlecomb hesitated, just for an instant, but he could see in the officer's eyes that he had lost him. The officer straightened and slid his sword back in its scabbard.

'Get these men on deck,' he said to the boarding party. 'And our sea lawyer here is to speak to no one.'

He turned to Fry. 'Send a man to collect their dunnage and bring it topside.'

Biddlecomb and Rumstick emerged on deck, blinking and shielding their eyes from the brilliant winter sun. In the light Biddlecomb could better see the considerable damage that Rumstick had inflicted on the British sailors. Two men were bleeding from the nose and Harland had a nasty cut on his lip and seemed to be limping.

Standing by the mainmast, flanked by seamen with drawn cutlasses, stood John Haliburton.

'How . . . ?' Biddlecomb asked, turning to the carpenter. 'I thought you had a good . . .'

'That bastard,' Haliburton said, gesturing toward the quarterdeck, his voice barely under control. 'That bastard Fry, the whore's son, led them to me.'

Fry stood at the break of the quarterdeck staring out at the brig lying hove to, three cables to weather. 'I'm sorry,' he said to the prisoners, 'but they managed to find you, and, well, someone had to be taken. You understand.' The expressions of pity and triumph that played across his bird face were intolerable.

'I'll kill you, you bastard!' Haliburton shouted. He lunged for the quarterdeck, but the sailors on either side of him grabbed his arms and held him back.

'Don't you worry about that,' Rumstick said in a voice loud enough for Fry to hear. 'I got friends in Providence will hear about this. Friends that'll do that bastard up. Ain't that right, Larson? You know who I'm talking about.'

'Aye,' said Larson, 'I know.'

'You'll see that they hear about this, won't you? When you gets back to Providence, you see that they hear what Fry here has done.'

194

'Aye. I'll do that, as God is my witness. They have ways they deal with treachery, I know. They have ways.'

Biddlecomb looked over at Fry and saw the fear on his face, the fear of real reprisal. He remembered what the Sons of Liberty had done to the customs official, and he imagined that what they would do to the man who gave Rumstick over to the British would be worse, indescribably worse, but the thought did little to ease his own anguish.

Lieutenant Pendexter, Captain Pendexter now by courtesy, sat brooding in the great cabin of his first command. Through the glass of the tiny quarter galleries he could see his boarding party moving across the deck of the merchantman, three cables to leeward.

But he was not thinking about the boarding party anymore, having already convinced himself that he had made the correct decision. Pendexter was thinking rather about command, about discipline, matters he had never considered before, having always taken his lead from the captain or first officer of the ship aboard which he served. Now he had no one to answer to, and no one to lead him, and he was trying to invent his personal philosophies on these subjects.

He had been pondering these questions, and how they related to the bosun, McDuff, for the better part of the day. McDuff had no questions regarding discipline. To him discipline was enforced fast, brutally, and often. And, Pendexter admitted, the results were impressive. The men worked hard, they did not talk back, and they lived in mortal fear. How Dibdin could consider McDuff's behavior bad

195

for discipline was quite beyond him. But still McDuff had certain habits that made Pendexter uneasy, and that morning he had tried to address them.

'Mr McDuff, would you lay aft please,' he had said as McDuff struck with his starter the last man down from aloft. Pendexter was always polite to McDuff. It never occurred to him that he was frightened of McDuff, although he was.

McDuff stepped up to the quarterdeck with his odd gait, much like a barrel rocking from side to side.

'Mr McDuff, I wish to speak to you about your practice of starting the men.'

'Aye, sir. And what of it?'

'Well, I notice that you are in the habit of striking the last man down from aloft following a sail change.'

'Aye, that I do. And it keeps the bastards hopping, don't it?' said McDuff with a grin.

'Yes, I suppose it does. But it seems to me that the last man down must have necessarily been the first man up, don't you see? I do not want the men to hang back for fear of being beaten.'

McDuff cocked his head and looked at Pendexter with an expression of growing suspicion. 'Don't you believe it, sir. Them buggers – beg pardon, sir – they knows how to be last up and last down, the lazy sods, and I knows it and they know I knows it.'

'And when we pipe all hands,' continued Pendexter, giving voice at last to concerns that had been growing for several days, 'I notice that you and Longbottom start the last man on deck.'

McDuff did not seem to understand the line of questioning. 'Aye, sir. Of course we does, sir.'

'Well, it seems to me that someone has to be

196

last, what? I mean, does being the last man on deck necessarily mean that a man is being lazy?'

McDuff's expression was now one of full-blown suspicion. 'I've been in the navy twenty years now, sir, and I knows every one of their tricks, the lazy bastards, begging your pardon, sir. If a man is the last on deck, he's been up to something, count on it, and he needs a starting.'

Pendexter looked at his feet and considered these words. McDuff had entered the navy when he himself had been just one year old. And he could not say that McDuff's methods did not produce results.

'Well, Mr McDuff, I suppose that if you, in your professional opinion, feel that this starting is necessary . . .'

'Believe me, sir, we wouldn't have no discipline without I start the men. Like animals they is, sir.'

'Well, now, I'm not so certain . . .'

'And, sir? I wanted to ask you, regarding the new arrangements of the course lifts . . .' and with great relief Pendexter abandoned the subject of discipline for the subject of rigging.

Now Pendexter recalled that conversation for the hundredth time, and for the hundredth time he felt uneasy about it. But how better to maintain discipline? Would greater kindness engender greater loyalty, or would it be taken advantage of?

He watched the boarding party on the merchantman lead the pressed Americans down into the boat, and his thoughts went back to the total, unquestionable authority that he held over every man aboard. He could order any man on the *Icarus* flogged, at any time. Just say the word and they would be bound

197

up and flogged, right there, no trial, no asking a superior officer, he could just order it and it would be done. He was taken by a feeling of excitement and wicked delight. He had the power to do it. They had better figure out, he thought, that I'm a man who's not afraid to run a taut ship. Pendexter stood and collected up his coat and cocked hat and made his way to the quarterdeck. It was time to welcome the new hands.

He stepped up to the quarterdeck, cast an eye over the sails and down in the waist, acknowledged the master's greeting, then turned to leeward where the American lay. The merchantman had filled away already. Indeed, she was cracking on more sail as she fled to the south.

The longboat had covered half of the distance back to the *Icarus*, and even without a glass Pendexter could make out the individual occupants. Three men were sitting amidships between the men at the oars, and Pendexter assumed these to be the men that Smeaton had pressed. If they were prime seamen, then they would go far toward filling the holes in the quarter bill.

The longboat swooped alongside and Bloody Wilson in the bow hooked on to the mainchains. Smeaton stood up in the stern sheets and made his way to the boarding steps, pushing his way past the Americans and clambering aboard. He stepped up to the quarterdeck.

'Any problems, John?' Pendexter asked. One of the pressed men had a bloody bandage on his arm, he noticed, and another looked as if he had been beaten. What's more, a number of the boarding party were bleeding as well.

'Nothing to speak of.' Smeaton continued quietly, 'James, have you ever heard of a "Royal Decree"?'

'No. No, I have not. What is it?'

'It's nothing. Never mind.'

Biddlecomb's arm hurt much worse now, and his mind seemed unable to focus, as overwhelmed as it was with the pain and the new circumstances and what he feared was loss of blood. He looked up at the brig; it seemed enormous, as all vessels do when viewed from a boat alongside. No one had said a word on the way across. He wondered what kind of a greeting awaited them.

A man appeared at the gangway, an ugly face on a squat body. Around the man's neck was a silver bosun's call, and in his right hand was a long rattan cane. 'Right, you Yankee whores' sons, up and out. Get up here on deck, you sorry bastards!' he shouted, answering, to Biddlecomb's satisfaction, the question of their greeting.

Biddlecomb made his way awkwardly up the boarding steps, followed by Rumstick and Haliburton. The brig seemed extraordinarily crowded; Biddlecomb imagined sixty men at least were on deck or aloft. The *Adams*, half as big again as this vessel, had an entire complement of twenty men.

The officer who had led the boarding party was standing at the break of the quarterdeck. Beside him stood another man in an identical uniform, whom Biddlecomb guessed to be the captain. Their eyes met, just for a second, and then the captain looked away, running his eyes over the others. Biddlecomb assumed his neutral quarterdeck expression. He would say nothing; it was always best to

199

say nothing. He hoped the other two would follow suit.

The captain at last stepped up to the rail at the forward edge of the quarterdeck. 'My name is Captain Pendexter, of His Majesty's brig *Icarus*, and I—'

'Well, lookee here, Captain Pendexter,' Haliburton shouted.

Biddlecomb flinched. Please, Haliburton, shut your stupid mouth, he thought, but he knew that Haliburton would not.

'If you're the captain of this here brig,' Haliburton continued, 'then you best know it ain't legal to press Americans.'

Pendexter's mouth fell open, but before he could speak, he was cut off by the squeal of the boat tackles as the longboat lifted from the water.

Haliburton turned to the men on the tackles. 'Belay thay!' he shouted, and the surprised men obeyed him and ceased hauling.

Biddlecomb turned his head toward the carpenter. 'John,' he said in a low voice, but Haliburton was not one to listen to reason or anything else.

'Shut up, Isaac,' he said, then turning back to Pendexter continued, 'It ain't legal, I says, and you can be sure that Mr Brown, out of whose ship you pressed us, Mr Brown won't stand for it. So you best return us to the *Adams* and be right quick about it, mate!'

Pendexter recovered from the shock and found his voice again. 'You do not give orders aboard my ship, and you do not refer to me as "mate"! You address me as "captain" or "sir" when you are aboard my ship, and that will be for a great long time. You will—'

200

'We'll nothing, mate. You set us back on the *Adams* now, you bastard, or I'll have the law on you. You can't press Americans!'

The crew of the *Icarus* had abandoned even a semblance of work and they were all staring at the altercation aft.

'How dare you?' Pendexter spluttered. 'No Jonathan will come aboard my ship and—'

'Come aboard, hell! We was dragged aboard, you bloody son of a whore, and you ain't got the right!'

Biddlecomb glanced around him. The men were grinning, enjoying the show, no doubt wishing that they could stand up to an officer in this way. Haliburton was humiliating the brig's captain, and Biddlecomb wondered when the captain would put an end to it.

'You are subjects of the Crown and as such are liable to impressment!' Pendexter argued.

'No, we are not, you bloody rascal! You stupid bastard!'

Biddlecomb could hear snickers from the Icaruses. Pendexter's face was flushed red and his mouth was hanging open. The captain was losing contol of the situation.

'You will watch your mouth, you insolent bugger, or I'll have you triced up and flogged!' Pendexter shouted.

'You are breaking the law! How bloody many times do I have to tell you?'

'Right! Mr McDuff, Mr Longbottom, seize this man up to the capstan and give him a dozen to teach him manners!'

The two men were already moving before

201

Pendexter finished issuing the order. They grabbed Haliburton by the arms and yanked him toward the capstan.

'Hey!' the American shouted, surprised by the crushing grip and the sudden threat of corporal punishment. He struggled against them, trying to break free. Haliburton was strong, Biddlecomb knew, but he clearly was no match for McDuff, and with Longbottom's aiding, he was quickly tied to the capstan, spread-eagle and chest down. McDuff grabbed the collar of his shirt and jerked down, the fabric parting like gauze and the man's naked back exposed.

'What the hell is this!' Rumstick shouted, and as Biddlecomb turned to order him silent, Bloody Wilson elbowed him in the ribs.

'Shut your bloody gob, Jonathan,' he hissed, 'or they'll have a go at you next.' Rumstick scowled but he did not speak.

Longbottom burst through the forward scuttle clutching the red baize bag that held the cat-o'-nine-tails. He was grinning.

'Now, Brother Jonathan,' Pendexter sneered, 'I shall give you the opportunity to apologize, and to volunteer for the Royal Navy, in which case you shall receive a bonus—'

'You can't do this, you bastard!' Haliburton shouted, twisting to try to meet Pendexter's eyes.

'Very well. Bosun, a dozen lashes,' said Pendexter.

'This ain't legal, you fornicating, black-balling bastard!'

'Very well, two dozen. Bosun, do your duty.'

Haliburton opened his mouth but his words were replaced by a sharp intake of breath as McDuff

202

slashed the cat across his naked back. The flesh opened up in bright red ribbons as the whip smacked down again and again.

'Sweet Jesus,' Biddlecomb said, turning his head away. He thought he would be sick.

'He's using a thieves' cat, the bastard,' Bloody Wilson whispered.

'A what?'

'A thieves' cat. The tails is knotted to really tear a bloke up. It's supposed to be used only on them what's caught stealing, but bloody McDuff likes to use it on everyone.'

'Silence!' roared Smeaton. 'The next man to speak will be next on the capstan.' The watching men fell silent.

At a dozen lashes McDuff switched hands, he being equally capable of flogging a man with his left hand as with his right. The whip came down now at right angles to the first dozen and made a horror of Haliburton's back.

The bosun made it to number sixteen before Haliburton cried out in agony, a sharp, inhuman sound, like an animal being mutilated. Biddlecomb swallowed hard, struggling to keep the contents of his stomach down. Each crack of the cat tore more flesh from Haliburton's back, each scream was more horrible than the last.

And then it was over. A waiting seaman dashed a bucket of salt water over Haliburton's back. Pink trails of water and blood ran down the deck and into the scuppers. Longbottom cut Haliburton free, but the American had fainted by the twentieth stroke. Two of the *Icarus*'s men carried him below.

'Some take flogging harder than others,' Wilson

203

muttered to Biddlecomb. 'Your mate there took it about as hard as any I've seen.'

'That is what insolence will get you aboard this vessel!' Pendexter announced to the still-gathered men. 'There can be no disobedience of orders, no back talk to officers. Do your duty and you will be fine. Fail to do so and you shall dance with the cat. Mr Smeaton, put the new men on the books. Mr Dibdin, please get the longboat aboard and get the brig under way.' With that he turned and walked aft to the weather side of the quarterdeck.

The *Icarus*'s company moved silently to their stations as Smeaton called out the orders that would get the brig under way again. Biddlecomb and Rumstick were left standing by the gangway watching the maneuver, so familiar in principle but so foreign in execution. The men ran to their lines and stood there, waiting to do their single tasks. The bosun and his mate ranged up and down the deck, cursing and beating men with their rattan canes.

'O brave new world that hath such people in it,' whispered Biddlecomb.

'We've been dragged into hell.' Rumstick spoke for the first time since the flogging commenced. 'We've been dragged into fucking hell itself.'

The *Icarus*'s yards were braced around and the brig gathered way. Bloody Wilson ambled over to the two Americans, grabbed Biddlecomb's seabag, and slung it over his shoulder.

'I ain't carrying yours, brother, after the drumming you give me mates,' he said to Rumstick, but there was no malice in his tone. 'Here, follow me, and I'll show you where to stow your dunnage.'

Biddlecomb and Rumstick followed as Wilson led

204

them down into the cramped lower deck of the brig, explaining as he walked the protocol of life aboard a man-of-war.

'And one more thing,' Wilson said as they were preparing to go topside again. 'Don't you cross the bosun or his mate. They don't like no one, but especially they don't like Americans. And don't cross Pendexter, the captain. He says he don't love the cat, but that was the first flogging he ordered, what you just saw, and I think he's getting a taste for it.'

CHAPTER 14

The Man-of-War's Men

By the end of his first week aboard the *Icarus*, Biddlecomb had the number of his mess, which was six. What this meant, or so Biddlecomb came to understand, was that he ate at mess table six, which was the third aft on the larboard side. Rumstick in turn was assigned to mess nine, on the other side of the deck and one table aft. The man-of-war's men seemed to attach great importance to where and with whom they ate. And the men at mess six quickly accepted Biddlecomb into their ranks, showing him his duties as regarded the policing of the mess.

'This here is our kid, and our bread barge, and these here metal tags is for marking the mesh bags in the tubs,' Bloody Wilson explained. 'One week out of six you're the cook.'

This surprised Biddlecomb greatly. 'For all these men? Surely a man-of-war carries a cook! Even a coasting packet carries a cook.'

'Not for the ship, for the mess,' Wilson explained.

'I hope the mess isn't too discriminating, because I've never cooked anything without I've burned it.'

'This is what you do as cook for the mess,' Wilson continued. 'You get the meat from the ship's cook, put it in the mesh bag here, and remember to put the tag on it, then you give it back to the ship's cook for him to boil, and when he's done boiling it, he gives it back to you and you carries it back to the mess table.'

'Oh.' Biddlecomb was pleased with the simplicity of his duties but concerned with the quality of the fare served aboard the brig. He was used to poor food on shipboard, but this boiled meat, day in and day out, sounded even less tempting than merchant-man's rations.

'And on days when you's the cook, you cleans up the mess table and gets all the gear squared away. See here how all our gear's got the number six on it?'

It seemed to Biddlecomb that these elaborate precautions were created to defend against the possi-bility of a sailor in the Royal Navy starving to death for want of a little prompting.

The chief thought on Biddlecomb's mind, since he and Rumstick were first taken from the hold of the *Adams*, was how they would escape from the British. That was still first in his thoughts, but he needed time to survey their situation, to plan. He knew well enough that the best way to appear innocuous on shipboard was to do your duty well enough to avoid reprimand, but not so well as to attract attention. That was his goal.

Biddlecomb had spent more of his adolescence and adulthood at sea than he had on land, but he was a merchant seaman, and for all his experience he was quite ignorant of the ways of the navy. He was forced now to learn new ways of doing familiar things, and that order, repetition, and ritual were integral to every aspect of navy life, from eating to

207

sail evolutions. He was rated as foretopman and instructed that the larboard side of the fore topsail yard (and nowhere else) was his position when setting, stowing, or reefing sail. If, however, they were tacking or wearing, he was responsible for hauling the starboard fore clew garnet on rise tacks and sheets or assisting with the main brace if the foresail was not set. Such regimentation was unheard of in the merchant service, where ten men would sail a ship the size of the *Icarus*. But Biddlecomb was willing to concede that he had never taken a ship into battle, and he imagined that the seventy-five men aboard a brig would come in handy in that circumstance.

The sail evolutions that they did – tacking, wearing, setting and stowing sail – were poorly co-ordinated and clumsy. Biddlecomb imagined that this was due to a lack of experienced hands, and a lack of energy on the part of the first officer, though the boatswain more than compensated, at least where discipline was concerned. Sloppiness was not a characteristic of the British navy. He had seen enough well-handled ships to know that much.

It was on the morning of his fourth day aboard that Biddlecomb first felt the bosun's starter. He was at his station for tacking, manning the clew garnet, when he saw the fore topsail gear fetch up tight and heard the popping of the cordage under a great strain. The lines had been made off too tight, a common mistake but one that could tear things up aloft, and Biddlecomb raced forward to loosen them off.

And then something cracked across his back. He staggered forward and gasped with pain and surprise.

He turned, certain that something had fallen from

208

the rig and struck him. McDuff stood behind him, his starter raised to strike again.

'Your station's the clew garnet, Brother Jonathan.' McDuff jerked his starter back and Biddlecomb flinched.

'This gear was made off too tight—'

'Don't you give me lip, you whore's son bastard, or I'll give you worse than you got now, Jonathan!' McDuff shouted in his substantial voice. Biddlecomb edged back to the clew garnet, never turning his back, never taking his eyes off McDuff. He felt like a cornered animal. He vowed that from then on, until he escaped this cursed brig, he would never again act on an independent thought.

Added to Biddlecomb's torment was his increasing concern for Rumstick. He watched his friend closely, hoping to see him adapting, or making an attempt, hoping to catch a glimpse of his former joviality. But Rumstick was sullen and uttered not a word to anyone but Biddlecomb, and even those words were terse and few.

The other men avoided him, Biddlecomb could see that, and he could see how the bosun was infuriated by Rumstick's sullen attitude. Push him as hard as he could, beat him and scream at him, McDuff could not raise a flicker of reaction from the morose Yankee. Rumstick did his work silently, competently, like a machine, giving McDuff no concrete basis for his anger, and that made him angrier still. And Longbottom, the bosun's mate, followed McDuff's lead. It was clear to Biddlecomb that Longbottom was afraid of a man like Rumstick, a man who could crush him like a bug, and enjoyed beating him when he could do so safely.

McDuff was kind to no one, but he singled Rumstick out for special treatment, driving him toward a confrontation. Biddlecomb heard whispers among the men, incredulous discussions of how much abuse Rumstick tolerated. But he knew that Rumstick was not made of marble, as much as he might now appear to be, and it was only a matter of time before Rumstick broke and lashed out.

'I been fighting these bastards for ten years and more,' Rumstick had whispered one morning when he and Biddlecomb found themselves side by side, holystoning the deck. 'I won't work their ship, and I sure as hell won't fight for them,' he said, but his tone was more desperation than defiance. 'I'm sailing by the lee here, Isaac.'

Biddlecomb could see the storm gathering within his friend, and he knew it would soon break. And when it did, Biddlecomb knew that men would be killed, and doubtless Rumstick would be killed with them. Biddlecomb was desperate to find some escape for them before that happened. He knew it would happen soon.

By the end of his first week aboard, Biddlecomb felt that he had learned all there was to learn about sailing as a foremast jack on a British man-of-war, so he was much surprised at the faux pas he committed while shaking out a reef in the fore topsail at first light, after the *Icarus* had reduced sail for the night.

'I thought only merchantmen snugged down at night,' Biddlecomb said in a whisper to Bloody Wilson, who stood beside him on the footrope. 'I thought men-of-war carried all she'd bear all night.'

'Most do,' said Wilson, tugging at a recalcitrant reef point. 'Them what has a proper captain, and a

210

first officer who cares about the ship.' Wilson jerked the knot free. 'Them what ain't afraid,' he added, almost to himself.

Biddlecomb could see that Wilson did not wish to discuss the subject further. He thought of another question, one that would have seemed obvious, but had not occurred to him until that moment.

'Where are we bound for?'

'West Indies Station. Barbados.'

The words were like a magic incantation, come trippingly off the tongue of the foretopman, and Biddlecomb could have kissed him, could have sung for joy! Barbados! After Bristol it was the one spot on earth he would call home. He was well known in Barbados, and well respected.

Wilson looked at Biddlecomb, his expression uneasy. 'Keep shaking this reef out, mate, and don't let McDuff see you daydreaming,' he whispered.

Biddlecomb forced his attention back to the fore topsail. 'On deck!' he cried. 'Give us some slack in this inner buntline, about a fathom or two!'

It was then that Biddlecomb learned that calling out from aloft was one of the great violations of naval protocol. But neither Wilson's urgent whispers nor the horrified looks of his shipmates nor the quite shocking stream of oaths that McDuff directed at him could dampen the complete relief that Biddlecomb felt about his pending salvation.

'We are going to Barbados, don't you see?' Biddlecomb asked Rumstick, who was seated beside him in the main top, overhauling studdingsail gear. He hoped the news would draw the big man out. He had earlier snuck down into the cockpit where

211

Haliburton was still recovering from his flogging and told the carpenter the good news. He had seen hope in the man's eyes, not much, but enough to buoy Biddlecomb's spirits.

'Yes, you said that,' Rumstick said, 'but I'll own I don't see how that helps us. We're still in the goddamned brig.' Those were the most words he had spoken at one time in a week.

'Glacous lives in Barbados. He has more authority there than the governor, certainly more than any admiral. I'll send word to him, and as easy as kiss my hand, he'll have us off this wretched brig and safe and warm in his plantation house, a glass of port in our hands.'

Rumstick regarded him with suspicion. 'This is the same Glacous you was bragging to me you tricked into selling you molasses at nineteen sous a gallon. "Practically stole it from him" was your words.'

'It was eighteen sous a gallon, but that's business. Glacous knows that. I'll send him a note and he'll dispatch a coach and four to the landing to pick us up. Never doubt it.'

Rumstick was quiet for a moment. 'I hope you're right.' He glanced around. 'We got to get off this brig, Isaac. That bosun and his mate have it in for me. They use me awful hard. One of these days I'm going to break both their necks, I know it.'

'Hold your temper, brother, I beg you. I don't know what the punishment is for striking a . . . what is a bosun, an officer?—'

'A warrant officer.'

'—striking a warrant officer, but I bet it ain't pleasant. Flogging at least.'

'It's death, and no two ways about it.'

212

'Just hold your temper for a few more days. Then we'll be in Barbados and this nightmare will be over.'

Biddlecomb had only to write a note, he knew, and see that it was sent ashore, and Glacous would deliver them from the Royal Navy. He had intended to buy paper from the purser, but on finding that the purser was still in Boston, he approached the captain's servant, a hunched man named Bolton, who sold him the paper and the use of a pen and ink for two shillings.

During his watch below he crept into the hold and wrote by the light of a glim, wording the note with care and taking his time with the pen as he could not afford much paper at the going rate. At last it was done, and he folded the note carefully and tucked it in his shirt. He would pass it to Bolton the next day.

It was just past seven bells in the forenoon watch when the men were piped below for dinner. Bolton, as usual, stood to one side of the galley ovens waiting for the captain's dish to be cooked. From the smell, distinct from the odor of salt pork eaten by the lower deck, Biddlecomb guessed that it was lamb. He approached Bolton, pulling the note from his shirt.

'How are you today, Bolton?' he asked in a cheery voice.

'Fair, fair.'

'Tell me, are all meals like this aboard a man-of-war?'

'Like what?'

'Quiet. There doesn't seem to be much talk. That's strange for sailors at mealtime, isn't it?' This was something that Biddlecomb had wondered at since first coming aboard. The quiet was unnatural.

213

Bolton shrugged his shoulders and glanced around the deck. 'This lot's worse than most. Discontent, sullen buggers. Say, ain't you got a letter you wants me to send ashore?'

'Yes. Here it is. It's imperative that it get ashore in Barbados, as soon as we arrive.'

Bolton let out a low whistle. 'That ain't so easy, mate. I'll have to sneak it into the captain's mailbag; could get me flogged, you know.'

'Two shillings?' asked Biddlecomb, producing the money from his shirt.

'That's the price.'

Biddlecomb handed Bolton the money. It was a bad precedent, but he needed Bolton's full co-operation, and soon he would be gone.

'That note doesn't get read, you understand?'

'You can count on me, mate,' said Bolton, tucking the note away and feigning a sudden interest in the steep tubs.

Hunched over and pushing his way across the crowded deck, Biddlecomb made his way back to mess table six. Wilson was mess cook, and he was just laying the steaming, foul-smelling food on the table when Biddlecomb arrived. The low murmured conversation stopped, and all eyes were on him.

'Why was you talking to Bolton?' asked Bloody Wilson. 'What do you want with the likes of him?'

'Who, the captain's steward?' asked Biddlecomb, helping himself to the largest piece of salt pork. 'We were just talking. Why?'

'You give him something, I saw you,' said Harland. There was accusation and threat in his voice.

'Yes. A note. He said he could get it posted in Barbados. Is that all right?'

214

'You gave him a note? You give him money?' asked Wilson.

'Maybe.' Biddlecomb did not like this line of questioning.

Israel Barrett spoke. 'He tell you he'd have to put it in the captain's mailbag? Cost you a half bob?'

'Cost me two shillings.'

Suddenly the tension broke and the men at mess six smiled. 'God, you're a dumb bastard!' said Wilson. 'I thought you had more sense than that!'

'What's wrong with Bolton?'

'He's a bloody pigeon, a Billingsgate villain,' said Barrett.

'That's no surprise, but I didn't see what else I could do. I figure the captain's steward could get a note ashore. He will send the note, won't he?'

This prompted some discussion among the mess.

'Yeah, I guess he'll send it,' said Wilson at last. 'I just hope there ain't anything in it you don't want old Pendexter to read.'

The discussion continued with stories of past captains' stewards, but Biddlecomb did not join in. He felt his stomach seize up with anxiety. He stared down at the boiled salt pork and the biscuit. A weevil crawled out of the bread, and Biddlecomb was once again afraid he would be sick.

Capt. James Pendexter was anxious as well, though no one before the mast would have suspected it. He sat behind his elegant desk, his feet splayed out across the Oriental rug, swirling the wine around in his glass and considering the papers piled before him and spilling onto the deck. On the quarterdeck above his head Smeaton's pistols went pop, pop, and Pendexter

215

ground his teeth and squeezed his glass tighter. He wished that his first officer were more industrious and would do something other than fire his pistols all day. It was bad enough that he did not have a purser, but now he barely had a first officer, and Dibdin, who grew more sullen, and McDuff, who grew more brutal and capricious by the day, were having to take on a disproportionate amount of the work.

The thought of the absent purser brought Pendexter back to the problem at hand. He shuffled through the pile to his left, under which he was certain lay the records for purchase and consumption of beef, but before he located them his mind had drifted back to thoughts of the boatswain.

He would be lost without McDuff. McDuff did the work of three men. He drove the men the way they needed to be driven. McDuff had been right about discipline, Pendexter could see that now. The lazy foremast sods would always try to get out of one thing, shirk another. They had to be watched.

He would speak with Smeaton. A few tactful words, things will be fine, he thought. After all, this is his first go at being a first lieutenant. He'll do his share of the work like a good chap, not stand there all day long shooting at those damned bottles and relying on McDuff to keep the ship neat.

He set down his wineglass and picked up the purser's log once again. He was beginning to understand. The purser, it seemed, was writing down provisions before they actually arrived, which, as far as Pendexter could tell, accounted for the log's claiming far more in store than there actually was. Unless, of course, he was reading the log incorrectly.

He would have been able to match his own records

with what was left in the hold, he reminded himself, if he had kept records as he had intended, but now there was no way of knowing how much had been consumed. He tried to form a mental picture of the number of casks he had witnessed being broached, but soon abandoned that attempt. He would have to reimburse the purser for the entire ship's stores, that was the only way. And as that was the case, then technically he owned all of the stores aboard and could do as he wished, including abandoning record keeping. This gave him an enormous sense of relief, which was in turn swept away when he considered the difficulty of finding the purser to pay his debit.

Pop, pop. 'I say, don't throw them so bloody far outboard!' Pendexter could hear Smeaton clearly through the skylight. As he dropped the purser's log and turned to yell back through the skylight, Bolton slipped in the great-cabin door.

'Will you have the lamb cold for your supper, sir?'

'Yes, fine, Bolton,' Pendexter said, turning back to the papers on his desk. 'And straighten this cabin up a bit, will you, it's a disgrace.' Pendexter hated Bolton and Bolton's presence made him squeamish, as if there were a revolting smell in the room.

'Aye, sir. Oh, and, sir . . .'

Pendexter knew that Bolton had some illicit intelligence for him. He always introduced such information that way, and he always seemed to have information. That was why Pendexter kept him around.

'I have a note here, sir, that one of the men tried to bribe me to send ashore in your mail, sir. I thinks,

217

well, I thinks you best read it, sir.' Pendexter accepted the proffered note, noticing as he did that it was written on his own personal stationery.

'Glacous, my good friend,' the note began.

You will find this quite extraordinary, but as a quirk of fate would have it, I have been pressed into service as a foremast hand aboard His Majesty's brig *Icarus*, which now lies at anchor here in Barbados. The circumstances that have led me thus I shall not here relate, and they shall make a fine story over dinner. Suffice to say that I would be most grateful if you could employ your not inconsiderable influence with the admiral to see me and my friends Ezra Rumstick and John Haliburton, who were pressed with me, released from this bondage. Do hurry as I do not know when we shall sail again. I look forward to seeing you and have certain business concerns which I wish to discuss.

I remain your most Humble and
Most Obedient Servant,

Captain Isaac Biddlecomb, Esq.

Pendexter set the note down on his desk. '"Captain" Biddlecomb? So now he is "Captain" Biddlecomb? Of what does he presume himself to be captain?'

'That's why I thought I best show you.'

'And who is this Glacous? "Not inconsiderable influence with the admiral," he says.'

'I never did like the looks of him, sir, and the big

218

one, that Rumstick. Trouble, I says, as soon as they comes aboard.'

But Pendexter was not listening to the steward. Rather he was considering these implications. Biddlecomb was just a foremast jack, a creature of the lower deck. Or was he? His speech was not lower deck, not entirely. It was so hard to tell with these colonials.

'Come!' yelled Pendexter in response to a knock on the door, and Master Gunner Roger Hickman stepped in.

'Yes, what is it, Hickman?' Pendexter realized as he said it that he should have addressed the man as 'Mr Hickman,' but he was too annoyed to care. The gunner's face registered the slight.

'Well, sir, rats has got at the cartridges, sir, and we're precious low. I spoke to Mr Smeaton—'

'Oh, God damn it to hell!' shouted Pendexter as he glanced at the brass chronometer on the bulkhead. He snatched up his quadrant and pushed his way around the table. He had nearly forgotten the noon sight that would fix their position on the chart and officially begin the new day.

'I am sorry, Hick . . . Mr Hickman, this will have to wait. Bolton, I'll thank you to keep this . . . revelation quiet,' he called over his shoulder as he fled the cabin.

It was a perfect afternoon, a typical winter afternoon just below 15° north latitude with the sun high overhead and the few clouds brilliant white. Pendexter slowed his pace as he stepped up to the quarterdeck and jerked his watch from his pocket. He noted with relief that it was still three minutes until local noon.

He greeted Dibdin as the master fiddled with his

219

own quadrant and nodded to Smeaton, who paused in his target practice to return the salute. Then Pendexter turned and ran his eyes over his command.

The men were, as usual, hard at work, though today there was an atmosphere of excitement, and Pendexter noted smiles here and there among the men, who scampered apelike through the rig or hung over the side in bosun's chairs painting the hull. That was unusual, Pendexter reflected. He had come to the conclusion that this was the most sullen and uncooperative ship's company that he had ever witnessed. He imagined that it was tomorrow's landfall that had them excited. It made him feel good to see the men smile. He had not had any intention of giving the men a run ashore, but now he thought perhaps he would. The men who could be trusted to return.

Pendexter looked above his head to the main top, and the good feelings vanished. 'Captain' Biddlecomb was there, with Wilson and Mr Midshipman Appleby. Pendexter caught the stench of the slush that they were applying to the masts – old rancid beef and pork fat scraped off the surface of the water in the copper kettles in which the meat was boiled. It was a revolting smell, made worse by the warm air, which melted the slush into a runny consistency.

The men in the main top talked softly as they worked. Pendexter could see their mouths moving but could not hear the words, and suddenly he was desperately anxious to know what they were saying. He searched their actions for a sign of something conspiratorial, but there was nothing. Nothing that he could see.

220

Behind him Dibdin cleared his throat, a signal that it was time to shoot the sun. Pendexter leaned against the bulwark and brought his quadrant to his eye. This was the worst moment of his day, when he and the master took their noon sight and calculated their position on the globe. When they had each worked out a fix, Pendexter pretended to compare the results, though in fact he simply checked the master's answer, agreed with it, and plotted it on the chart, ignoring his own, which was always very different. Pendexter had never mastered the art of celestial navigation. He wondered if Dibdin had realized this, and the realization that he probably had humiliated Pendexter.

He was so engrossed in bringing the sun down to the horizon that he did not hear the frantic cry of 'On deck!' – and then Pendexter was covered with a warm and liquid substance. At first he took it to be spray, until the horrible smell of the slush reached his nose.

He lowered the quadrant and looked down at the deck. At his feet lay the canvas slush bucket that had plummeted from the main top and landed beside him, spraying him with its contents. He was aware of an unnatural silence. He looked up and saw that the entire ship's company was looking at him. Some men were suppressing grins, he could tell. The rancid smell assailed his nostrils again.

He looked up to the maintop. Biddlecomb was halfway up the topmast shrouds, his bucket in his hand, and Wilson was below him. Mr Midshipman Appleby stood on the edge of the fighting top, staring back at him. His face was bright red and his mouth opened and closed like a fish, but he made no

221

sound. Somewhere forward a man broke out in open laughter and was quickly stifled.

'Appleby! Get down here on deck this instant, God damn your eyes!' shouted Smeaton, but Wilson was already on the backstay, sliding to the deck.

CHAPTER 15

Barbados

By noon the following day Mr Midshipman Appleby was still walking with difficulty, eating his meals standing, and sleeping prone, so thoroughly was his bottom thrashed by Mr McDuff while the young man lay screaming over number-ten gun. And while the men had sympathy for Appleby – they liked him as they might a younger brother – they had more sympathy for themselves.

Pendexter, spluttering and stamping in rage, had ordered their rum, their chief source of pleasure in a world of toil and brutality, withheld for a week. There was no greater punishment, save for stopping their rum entirely, that Pendexter could have inflicted on the men. With the issuing of one order the *Icarus* was transformed from an unhappy ship to a very unhappy ship.

These thoughts occurred to Biddlecomb as he looked around the brig from his vantage point high on the foremast.

'Give me a piece of that spunyarn, Isaac,' said Rumstick, standing on the crosstrees opposite Biddlecomb. 'You remember how to seize on these ratlines here, or are your hands too soft to tug that small

223

stuff?' It was the closest to a joke that Rumstick had come in two weeks, and Biddlecomb was encouraged.

'You're some chipper for a seaman on this bucket.'

'And why not? Ain't this the day that Glacous rescues us?'

The two men turned and looked out at Barbados. The island was less than ten miles away, a brilliant green mass in the blue sea and the blue sky. Biddlecomb could see the headlands that delineated Carlisle Bay, a great indentation in the lush coast. With the *Icarus* to leeward of the island they could pick up the scents of land, the smells of dirt and vegetation. There is little smell at sea, rarely even a salt smell, and the perfume of the island stood out like a tar stain on a white sail.

'Yes, this is the day that Glacous will rescue us. If he gets my letter, and if he's on the island.'

'You don't sound so sure now. A few days ago you said we'd be off of here and no two ways about it.' Rumstick sounded worried.

'We'll get off,' said Biddlecomb, smiling. He glanced down at the deck, a habit by now, to make certain that neither McDuff nor Longbottom was watching, then turned his attention back to Barbados.

This landfall was like a homecoming to him, so often had he entered that wide harbor over the past decade and a half. It had been eight years at least since he had seen it from a masthead, having been, since that time, either the first mate on the foredeck supervising the preparation of the anchor or the master on the quarterdeck, conning the ship. But this was fine. Barbados was always beautiful, and with even a little luck he would never again see it from aloft on a man-of-war.

224

Half an hour later Biddlecomb stood in the fore top, now crowded with Harland, Wilson, and the other foretopmen, standing ready to get their sail in quick, while on the deck below the Icaruses prepared the brig for anchoring. The atmosphere was tense, volatile, even beyond the general air of tension that hung like a cloud over the vessel. Not even McDuff and Longbottom were immune, and they beat with particular malevolence those men they deemed lax.

The steep, jungle-shrouded hills rose out of the sea just half a mile to starboard. The warm-earthy smell was all around them now, and the men in the fore top breathed deep, enjoying the luxurious scent.

Biddlecomb was startled by a new sound, a low rumbling. He looked down to the deck. On the starboard side the guns had been cast off and gun crews were rolling their charges back. The ship's boys stood at a distance, the black, cylindrical containers for powder cartridges in their hands.

'Are we loading the guns? Might there be trouble?' Biddlecomb asked Wilson, who stood beside him.

'There'd be some bloody trouble if we didn't give the admiral his salute, mate,' he said, smiling.

'Oh, the salute, of course,' Biddlecomb said, watching with interest the loading of the guns. It occurred to him that this was the first time that he had seen the guns being used. 'Say, I'm supposed to handle the rammer and sponge on number-five gun. Shouldn't I be there?'

'That's at quarters,' Wilson whispered. 'We're at stations for anchoring now.'

'Oh.'

Wilson and Biddlecomb and the other foretopmen waited in silence as the brig raced through the

225

approaches to the harbor. The wind was still brisk, and the tide was ebbing fast; Biddlecomb could see eddies around the rocks near the shore. He worked out in his mind where and how he would approach the anchorage. It would be tricky under these conditions. He wondered how good a ship handler Pendexter was.

Israel Barrett clambered up onto the fore top and began to unhook the stay tackle. His expression was grim.

'A bit early for the boat tackle, isn't it?' Biddlecomb asked.

'Pendexter's coming it the showman. He's going to fire the salute, round up, and drop in the smoke,' Barrett said ominously.

'What do you mean by that?' Biddlecomb asked.

'Means we sail up to the anchorage, fire and salute as we round up, then drop anchor and clew up and get the boat over the side before the smoke from the guns has cleared.'

'So when the smoke clears, they find us anchored and secure with the boat in the water. Like a curtain lifting on a stage.'

'Yeah, like that.'

Biddlecomb considered the maneuver. It would be a pretty thing if brought off well, and it would make Pendexter look like quite the ship handler to the admiral and the others watching from shore. 'Can Pendexter pull it off?'

'Dunno. I ain't seen him try before.' Barrett eased the stay tackle away to a man standing in the longboat. Mr Midshipman Appleby, who was apparently charged with seeing the boat launched, was issuing superfluous orders in his high-pitched voice.

226

Biddlecomb turned his attention back to the island. They were inside the harbor now, but there was no shelter from the wind that funneled over the land. The *Icarus* was sailing close-hauled toward the island, straight into the wind and the current. Once Pendexter rounded the brig up into the wind to anchor, they would start making sternway fast. Biddlecomb considered the problem of anchoring in the strong breeze and the ebbing tide. They would have to be certain nothing was downwind of them when they dropped the hook. Then he reminded himself that these were not his problems.

In the distance he could see the town of Bridgetown like a rocky white outcropping in the jungle. It seemed unchanged from the first time he had seen it, fifteen years ago. The anchorage was not crowded, not as it had been in years past. In the roadstead by the town lay the ships of His Majesty's navy, a larger force than Biddlecomb was accustomed to seeing there. There were three 74s, one with its rig sent down to a gantline, but the other two appearing ready for sea. There were two frigates as well, and a variety of sloops, brigs, and schooners. At the other end of the harbor lay the merchantmen, British, French, Dutch, and American. The world was at peace, albeit an uneasy peace, and all maritime nations came to Barbados to trade. Biddlecomb looked longingly at the Americans. One ship he thought to be the *John Stanton*, but he could not be certain.

'Take a good look,' said Wilson. 'This is the closest you'll get to them Yankee ships.'

'Then you don't think we'll get a run ashore?'

'I don't think we will. I know you won't. They

227

don't give leave to pressed men. You can guess why that is.'

Biddlecomb could indeed guess why he would not be allowed off the ship.

Wilson continued to voice Biddlecomb's thoughts. 'Bet you wish you was aboard one of them,' he said, jerking his head in the direction of the American ships.

'Yes, I do.'

Wilson was quiet for a moment. 'There are times I wish I was aboard one of them too.'

The bow of the *Icarus* swung more northerly, and above and below the fore top the foreyards were braced around. They were on a beam reach now, running down on the anchorage at six knots at least, but there was no knowing for certain what the fast ebb would do. If I were in command, Biddlecomb mused, I would be damned nervous about all this.

He looked down to the deck below. The stay tackles and yard tackles were rigged to the boat and well manned, and Mr Appleby was pacing the gangway, apparently anxious for the moment that he would play his part. The gunner walked down the length of the guns, now loaded and run out. Biddlecomb realized that he would be leaving the *Icarus* without ever having drilled with the great guns, and he was almost sorry to miss the experience.

Biddlecomb moved his attention outboard. He knelt and looked under the foot of the fore topsail and was startled to see one of His Majesty's schooners anchored two cable lengths ahead, directly upwind and directly in the brig's path.

'Look here,' he said to Wilson, and Wilson knelt beside him.

'Jesus Christ! I wonder if Pendexter means to turn before we cut them into two bloody parts.' The captain clearly could not see the schooner beyond the *Icarus*'s foresail.

If the *Icarus* had been a merchantman, Biddlecomb would have called down a warning, but he knew better than to do so aboard the man-of-war. 'If he turns right now, it'll still be a close thing,' Biddlecomb observed.

And then they heard Pendexter's voice. 'Commence with the salute, Mr Hickman!' he shouted from the quarterdeck, and instantly the forwardmost gun on the starboard side went off, expelling smoke and flame from its muzzle as it flew inboard.

'If I wasn't a gunner, I wouldn't be here,' came the singsong chant as the gunner timed his shots. 'Fire two!' and the next gun went off. 'If I wasn't a gunner, I wouldn't be here . . . fire three!'

Biddlecomb listened to the rhythm and anticipated the fourth gun, but it did not come. The gunner, who had already marched past number four, turned and ran back, his cadence ruined.

'Mr Hickman, God damn your eyes! What is the problem?' shouted Pendexter. Biddlecomb could see him now, leaning over the rail at the break of the quarterdeck.

'Slow match is out!' the gunner replied, reaching out for the slow match from number-three gun.

'I don't give a goddamn, just get on with it!' Pendexter replied, and even as he spoke, Smeaton hurried to his side and grabbed his arm and pulled him to the weather rail, pointing forward around the foresail. Biddlecomb saw the captain's eyes open

229

wide and his mouth drop as he caught sight of the schooner. He turned to the helmsman, but if he issued an order, no one aboard the *Icarus* heard it, for in that same instant Hickman fired number four and Pendexter's voice was lost in the report.

'Hickman! Belay the goddamned salute!' Pendexter cried.

'Turn to starboard,' Biddlecomb muttered, 'go downwind of the schooner.'

Pendexter turned to the helmsman. 'Larboard!' he shouted. 'Hard a'larboard!' and the *Icarus* began to round up into the wind.

Biddlecomb could see the schooner now as the *Icarus* passed twenty feet to windward of her. Her crew was running around the deck, waving their arms. Four men were wrestling with a giant fender, trying to get it over the side as the *Icarus* continued to turn into the wind.

'That was bloody close,' whispered Wilson.

'He should have turned and run to leeward of her,' Biddlecomb said. 'If Pendexter thinks he can drop the anchor now, with the schooner right down wind and current, we'll be all over her before he has enough cable out.'

The fore topsail began to collapse and flog in loud confusion as the wind ran down the edge of the canvas. The brig continued its swing into the wind, and suddenly the sails were hard aback, the beating canvas was silent, and the *Icarus* came to a stop, the schooner now forty yards astern and directly down wind and tide.

'Let go!' Pendexter shouted, and McDuff, standing on the cathead, let fly the ring stopper. The best bower plunged into the harbor, and the anchor cable,

230

flaked out along the deck, began to fly through the hawsepipe.

The *Icarus* was moving faster and faster astern with all plain sail set and fully aback. Biddlecomb watched the distance to the schooner falling rapidly away.

'Get the sails off of her! Get the damned sails off!' Pendexter shrieked, glancing over his shoulder at the schooner.

'Cast off the topgallant sheets!' Dibdin shouted, his voice loud and even. 'Cast off topsail halyards! Clew down!' The men on the deck below tumbled over themselves to get to the running gear. Knots of men sweated the topsail clewlines, struggling like demons to haul the big sails down. But their efforts were hampered because the sails were aback and pressed hard against the mast, and because no one had obeyed Dibdin's first order to cast off the topgallant sheets, which were now holding the topsail yards in place.

Biddlecomb glanced up at the main topsail yard. The spar was bending in the center, threatening to burst from the forces acting upon it.

And then with a rending sound the corners of the fore and main topgallant sails tore out. The canvas fluttered in the breeze like a tattered ensign, and the topsail yards fell ten feet down the mast.

Biddlecomb looked aft again. The *Icarus* was still making sternway, still moving fast, and the schooner was no more than twenty yards astern. He looked down at the deck. The anchor cable was still snaking out of the hawsepipe.

'McDuff!' Dibdin shouted from the quarterdeck. 'Clap a stopper on that anchor cable or we'll be aboard that schooner!'

231

McDuff stared at the anchor cable, eight-inch-thick hemp lifting off the deck as it flew out the pipe, and Biddlecomb guessed that McDuff did not cherish the thought of trying to stop it. He glanced around, then seized a coil of line from the pinrail and tossed a midshipman's hitch around the anchor cable that still lay on the deck, making the stopper fast to the fife rail.

At that moment Mr Appleby, apparently considering the *Icarus* to be anchored, issued his orders to the men waiting anxiously at the boat falls. The longboat flew from the booms and swung out over the side. The boat was fifteen feet outboard before Pendexter could issue an order.

'Belay that, you idiot, you whore's son!' he shrieked at the confused boy. 'Get that boat back on the booms!'

Before Appleby could countermand his orders, the last turns of the anchor cable spun out. The cable lifted off the deck as the stopper took the strain, and the fife rail and the line groaned together with the shock as the *Icarus*'s sternway was checked. The brig hung there for a moment, the creaking of the fife rail and the popping of the straining cordage loud in the silence. Then the stopper parted and the anchor cable spun out again and the brig slewed to starboard as it once more gathered sternway.

The schooner was only fifteen yards away, the distance dropping fast. Her panicked crew was lining the side with anything that they could employ as a fender. The *Icarus* continued to slew around until she was hurtling down broadside to the schooner.

Biddlecomb knew that nothing could prevent the collision. 'Grab hold of something, you men,' he said

232

as he grabbed a fistful of running rigging. The other foretopmen grabbed on to any handhold that they could find.

The *Icarus*'s longboat, hanging outboard as it was, was the first thing to strike the schooner. It passed just abaft the foreyards and fetched up on the mainstay, tangling in the braces. And then the boat falls parted and the longboat fell to the schooner's deck, breaking its back and stoving in the main hatch.

The actual impact was softened by the fenders, but still the two vessels came together with a crunching sound like a giant beam splitting, and a cacophony of smaller snapping and popping noises. The high-sided brig rode up on the smaller vessel, crushing twenty feet of bulwark and splintering the main channel. The lanyards on the schooner's main shrouds parted one at a time, and the shrouds swung inboard. Biddlecomb wondered if the mast would go.

The grinding sound of the two vessels, loud though it was, was merely a backdrop to the shouts and curses that flew between the ships. It was clear to Biddlecomb that the two vessels were locked together now, and the greatest danger was that the schooner would drag her anchor and both vessels would be driven ashore. He imagined that that point was being discussed, though he could not hear anything other than cursing from the deck of the schooner.

And then it was quiet again, save for the low sound of the vessels grinding against each other. The topsail yards were lowered away and the sails clewed up, and the topmen layed out to furl their sails. Biddlecomb reached over the yard and grabbed a fistful of canvas

233

when number-one gun, larboard side, went off with a shattering roar.

'What in the hell . . . ?' shouted Pendexter from the quarterdeck, and Biddlecomb saw the gunner spin around and face aft.

'Hickman, what in hell are you doing?' Pendexter shouted.

'But, sir,' the gunner stammered. 'The admiral's salute . . .'

Ten yards away the schooner's crew burst into a wild and derisive laughter.

234

CHAPTER 16

Repair to Sea

The flag had been flying above the admiral's house for some time before Mr Midshipman Appleby noticed it. He grabbed his signal book and thumbed through the smudged pages until he found the correct interpretation.

'Signal from the admiral, sir,' he said brightly. '"Captain to report aboard flagship." He must mean to go ashore, sir, since there is no flagship.'

Midshipman Appleby's observations were terminated with a sharp blow to the ear, delivered by Captain Pendexter, who had seen and interpreted the flag fifteen minutes prior.

'McDuff, God damn your eyes!' he shouted to the bosun, who at that moment was trading obscenities with the bosun aboard the schooner. 'McDuff, get a boat in the water and get it now! The admiral will not wait for you.'

At the sound of Pendexter's voice McDuff broke off and hurried back to the quarterdeck. 'It's them whore's sons on the schooner, sir. The launch is kindling now, sir, and them bastards won't cut away their rig so's we can get the gig out, sir.'

'So you are telling me that there is no boat to take

235

me ashore?' Pendexter's voice was taut, like a line about to break.

'Not right now, sir, no, there ain't. And, sir? I thinks it would be best if you called me "Mr" in front of the men. Discipline and all, sir.'

'You blackballing, impertinent philistine! I'll break you! I'll send you forward if you dare lecture me again, you villain!'

McDuff's face turned a deep red, and then pale. Every member of the *Icarus*'s company was watching the drama aft.

'Very well, sir,' McDuff said at last, then turned and walked slowly forward.

Pendexter stepped up to the rail, ready to hurl more threats at the warrant officer, when the master's voice, roaring across the deck, cut him off.

'Avast there! Stand off, you! Keep away from this ship! Barrett, fetch a sweep and fend them bastards off!'

Pendexter looked over the larboard side. A bumboat with two huge black men at the oars was rapidly closing with the *Icarus*. In the stern sheets stood a portly black woman, her head bound in a colorful cloth. In one hand she held aloft a limp and plucked chicken, in the other a small bunch of bananas. The smell of fried fish and perspiration wafted across the water.

'I say,' observed Smeaton, 'here's a boat that could take you ashore.'

'A bumboat? Are you mad? I can't arrive ashore in a bumboat, you idiot!'

'Well,' said Smeaton, as much to himself as to Pendexter, 'it would be better than keeping the admiral waiting. Any longer than he already has.'

236

'Stand off, there!' shouted Dibdin again. 'They have rum, sir, and they'll slip it to the men if they get a chance.'

'Well, see how much they want to take me ashore,' Pendexter said to Smeaton.

The first officer leaned over the larboard rail. 'I say, there,' he shouted.

'You want fresh chicken? Banana? Plantain I got too, mister!' the fat woman yelled through huge and brilliant teeth. The bumboat thumped alongside the *Icarus*, and Pendexter could see that it was more filthy than he had first imagined.

'Stand off there, you!' Dibdin shouted. 'Sir, tell them to stand off.' The men of the *Icarus* drifted toward the larboard side, and each seemed to find work that needed attention there.

'How much to take captain ashore?' Smeaton continued. 'Captain, big man, big important! Must go ashore.'

'I don't think captain of little ship such a big man, not so important. You pay me five sous, I take lieutenant ashore.'

'You there, Smith, what did you take from that man?' Dibdin shouted.

'Five sous? To ride in that filthy scow? Five pence, no more!'

The fat woman laughed. 'Your boat is all broke, mister, and the admiral, he don' like to be kept waiting. I know the admiral, he don' like to be kept waiting.'

'God damn it! Just pay the damned money!' shouted Pendexter, snatching up the bag of dispatches. The crowd of men parted before him as he made his way to the boarding steps.

237

Smeaton tossed down the coins as Pendexter settled in the stern sheets. He gritted his teeth and wrinkled his nose at the overpowering smell. Barrett shoved the bumboat off with the sweep, and the two oarsmen fell into a steady rhythm.

'You want chicken, Mr Captain?' asked the fat woman, thrusting the dead bird into Pendexter's face.

From the foretop Biddlecomb watched the bumboat pulling away from the *Icarus*'s side. He could see the mailbag between Pendexter's legs, which contained, he hoped above all things, his letter to Glacous. Biddlecomb roughly estimated the time it would take to get word to the plantation and back. Three or four hours. And then he and Rumstick would be free again.

'All hands on deck, now, you lazy, motherless bastards, now!' McDuff shrieked from the deck. His voice had a hysterical, animal quality far worse even than his normal beastly tone. Biddlecomb imagined that the bosun was still smarting from Pendexter's threats and his humiliation before the ship's company.

'We're bloody in for it now,' whispered Wilson as he reached out for a backstay and slid to the deck. Biddlecomb knew he was right. McDuff would worry that his dressing-down had made him less terrible in the men's eyes and would try to prove that he was, if anything, more terrible than before. Biddlecomb reached out for another backstay and slid reluctantly to the deck.

The gang forward, ostensibly led by Longbottom but in fact following Barrett's direction, was rigging

238

the capstan to take up on the anchor hawser, which lay like a dead serpent across the deck. Along the starboard side the crews of the *Icarus* and the schooner labored to untangle the two vessels.

The schooner's main brace was tangled in the brig's main shrouds, and Paul Harland was wrestling with the Gordian knot that had developed.

'What in bloody hell are you about?' McDuff snarled.

'Trying to free the schooner's main brace—' Harland began, but McDuff clapped his huge hand over Harland's face and shoved him to the deck. Then he pulled his sheath knife from his belt and cut the schooner's main brace in two.

'Hey . . . !' the schooner's boatswain began, but the protest died on his lips when he saw the black scowl on McDuff's face.

'Get up off the goddamned deck, Harland, and get an ax and cut the schooner's main channel away,' McDuff ordered over his shoulder as he stamped away.

For two hours the men of the *Icarus* labored as Biddlecomb had never seen a ship's company labor. With flailing axes and slashing knives the brig was disentangled from the schooner. A strain was taken on the limp anchor hawser and the *Icarus* was hauled to windward, where she lay peacefully at anchor while the damage was repaired.

The multitude of broken running gear and torn sail was replaced, while the carpenter and his mate swarmed over the side, replacing the chunks that had been torn from the hull. During the few instances that Biddlecomb was able to glance around, he was astounded at the speed with which the men worked.

239

They had been well trained under Bleakney. Each man knew his job, and there were a lot of men. He had to admit the efficiency of this naval practice, which he had never seen in the merchant service.

But military efficiency alone did not account for the pace with which the men worked. In this instance it was fear, mostly fear, that drove them, for they knew that McDuff was looking for an excuse to beat someone half to death. They could see it in the way that he stamped around the deck, and the way he kept his starter in constant motion, slashing at one man, then another. With Dibdin below and Smeaton staring wistfully ashore and taking the occasional shot at floating debris with his dueling pistol, there was no one to stop McDuff. He cursed and yelled and kicked until the men worked as fast as they were physically capable of working, but still he did not ease up. Even Longbottom stayed out of the bosun's way.

It was past noon, with the men working through dinner, when Smeaton spotted the *Icarus*'s gig, which had at last been cleared away and sent after Pendexter, putting off from the shore.

'I say, Mr McDuff!' Smeaton shouted from the quarterdeck. 'I do believe that the captain is on his way back.'

McDuff squinted in the direction of the shore just long enough to see for himself, then began alternately shouting orders and kicking men out of his way.

'Side boys! Get those motherless side boys up here!' he shouted. 'Man the sides! Rig side ropes, and get those goddamned gloves for the side boys! Get this deck squared away, now!'

Men rushed in every direction as the deck was

240

tidied and the sides manned as if to welcome an admiral. Israel Barrett scooped up the last balls of marline and tossed them down the forward scuttle just as Mr Midshipman Appleby, steering the little gig, called for the boat's crew to toss oars.

The boat crew had pulled with a will, and Appleby had waited too long to toss oars. Biddlecomb grimaced as Appleby, now pale with fright, turned the boat a second too late. The gig struck the *Icarus*'s side with a force that made the brig shudder. Biddlecomb braced himself for the tirade that Pendexter would unleash on the boy, but nothing came. Bloody Wilson in the bow hooked on and the gig rode at the ship's side.

As soon as Pendexter's head came level with the *Icarus*'s deck, McDuff and Longbottom let loose with their bosun's pipes. Pendexter stepped up the boarding steps into all of the pomp and circumstance that the *Icarus* could muster.

'Stop that damnable noise, McDuff, and get us to short peak, now,' the captain said as he brushed past, his eyes on the deck. Biddlecomb could see that his hands were trembling. 'Smeaton, get us under way. Get us out of this damned harbor!' he shouted as he passed the stunned first officer. He jerked open the door to the after scuttle, slamming it against the quarterdeck rail, then disappeared into the darkness below.

Biddlecomb felt sick, profoundly sick. They were getting under way! Even if Glacous had received his note, they would be gone before he could respond. He looked desperately around, as if help would come from some hidden corner of the deck.

But there was no one who could help him, and

241

already the gig was rising from the water and swaying inboard as the hands tailed on to the boat falls, and amidships men began to walk the capstan around, hauling the *Icarus* up to her anchor.

'We're getting under way . . .' Biddlecomb heard a voice behind him, familiar but weak. He turned around. John Haliburton was standing there, his bare chest and shoulders still flaked with blood, two weeks' growth of beard on his face, his skin white from his time below. He stared around the deck as if unsure of where he was.

'Yes, John, I'm sorry,' Biddlecomb said, trying to comfort his shipmate even while he himself felt overwhelmed with despair. 'I thought I could get a note—'

'You said you could get us off this brig. You said you had a friend,' Haliburton interrupted, his voice low and choked as if he were on the verge of crying.

'I thought I could, but . . .' Biddlecomb began again, and then McDuff loomed up behind them. Biddlecomb reached out to jerk Haliburton out of the way, but before he could, McDuff's starter came down across Haliburton's raw back. Haliburton gasped and staggered forward. Biddlecomb could see blood running down the length of McDuff's starter.

'Glad you're up and about, you Yankee bastard,' McDuff sneered. 'Now get on that capstan and heave around.'

Haliburton stared at McDuff, his eyes wild, but the strength and contentiousness that made Haliburton himself were gone. He staggered back one step, then two.

'John, please, just follow orders,' Biddlecomb said, and McDuff rewarded him with a slash of the rattan

242

cane across his face. Biddlecomb could feel the blood running down his cheek.

McDuff turned back to Haliburton, starter raised over his head. 'To the capstan, Jonathan.' Haliburton looked at Biddlecomb, then at McDuff. He shook his head slowly, then turned and leapt through the gangway into the harbor, flailing in the air and smacking down in a shower of spray. He went under, then regained the surface and with awkward strokes began swimming toward the shore.

'You son of a whore!' McDuff shouted. 'Avast heaving the capstan! Clap the boat falls on that gig! Gig crew—'

The crack of a pistol drowned out his voice and silenced the chaos on deck.

Biddlecomb spun around and looked aft. Smeaton was standing there, a faint smile on his face, the smoking gun in his right hand. Through the red-tinged water Biddlecomb could see Haliburton's body sinking slowly to the bottom, arms outstretched, half of his head blown away. Biddlecomb looked back toward the quarterdeck, and Smeaton was smiling down at him. He held up the other pistol and pulled the cock back. The click was loud on the silent deck. 'Anyone else care to try for a run ashore?'

Biddlecomb clenched his fists at his sides as he fought the urge to charge at the quarterdeck, and then he was struck from behind, a line of pain shooting across his back.

He turned. McDuff was there, his starter dangling in his hand. ' "You said you could get us off this brig," ' he mocked Biddlecomb with Haliburton's words. 'You was a real help to him, wasn't you, you worthless bastard.'

243

Biddlecomb blinked and stared at McDuff.

'Get your arse down in the cable tier and see if that cheers you up,' the boatswain said, and raised his starter again. Biddlecomb fled aft down the hatch.

Biddlecomb stood in silence, in the dark, sweltering cable tier. He had let himself believe that the nightmare would end in Barbados, that he and Rumstick would escape before Rumstick killed someone, before he himself or Haliburton lost his mind.

But there was no chance of that now; they were still in bondage, heading for sea again, and Rhode Island and Virginia were farther away than ever. Overhead he heard the capstan turning, and slowly the cable came down to him, wet and coated with mud and stinking of all the filth on the bottom of the harbor. Biddlecomb took up the heavy line and laid it out in the cable tier as it came in, grateful for the darkness below that would hide his angry and desperate tears.

244

CHAPTER 17

The Privateersman

The pistol shot and the groaning of the capstan and the click of the pawls at last made Capt. James Pendexter raise his head off his desk. He stared around the great cabin, as if seeing it for the first time. His eyes rested on the wine rack and he recalled that he still had one bottle of the excellent port left. For an instant he was cheered by that thought, and then his misery and humiliation flooded back.

The admiral, as it turned out, had waited forty minutes from the time his flag was flown to Pendexter's arrival, a geological age for an admiral. And he had witnessed the entire botched anchoring from his third-story balcony, from the moment the *Icarus* had entered the harbor with all plain sail to the moment she had come to rest on the schooner's side. It was Pendexter's bad luck that the schooner had already captured a number of small but quite valuable prizes, greatly increasing the admiral's wealth, and he was more than disappointed to see it rendered unseaworthy for the sake of Pendexter's showing off.

For nearly an hour the admiral had shrieked and cursed. He had called Pendexter all manner of names,

245

questioned him on his naval experience, and even quizzed him on points of seamanship. And Pendexter could do nothing beyond nodding, answering, and saying, 'Yes, sir.'

At last Pendexter had decided to offer up an excuse, which made the admiral more furious still, and his excuse of being shorthanded was, as it turned out, the stupidest thing he could have said. If he was shorthanded, why had he tried such an idiot stunt? That in turn led to questions of how he had come to be shorthanded in the first place, and further recriminations about giving unreliable men a run ashore. The hour-long harangue became ultimately an hour-long review of the legion of failures that comprised Pendexter's first month of command. Laid out at his feet that way, Pendexter was forced to admit to the admiral, and worse, to himself, that it was not an auspicious start.

And there was the admiral's daughter. She was just as Smeaton had described her: young and beautiful, her hair curly and blond, and her skin glowing brown as a healthy young girl's skin will do in the tropics. She was in real life more beautiful than she had been in the amorous fantasies that Pendexter had entertained for the past week. And she had been there, smiling pertly, as the admiral stripped Pendexter of the last syllable of his dignity and stomped on the pathetic creature that was left. It was the greatest humiliation that Pendexter had ever suffered, and now he was cruelly mocked by the memory of his fantasies of impressing the admiral and winning the favors of his daughter.

'Short peak!' Pendexter heard McDuff through the skylight yelling from the bow, and then Dibdin's voice, loud and confident, yelled out, 'Let fall top-sails! Sheet home!'

What must Dibdin think? That old man always had a smirk just under the surface, was always ready to criticize. He would have anchored safe, but he didn't have the courage to try anything with flash.

The capstan creaked again. 'Anchor's aweigh!' shouted McDuff.

Dibdin would know, of course, that the admiral had humiliated him. It was the only explanation for their hasty departure. Smeaton would know as well. There were no secrets in the navy. The story of their botched anchoring would make the rounds of the fleet, be told in gaming rooms and taverns, in great cabins and lower decks. He would be the laughing-stock. This tale would follow him to the grave. The realization made him feel sick to his stomach.

And then he remembered the admiral's promise to send word to Admiral Graves delineating what a fool Pendexter was. If he lost favor with his uncle, he would remain commander of a brig until he retired. Or worse. He would be sent back to a ship of the line as a fourth or fifth lieutenant, there to eke out his days in obscurity until he was an old and drunken wretch. Graves would do that too, the villain.

Below the great cabin's window the rudder pintles groaned in the gudgeons, and the *Icarus* heeled a trifle to larboard as she gathered way. A small pile of paper slid off the desk and landed in a heap on the deck. Pendexter stared blankly at the piles that remained. Reports on powder and shot and cordage and sailcloth and barrels and the endless purser's logs that he could not understand.

I have no purser. I have no first officer. Dibdin

247

fights me at every turn, Pendexter reflected. McDuff, McDuff is an animal. But those bastards, dropping tallow on me and ruining my anchoring, an animal is what they deserve.

Dibdin's voice, no longer a shout, came down through the skylight. 'Shall I get the topgallants on her?'

Smeaton's voice came next, with a peevish note. 'I am certainly capable of setting the topgallants, Mr Dibdin!' he said, and then in his best voice of command, 'Hands to the topgallant gear!'

Pendexter's eyes moved over the piles of paper on his desk and on the deck below, and he let out a low moan. He had to get things organized to prove that he ran an efficient ship. Logs to fill out, reports to write . . . his eyes settled on a folded note on the corner of his desk. He snatched it up and unfolded it, and as he did, a new understanding flooded over him. 'Glacous, my good friend,' he read again. The American. This . . . 'Captain' Isaac Biddlecomb. And Ezra Rumstick. It was when they came aboard that the trouble had started.

It was clear to Pendexter now. Things had been fine until those two had infected the *Icarus*. Well, the men were fools if they were following the Americans, and they would see what divided loyalties got them. And as for this Rumstick, and this Biddlecomb, a lower-deck villain who dared call himself captain, he would turn McDuff loose on them. Pendexter flung the letter aside and sank his head in his arms, relishing the vengeance he would let ship on this disloyal company.

'Come!' shouted Pendexter as the pounding on the door brought him out of his reverie.

Appleby opened the door and peeked in. 'Beg pardon, sir, but Mr Dibdin says we're clear of the harbor and what course should we steer?'

'Steer the goddamned direction we are going, tell him that!' Pendexter shouted. 'Wait!' he yelled as Appleby withdrew his head. The midshipman appeared once more. 'You were the one that dropped the slush on me, weren't you?'

'It was an accident, like I said then, and I was beat something awful already, sir,' Appleby stammered.

'And that Biddlecomb was with you aloft, wasn't he?'

'Uh, yes, sir, but he didn't have anything to do with the slush, sir.'

Pendexter was silent for a long moment. His thoughts were interrupted by Appleby's nervously shuffling feet. 'All right, Appleby. Tell Dibdin to assemble the men aft.'

Appleby hesitated, expecting more, but when it did not come, he turned and fled the great cabin.

Pendexter listened to the sounds of the men assembling, the bosun's calls and the shouted orders, and the stamping feet, which quickly settled into silence. He pictured them all there, waiting, wondering what was to come. He let them wait. For ten minutes, then fifteen, then twenty, he let them wait and fester with their thoughts. He wanted the men to have time to think about their crimes.

At last it was time and Pendexter stood up and marched out of the great cabin, through the gunroom, and out on deck. The sun had just set, but enough light remained for him to see the men assembled in the waist.

He stepped up to the quarterdeck, ignoring the

249

salutes of the officers, and turned and surveyed the men. They looked back, anxious, eager to hear what Pendexter would say.

'You men,' Pendexter began at last, 'have disgraced this ship and its officers, and you have disgraced yourselves. Up until now I have been a strict captain, but a fair one, and I've run a crack vessel. But you men have chosen to thwart me, to be seduced by the influence of others, and to make me the laughingstock of the Royal Navy. Don't think that I do not know who among you is plotting this, is filling your heads with sea-lawyer talk, because I do. But you are all ultimately guilty of plotting against me, and you will now see who holds the legal authority aboard this brig! You will see just who your God is! There shall be no more Sunday service, and Sunday shall be a workday like all the rest. There'll be no make-and-mend day and no plum-duff pudding. And there shall be no more rations of spirits, none at all.'

He waited as the murmur ran through the ship's company, let it swell and subside. He knew that he had just stripped these men of every tiny comfort that made their hard life bearable, and he wanted to savor the moment. They had ruined his life, but he would take them with him to hell.

He waited until the men were quiet again before he continued. He was ready to demonstrate the godlike power he possessed as captain of a man-of-war at sea.

'Hickman! I hold you primarily responsible for this late humiliation, with your incompetence and your stupidity. I am stripping you of your warrant as gunner and placing you under arrest. You will receive a dozen at the capstan at first light!'

250

The men were silent for a second, and then as one they shouted their protest.

'You can't do that!' shouted Hickman. 'You have no power over my warrant! That's—'

'I have power over everything aboard this brig. Mr McDuff, Mr Longbottom, place Hickman in irons.'

The boatswain and his mate shoved their way through the protesting men and grabbed Hickman by both arms.

'Silence!' Pendexter roared, and the deck was quiet. 'You men will stand down to the watch on deck. Go!'

Slowly, sullenly, the men shuffled off, and the unfortunate Hickman was dragged below, his shouted protests audible until he was in the hold and his legs were bound by the heavy irons.

The brig was cleared for action, the first time since Biddlecomb had come aboard, and high aloft McDuff stood on the main crosstrees focusing a telescope on a distant unidentified vessel, a vessel that was still invisible from the deck. Pendexter and Smeaton were below, eating a dinner that the brig's company, standing at quarters, had been forced to miss. Before going below, Pendexter had sent McDuff aloft for the sole purpose, Biddlecomb was certain, of demonstrating to the boatswain that he, Pendexter, was still the lord and master. McDuff would be in a black mood when he regained the deck.

Biddlecomb looked aft. Dibdin had the deck. With the lieutenants below and McDuff aloft the atmosphere on deck was less tense than it had been in days.

251

Biddlecomb leaned heavily on the rammer he held in his hand. He blinked slowly, then blinked again, and his eyes remained shut and he felt his head swirl with fatigue. He shook himself awake and looked out toward the horizon. He shifted in his stance to try to ameliorate the pain. His legs were covered with welts from McDuff's starter, as was most of his body. He looked at his arm resting on the rammer. The dark bruises made him look as if he had been tarring the rig.

His eyes began to close again, and this time he slapped himself across the cheek. The welts and open wounds on his back did not allow him to sleep easily in a hammock, and it seemed as if every time his exhaustion overwhelmed the pain and he did fall asleep, Pendexter turned all hands out to tack or wear ship. Several times they had been turned out in the middle of the night just to be mustered and sent below again. It was just another form of torture. Biddlecomb did not know what had happened on Barbados, but it seemed to have made Pendexter go completely insane.

Bloody Wilson, captain of number seven gun, took a step in Biddlecomb's direction. 'You see you don't fall asleep, there,' he said in a low voice, his eyes still locked on the horizon. 'That whoremonger McDuff's up there running his glass over the deck as much as he is the horizon. You got to watch your arse. I wager your back ain't been scratched by a cat before.'

'Why should I watch my arse? More than anyone else, I mean.'

'McDuff's got it in for you, mate. You ain't noticed how hard he rides you, how he's always

252

watching you and pushing you, waiting for you to do something? You and Rumstick?'

Biddlecomb had indeed noticed that he and Rumstick seemed to be getting the brunt of McDuff's and Longbottom's sadistic natures, but until that point he had told himself that it was his imagination, that every man aboard felt the same way.

'Sure, I guess we've been ill-used by that whore's son, but so has everyone else.'

'That's no lie. But just watch your arse. I don't know why, but he's lying for you.'

The two men fell silent again, then Biddlecomb glanced around and, satisfied that they were attracting no attention, asked in an even softer voice, 'So what's to be done?'

'About what? What do you mean?'

'Well, it seems like Pendexter has gone mad. McDuff and Longbottom are like rabid beasts. The men are desperate. How's this situation to be solved?'

Wilson looked at Biddlecomb with an expression one might use on a confused child. 'We don't "solve" nothing, mate. There ain't a thing we can do.'

'But yesterday you said Pendexter was breaking the law by disrating and flogging the gunner. Can't he be reported to the Admiralty?'

Bloody Wilson laughed, though he was careful not to make a sound. 'Pendexter is a gentleman and a commissioned officer, and you and me? We're lower-deck bastards. There's nothing we can do. Nothing legal.'

'All right, then. What is there illegal that we can do?'

253

'You can smoke that one yourself, mate.'

'Pendexter goes overboard on a dark night?'

'What bloody good is that? Then you get Smeaton as lord and master.'

'Of course. So the only option would be . . .'

'We take the ship,' Wilson said, his words barely even a whisper.

Mutiny, of course. Would it work? Biddlecomb wondered why he had not thought of that.

'Is there talk of that?' Biddlecomb asked, just breathing the words.

'The lads always talk about it, but they'd never do it. They ain't got the balls. And there's nowhere to run.'

'What do you mean?'

'Nowhere to run. We ain't at war with anyone, in case you didn't know. In war you just take the ship and go to whoever you're fighting and you're safe. But now there's nowhere, and the Royal Navy's damn good at running men to earth.' There was an odd tone of pride in his words, and he added, 'It ain't no use. But that don't stop the lads from jawing.'

Biddlecomb turned and ran his eyes along the horizon once again. So the men were thinking about mutiny, but Wilson did not credit them with the courage to attempt it. The question of where to take a stolen man-of-war was a thorny one and would require some thought. We are at the stake and bayed about with many enemies, Biddlecomb thought, the line from *Julius Caesar* rising like a bubble from the depths of his memory. He had not thought of that line in years.

Biddlecomb looked across the deck to number-four gun, opposite his on the larboard side. Rumstick

254

was standing there, stripped to the waist, the rammer he held looking like a twig in his huge hand. Biddlecomb shook his head as he looked at the angry welts that stood out in many places on Rumstick's back, all courtesy of McDuff and Longbottom. Longbottom in particular seemed the type of deviant who enjoyed beating a man who was far more powerful than himself, but helpless to strike back. But Rumstick, Biddlecomb knew, was entirely capable of striking back, and Biddlecomb prayed that he would not.

Rumstick turned and their eyes met, but not a hint of recognition was on Rumstick's face. To Biddlecomb's knowledge Rumstick had not spoken a word since the *Icarus* had cleared out of Barbados, and Biddlecomb could only guess at the depths of his friend's despair. Then a thin smile played across the big man's face and he shook his head. Biddlecomb realized that his back must look as bad as Rumstick's.

'Listen here, you men!' Mr Dibdin shouted from the quarterdeck. 'We shall remain at quarters until we see what this strange sail to weather is about. Larboard guns will reinforce starboard. You may stand easy.'

To Biddlecomb's surprise most of the men at the larboard battery deserted their charges and crossed over to the starboard side. Then he realized that, as comparatively large as the *Icarus*'s crew was, there were still not enough men to effectively man both batteries. That being the case, the men were taken from the unengaged side to reinforce the engaging side. Biddlecomb wondered what they would do if they engaged on both sides, and how often that occurred.

'Well, Isaac, perhaps we'll be killed in a fight

255

today,' said Rumstick, who had joined Biddlecomb's gun crew, 'and that'll be an end to it.'

Biddlecomb was happy to hear Rumstick talking again, as morbid as his words might be. 'A fight would be a welcome change. One can strike back, at least,' said Biddlecomb.

'Aye. And if we get into it, like hand to hand, I'm looking for my chance to get that fucking bosun and his mate.'

'Please don't do anything stupid.'

'Whatever I do, you can be certain that that bastard Longbottom comes with me. Look, here's the chase.' Rumstick leaned low and peered out of the gunport, as did Biddlecomb and the rest of the brig's company along the starboard side. The strange vessel, which only fifteen minutes earlier had not been visible from the deck, was now almost hull up as its course converged with that of the *Icarus*.

'Schooner, looks like,' said Biddlecomb. 'Yankee built, I'd venture.'

'She's a right tub. You must be right,' said Harland, who was filling out the crew on number-three gun.

'Tub, my arse. She's a Yankee to be sure, look how she flies,' observed Rumstick, sounding happier than he had been since coming aboard the *Icarus*. It was as if he were getting a glimpse of home.

'Well, wherever she was built, she ain't no Yankee no more,' Harland continued. 'No Yankee would run down on a British man-of-war like that.'

Harland's point was valid and was at the heart of the speculation that ran the length of the *Icarus*'s weather deck. The schooner was on a course to intercept the brig. It made no sense for any vessel

256

to do that, unless the schooner was also a vessel of the British navy wishing to communicate, which the older man-of-war's men asserted it was not. What then was the schooner's intent?

The two vessels were closing fast, with all of their plain sail spread to the trade winds. The schooner was less than a mile away, her course not altered a degree, her wake stretching out in a long straight line behind her.

'What in hell is she about?' muttered a man who held the handspike to Biddlecomb's left.

'I know this schooner, Isaac,' said Rumstick. 'I'm certain I know this schooner. She's the *Elizabeth* out of Falmouth. Joseph Page's ship. You remember Joe, I'll warrant.'

'Joseph Page. Certainly, I remember him.'

'He bought the *Elizabeth* two years ago.'

'But what in hell is he doing?'

'Ensign's going up,' observed Harland. The others crouched and peered through the gunport. A flag was breaking out at the schooner's gaff, but over the distance they could not identify it.

Biddlecomb glanced back at the quarterdeck. Pendexter and Smeaton were back and Dibdin had moved aft, looking as if he were trying to put as much space as the small quarterdeck would allow between himself and the lieutenants.

A signal flag fluttered from the gaff and another from the main truck, and Biddlecomb imagined they must be orders for the schooner to heave to. He had seen those flags before, from the deck of the *William B. Adams*. But the flags were a naval code and Biddlecomb wondered if Pendexter knew that they were meaningless to a merchant captain.

257

Pendexter stood alone, as was now his habit, at the quarterdeck's weather rail, his telescope trained at the schooner. He took the glass from his eye and beckoned to the officers behind him. Smeaton and Dibdin stepped across the deck, and the three officers together brought their telescopes to their eyes. They stood for a moment, swaying to the rhythm of the ship, then as one they lowered their telescopes again. Each spoke in turn, and though Biddlecomb could not hear their words, he could see them shake their heads. Apparently the telescopes were no help in identifying the strange ensign.

Pendexter waved his arm again and Appleby hurried to his side. Pendexter pointed to the bow and spoke a few words, which sent Appleby racing off the quarterdeck and down the weather side. He rushed past Biddlecomb and Rumstick and up to the number-three gun, where that gun's captain stood with his foot on the cascabel.

'Please, sir, the captain says, "Would you be so good as to put a shot across her bows?"' Appleby blurted out. The gun captain nodded and crouched over the gun, signaling with his hands to the hand-spike men.

The schooner had closed to half a mile, and Biddlecomb could see the trace of a smile on Rumstick's lips. 'Well, Ezra, who is she? What is that ensign?' Biddlecomb asked.

Rumstick jerked his head and stepped away from the others, and Biddlecomb followed. 'She is the *Elizabeth*, like I thought. She's flying a new ensign. An American privateer's ensign. I heard tell of it, but I didn't know anyone was using it. Page might be the first.'

258

Biddlecomb was struck dumb, and before he was able to speak again number-three gun roared out and leapt back against its breeches. 'The "American privateer's ensign"?' Biddlecomb asked when his ears had recovered sufficiently for him to hear his own whispered voice. 'Since when does America have "privateers"? Who in America has the authority to issue a letter of marque?'

'Well, they ain't exactly issuing letters of marque just yet. There's talk the governor of Massachusetts will soon. Some of the boys are just starting a bit early.'

'Starting early? This is piracy, and nothing less. How can you call yourself a privateer if there is no war on?'

'Look around you, Isaac. Look where you are. You still say there's no war?'

Biddlecomb was struck with a thought that made him grin. 'I believe, Ezra, that you are right, and it's high time I joined in the fight for liberty.'

'Good Christ!' Harland shouted before Rumstick could reply. The two men crouched and peered out of the gunport. The *Elizabeth* was lost in a cloud of smoke. A flat rumble rolled down on the brig, and thirty-six pounds of American iron crashed into the *Icarus*'s hull.

259

CHAPTER 18

Chase to Weather

'God damn it!' Pendexter shouted as a section of the quarterdeck caprail shattered and oak splinters whistled past his head.

Biddlecomb crouched down and peered through the gunport. The *Elizabeth* was still wreathed in smoke, though most of it had been carried away by the wind, and Biddlecomb was surprised to see that she was now on a taut bowline, moving away from the *Icarus*. She must have fired her broadside and put her helm up at the same time. A neat trick.

'She's smartly handled,' he commented.

Rumstick was grinning broadly. 'Spun her like a top in her own gun smoke! And every shot told, it seems.'

'God damn your eyes, fire! Fire!' Pendexter's voice, high-pitched with tension, cut through the chatter of the waiting men.

'Fire! Fire when you bear!' Smeaton shouted, and Appleby took up the cry, screeching with excitement. Gun captains leaned over their charges and waved their crews out of the way. Some called for handspikes to train the guns fore or aft, but most just looked down the length of the barrel, stepped back,

260

and drove the slow match into the touchhole.

The broadside was ragged at best, with nearly a minute elapsing between the first gun and the last. Biddlecomb stood back and peered over the bulwark. Within a half-mile radius of the schooner the sea was marked with spouts of water where the shot fell, but as far as he could tell, the *Elizabeth* was unscathed.

'Not even close!' Rumstick said, too loud for Biddlecomb's comfort.

'Ezra, shut up, please. It'll go hard on you if they hear you celebrating our failure.'

'Sorry. I'll keep quiet.'

'What's he doing? If he's a privateer, why attack a man-of-war?'

'Probably wanted to see if he was escorting a convoy. He sees we ain't so he takes a shot for fun and he's gone.'

'Has it occurred to you that if we catch them, we'll be forced to fight them? Our own countrymen?'

'We won't catch them. See how he gets his squares in?'

'Sponge!' cried the number-five gun captain, and Biddlecomb realized with a start that that meant him. He was finally getting a chance to fire the guns and he was not even paying attention. He plunged his swab in the water bucket and drove it hissing down the barrel, stealing a glance at the fleeing schooner as he did. Her square sails, topsail and topgallant sail, were clewed up, and already men were laying out on her yards and fisting the canvas.

The *Icarus* could have outsailed the schooner on any point of sail, save this one. In the present circumstance, sailing close-hauled, the *Elizabeth*'s massive fore and aft sails would allow her to point

261

several points higher than the square-rigged *Icarus* could ever hope to make. As long as the chase was to weather, the Yankee was safe.

'You're right,' Biddlecomb said to Rumstick. 'Unless something carries away, we won't catch her now.'

'We sure as hell ain't going to catch her if Pendexter don't turn the bloody ship!' Harland grumbled as he shoved a fresh cartridge down the barrel of the gun.

He was right in that. The *Icarus*, still on its old course, was moving perpendicular to and away from its quarry.

'Silence fore and aft! Shut your bloody gobs!' McDuff, now down from the masthead, fairly screamed. 'Who give you bastards leave to talk?' He wound up with his starter and struck hard at the man nearest to him. Silence fell over the deck.

'Hands to braces!' Dibdin shouted from the quarterdeck, and the men scrambled to their lines, casting off coils and taking turns off belaying pins. 'Starboard tack, sharp as she'll go! Let go and haul!'

The yards squealed as they came farther around, and the *Icarus* heeled hard over through the turn. The men sweated and heaved to the accompaniment of curses and lashings from the bosun and his mate until the yards would come no farther.

'Lay into those bowlines!' Dibdin shouted. 'Put some weight in them, as much as they'll take! Come, Mr McDuff, mind your business!' and the men hauled until the bowlines were as taut as harp strings and the *Icarus* was sailing as close to the wind as she was able.

Biddlecomb looked over the starboard bow. The

262

Elizabeth was sailing closer still, not much, but enough that she would inch away from the *Icarus*. By nightfall she would be gone, and Pendexter could do not one thing to prevent it.

For half an hour the *Icarus* was silent in an unnatural, anxious way. The men stood at their stations, no one daring to make a sound, watching the schooner draw steadily away. Once Smeaton fired his pistols at a passing turtle, the crack of the guns making the men leap. That and the clumping of McDuff's boots as he prowled the deck were the only sounds to be heard above the rush of water down the side.

'Mr Smeaton!' Pendexter shouted at last, his voice sounding odd after the silence. 'We shall fall off to present a broadside. Every man is to aim with care. I want that pirate crippled!'

Orders flew down the deck and the sail trimmers prepared their lines as the gun captains again crouched low over the guns and the handspike men stood ready. Every man aboard was greatly relieved to have a job to do, something to break the terrible silence.

Biddlecomb looked down the deck and saw that all was in readiness, every man concentrating on his task. On the quarterdeck Pendexter held his glass to his eye. He nodded his head and Dibdin stepped up to the rail.

'Helm's a-weather!' he shouted, and the *Icarus* swung round, her starboard battery coming to grip with the enemy. Biddlecomb tensed, waiting for the moment when the guns would bear, anxious for the men to do well and so avoid Pendexter's wrath, but not so well that the *Elizabeth* would be caught.

And then number-eleven gun fired, a deafening

263

blast. Biddlecomb dropped his swab in surprise, and he saw Pendexter drop his telescope, glass spewing from the end. The gun leapt inboard, over the foot of the handspike man, who fell, shrieking in agony. Blood poured from his shattered foot and spread across the deck.

'God damn you to hell!' screamed Pendexter at the stammering, frightened gun crew.

'Sorry, sir, it were an accident,' said the gun captain.

'God damn your accidents!' Pendexter shouted. 'Mr McDuff, a dozen for each man on this gun crew at first light tomorrow, do you hear?' McDuff nodded.

'Now,' Pendexter continued, gesturing toward the sobbing man on the deck, 'get him below and get back to your gun, or God help me it shall be two dozen each!'

Three men from number-eleven gun picked their fallen mate off the deck and carried him below, the motion making him scream with renewed vigor.

Biddlecomb glanced over the starboard side, looking for the *Elizabeth*, and was surprised to find her gone. He was confused for a moment, then realized that all the while the brig must have continued to turn. He looked aft. The *Elizabeth* was now broad on the starboard quarter, and the two vessels were moving in opposite directions.

'Round up! Round up, God damn you, Mr Dibdin, are you an idiot?' Pendexter shouted. The helm shifted and the *Icarus* began the turn to weather. 'Now, you motherless imbeciles,' Pendexter addressed the men, 'fire as your guns bear, and not a moment before or after.'

264

The *Elizabeth* came into sight once more as the *Icarus* turned in her wake. Number-thirteen gun was the first to bear and it fired at the schooner, then number eleven, which remained silent, half her gun crew below tending their mate. Number nine came to bear and went off with a crash. Biddlecomb could see the fall of the shot, three cable lengths short of the schooner. Number seven fired, and five, all down the starboard side, each gun laid as well as its out-of-practice crew was able, each gun missing by a cable length or more. When at last the *Icarus* came up in the *Elizabeth*'s wake, still unable to point as high as the schooner, she had lost half a mile in the chase.

'Mr McDuff,' Pendexter yelled, his voice calmer than it had been, 'start the fresh water please.'

Biddlecomb was surprised by this order. By 'start the water' Pendexter meant that all the fresh water should be let to run into the bilges where it could be pumped overboard to lighten the vessel. This seemed excessive, considering that they would still never catch the schooner.

Ten minutes later the fresh water was streaming over the side. Ten minutes after that the carpenter was knocking the wedges out of the mast. And in another ten minutes the sail trimmers were sent below to carry round shot to the windward side, all in an effort to coax an extra half a knot out of the flying brig. And Biddlecomb admitted to himself, reluctantly, that they were moving faster. But the *Elizabeth* was still pointing higher.

He was running his eye over the trim of the *Elizabeth*'s sails, noting how Page had let the main out just a hair farther than seemed right, when the

265

stern of the schooner coughed gray clouds of smoke and two plumes of water shot out of the sea, two hundred feet in front of the *Icarus*.

'He's rigged stern chasers, by God!' Rumstick marveled.

'Don't look so pleased, Ezra. We're being shot at,' Biddlecomb reminded him.

'Didn't take too bloody long to get them guns aft, either,' Rumstick noted in a softer voice.

The *Elizabeth* fired again, and this time the shot fell so close that the spray was blown across the deck.

Biddlecomb wondered what Pendexter would do now. The brig would have to fall off for her guns to bear, and that had not proved successful before. Pendexter's other choice was to continue the chase and ignore the impudent fire of the schooner in hopes of closing to a distance from which the gunners could not miss. Biddlecomb looked back at the quarterdeck. Pendexter stood at the weather rail, motionless like a statue, staring out at the schooner.

The *Elizabeth* fired again. A plume of water shot up from the larboard bow and a black hole appeared in the fore topsail.

'Getting their range now,' Rumstick commented.

'Who in bloody hell is this? What are they doing?' asked Harland in a voice filled with exasperation.

'She's American. The *Elizabeth*, out of Falmouth, Massachusetts,' Biddlecomb said matter-of-factly.

'You know what boat that is? What the hell is he doing?'

Rumstick opened his mouth to speak, but Biddlecomb shot him a look that Rumstick knew from long experience meant he was to let Biddlecomb do the talking now.

'I have my ideas,' Biddlecomb said, and then, looking furtively around the deck, added, 'Not here.'

Harland nodded, glanced around himself, then peered through the gunport once again.

For another twenty minutes they continued in pursuit of the schooner. Not a line was touched, nor a sail trimmed, as nothing, short of jettisoning the guns, would make the brig move faster through the water. The *Elizabeth* continued to pepper them with shot, getting off a dozen in that time, over half of them telling and inflicting minor damage. And it was clear to everyone aboard the *Icarus* that slowly, inexorably, the Americans were pulling away.

'Listen here, you men,' Pendexter shouted from the quarterdeck. 'We are going to fall off and fire a broadside. I want no stupidity, for once. Make your shots count, or God help me there will be more than one gun crew dancing with the cat tomorrow.'

Overhead Biddlecomb heard the sound of tearing canvas, followed instantly by the dull report of the *Elizabeth*'s stern chasers. He looked aloft. The fore topsail's weather clew had been shot out, the shredded canvas flapping out to leeward.

'Let go your halyards!' Dibdin shouted, and the yards were eased down the mast. Biddlecomb saw Dibdin address a question to Pendexter, saw Pendexter nod and then disappear below.

'Draw your charges and secure your guns,' Dibdin said. The chase was over.

It was six bells in the afternoon watch before the weary and famished men were sent below for dinner. As hungry as he was, and as tempting as even the cold salt pork and weevily biscuit were to him at that moment, Biddlecomb did not repair to mess table

267

six. Instead he clambered over the bulwark at the bow and down to the beakhead, positioning himself on one of the seats of ease there and trying to guess when ten minutes had elapsed.

He wanted his messmates to have a moment to themselves, a moment in which they could speculate about the identity of the bellicose schooner and give free rein to their imaginations. After years of negotiating for ship's cargoes the world over, there was little that Biddlecomb did not understand about manipulating his fellow man.

At last he judged that the time was right. He pulled his trousers up and buckled the wide belt around his waist, then climbed back over the bulwark and made his way below. He pushed through the crowd of hungry men and slid in next to Bloody Wilson at mess table six.

'Where the hell you been?' Harland asked. Biddlecomb glanced around the table. All eyes were on him. That was good.

'Head,' Biddlecomb said, and with some difficulty he stabbed the last piece of salt pork with his sheath knife and transferred it to his plate.

The table was silent, save for the sound of Biddlecomb noisily ripping meat from the bone.

'Well?' Harland asked at last.

Biddlecomb looked up and glanced around. He appeared surprised that all eyes were still on him. 'What?'

'Harland says you know what schooner that was,' Wilson took up the questioning. 'He said you said it was a Yank.'

'Sure. She's the *Elizabeth*, privateer out of Falmouth.'

268

His messmates were silent, but Biddlecomb was not unaware of the glances being shot back and forth.

'Privateer?' asked Israel Barrett. 'We ain't at war with the colonies. Are we?'

'Close enough that the Continental Congress is issuing letters of marque. They started about six months after the *Gaspee* mutiny.'

'*Gaspee* mutiny?' Wilson asked. 'You mean the *Gaspee* what was burned by them Yankees in Narragansett Bay?'

Biddlecomb chuckled and scooped a knifeful of dried peas into his mouth. 'That what they told you?'

'Ain't that what happened?' Wilson probed.

'No, that ain't what happened. The crew of the *Gaspee* mutinied.'

'I heard that Dudingston what had her was a foul-mouthed bastard,' Harland supplied.

'Shut up, let Isaac talk,' said Barrett.

'The crew mutinied, that's all. No killing, just took the ship and sailed her to Providence. They sold her as a privateer, for a damn lot of money, I'm told.'

'We heard tell the *Gaspee* was burned whilst she was aground,' said Barrett.

'You don't think the navy's going to tell you there was a mutiny and the crew got clean away, do you?'

'How did they get away? They would've been hunted down, hung in public,' said Wilson.

'America's a big country, settlements back to the Ohio River. The crew wasn't stupid enough to stay in Providence or go to sea where the navy'd catch them. I hear a fellow with a little money in his purse can set himself up real nice in the Ohio Territory.'

269

The table was silent again, and Biddlecomb knew that he had said enough.

'Tell me this,' Barrett began, but Biddlecomb cut him off.

'If it gets out I'm telling you this, it'll go damn hard on me. I've said enough,' and with that Biddlecomb turned to his food in earnest.

The mess fell silent again, and Biddlecomb knew that each man was considering this new information. If anyone could move the men of the *Icarus* to action, these three could. He had planted the seed of mutiny, and he knew it would grow fast and spread far in such fertile soil. Biddlecomb thought of another line from *Julius Caesar*. They were Antony's words: 'Mischief, thou art afoot, take thou what course thou wilt.'

270

CHAPTER 19

The Watering Party

It was hot in the cay, miserably hot, as the morning breeze that had wafted the *Icarus* in through the reefs died away and the brig sat motionless, anchored above her own reflection. The men worked silently, refilling the water casks that in the chase with the *Elizabeth* had been pumped dry. Tempers were brittle, like crystal, ready to shatter, as gangs filled the barrels from a spring ashore and others rowed them out to the brig where they were swayed aboard and stowed down below.

The day had started with the flogging of the crew of number-eleven gun, a horrible and macabre spectacle. One by one they were lashed to the capstan and flogged, the blood puddling on the deck. The man whose foot had been crushed was carried to the capstan between McDuff and Longbottom, the lashings at his wrist holding him up as much as holding him in place. The Icaruses seethed and stared outboard and clenched their fists. Their hatred was a tangible thing, and it still smarted in each man like the swollen wounds on the gun crew's backs.

On deck, in the still air, the heat was almost unbearable, but down below in the hold where the

271

barrels were stowed in tiers, it was much, much worse. That was where McDuff had sent Biddlecomb, Wilson, Barrett, and those others that he had singled out for this most unpleasant task. The men worked stripped to the waist, guiding the full casks down as they were lowered on the stay tackle and rolling them into position. They were soon lathered in sweat, which poured off their brows, blinding them, and making their hands slick and unable to grip the awkward barrels. Despite the unlimited fresh water available Pendexter allowed the men only their standard ration and not a drop more.

'Here, Isaac.' Wilson turned to Biddlecomb as the men struggled to stow the heavy barrels in the forward end of the hold. 'Some of us have been talking about this *Gaspee* mutiny, and we decided that, you being a proper seaman, and a messmate to some of us, that you wouldn't steer us wrong. And then some of us were thinking, "Well, why couldn't we do the same with *Icarus*?" '

That's the idea, Biddlecomb thought.

'I been in a score of ships,' Barrett interjected, 'and ain't none was a hell ship like this one. And there ain't nothing we can do. We could take care of McDuff, sure, and Longbottom, but there'd be others. Pendexter's gone mad, that's all.' The others nodded and murmured consent.

'Well, it's a damned thing . . . mutiny! But I don't see why it couldn't be done. I have friends in Providence, people that can sell a ship with no questions asked, people that can help a man disappear into the Ohio Territory. But when? When can we do it?'

'It ain't that easy, Isaac,' Wilson said. 'We got to

272

talk to the others. Everyone's got to agree. We need to vote.'

Biddlecomb's heart fell. 'It should be done quick. With talking and voting and such there's more chance we're found out. If you wait, people lose the fire in the belly.'

'I know that, Isaac, but, faith, we ain't pirates and we ain't murderers. All of us . . . well, most of us volunteered to fight for our king. We ain't criminals. We just can't take no more. But we got to make this legal.'

Biddlecomb resisted pointing out that they were unlikely to make the mutiny legal, by vote or otherwise. 'Let me know what you decide, and I'm for you.'

For the next two hours the men sweated and cursed as they rolled the casks around the hold and lifted them in place.

Biddlecomb worked in silence, agonizing over his disappointment. He had thought they were ready, thought they were desperate enough for anything, but now he saw that he had misjudged them. Perhaps they were too afraid, or perhaps their loyalty to king and country was too strong. Whatever it was, Biddlecomb could see now that there would be no mutiny. Once men crowded together in quiet parts of the ship, or high in the rig, and debated the question and took furtive votes, then regardless of what they decided they would not do it. It had to be a moment of insanity, like a spark that ignites a powder keg. A mutiny was a mob event and it happened spontaneously, or it did not happen at all.

It was halfway through the first dogwatch when the last of the barrels came aboard and Biddlecomb,

273

bruised, with at least one toe that he knew of broken, made his way topside for his first breath of fresh air in hours.

The men who had remained above, who had spent the day swaying barrels out of the boat and down into the hold, had had at least as bad a time as he had. Worse, he imagined, as they had McDuff and Longbottom to contend with. They looked drawn and exhausted, stooping and leaning when they could, the few rags they wore quite soaked through with sweat. Their faces were set and tense and they kept their eyes on the deck.

Biddlecomb saw Rumstick leaning on the bulwark by the fall of the stay tackle. McDuff had not sent him below. The boatswain did not want Rumstick out of his sight, beyond the reach of his starter. Rumstick's face was expressionless, but on his shoulder was an open cut and the blood had run down his back unattended.

Something about Rumstick's expression was familiar, and Biddlecomb realized to his horror that it was not unlike the expression that Haliburton had worn when he dove over the side. Rumstick was close to the edge; Biddlecomb knew it and he was certain that McDuff knew it as well. Biddlecomb thought of the men's indecision about the mutiny, and he felt impotent and angry. It ws the second time he had failed to get them out of this nightmare, and he was running short on time. He thought of Haliburton's body sinking in a cloud of his own blood. Rumstick was following his old adversary down.

The gig pulled alongside, one last barrel in the stern sheets. 'All right, you sods, one more to come aboard,' shouted McDuff, and the men shuffled to

274

their stations, bending with some effort to pick up their lines.

'Sway away on the yard tackle!' McDuff bawled, and the barrel rose out of the gig to the groans and muttered curses of the men heaving on the fall. 'Avast! Haul away the stay tackle!' McDuff ordered, and the barrel began to sail inboard. 'Ease away smartly, the yard tackle!'

Biddlecomb caught a flash of motion from the corner of his eye, where Rumstick and a dozen others tended the yard tackle. 'Hold fast! Damn!' a young waister tending the line at the pin shouted, and then everyone shouted at once and the fall of the yard tackle went spinning out of control.

Biddlecomb turned in time to see McDuff leap from under as the barrel fell to the deck, smashing the wheel off a gun carriage and shattering on impact. Fresh water ran in rivers along the dry planking and poured out of the scuppers. The brig fell silent.

'Mr McDuff, I want the name of the man who . . .' Smeaton called from the quarterdeck, but McDuff did not seem to hear him. His eyes were fixed on the waister, who in turn shook his head and took small steps back.

'So, think you can kill me just like that, eh? Saw your chance to do me with the barrel?'

'No, by God, I vow it ain't true,' the waister pleaded. He was terrified. Biddlecomb knew him to be no more than sixteen, and with his eyes wide and his hands shaking he looked much younger than that. 'I thought they had it,' he stammered.

'We thought he had wraps on the pin, Mr Bosun,' said Rumstick as contrite as he could manage. 'It weren't his fault, it was an accident.'

275

'You shut your gob, Brother Jonathan, I'll have time for you later!' McDuff advanced on the waister, who held his hands before him as if to fend the bosun off.

'You thought the line was belayed? To this pin?' McDuff asked, pointing to the belaying pin in the rail. The waister nodded. Then in one fluid motion McDuff yanked the pin from the rail and crashed it into the side of the young man's head. The seaman went down like a bundle of rags, rolling on the deck and clutching his head.

'You tried to kill me, you miserable bastard!' McDuff cried as he drove his leather shoe into the boy's stomach.

'God damn you, it was an accident!' Rumstick cried.

McDuff looked up at him, a faint smile playing on his lips. 'God damn me?' he said, his voice almost conversational. 'Fine, Rumstick, you rutting bastard, I'll see to you in a moment,' and with that he stepped back and kicked the boy in the face. The boy's head snapped back and blood spewed from his shattered nose. Then McDuff kicked him in the stomach again, then again in the face.

'You'll kill him, you bastard!' Rumstick shouted. Biddlecomb stepped over and put his hand on Rumstick's shoulder, but Rumstick shook him off.

'You mind yourself, Rumstick!' Longbottom called from where he stood behind McDuff.

'And then I'll kill you,' added McDuff. He stepped aside and Longbottom kicked the waister hard, but the seaman was either unconscious or dead.

'Enough!' Rumstick roared, and pushed past the watching crowd.

276

'Ezra, God damn you, no!' Biddlecomb shouted, but he knew that it was too late. Rumstick had been pushed too far.

McDuff looked up in surprise at Rumstick's advance. He wound up with his starter and struck Rumstick across the face, opening his cheek wide, but Rumstick did not seem to notice.

'Get back there, you whoremonger, you son of a bitch!' Longbottom cried, pushing past McDuff and grabbing Rumstick by the collar. Rumstick reached down and grabbed a fistful of Longbottom's crotch, hard. Longbottom's eyes went wide and his mouth hung open. Rumstick grabbed him by the neck and with a swift jerk lifted him like a bread bag and hurled him overboard.

He turned toward McDuff and the rattan cane came down across his face again. 'You're a dead man, Jonathan, you hear me?' His starter sliced toward Rumstick's head, but Rumstick's hand lashed out and grabbed the cane in the middle, checking the blow. They stood like swordsmen with locked blades, and then Rumstick snapped the starter in two with his powerful hand. McDuff's confidence was shaken now. His mouth opened and closed, but he said nothing.

Then McDuff released the broken starter and wound up and swung his heavy fist, but still Rumstick was too fast for him. He caught McDuff's fist in his open hand, like a man catching a ball, and with the same jerking motion he had used on Longbottom, he twisted the bosun's wrist outboard. McDuff howled in pain and fell to his knees. Then Rumstick let McDuff's hand go and drove his fist into McDuff's face. Blood shot out like spray as

277

McDuff's nose collapsed under Rumstick's hand, and he would have fallen back if Rumstick had not caught him by the collar and yanked him to his feet. McDuff staggered, supported by Rumstick, and then Rumstick struck him again.

There was an audible snap when McDuff's jaw broke, and that sound seemed to bring the watching men from their reverie. They jumped on Rumstick and pulled him away from McDuff, whom they allowed to collapse on the deck. As Rumstick struggled and tried to shake them off, Smeaton, cocked pistols in his hands, and Dibdin burst through the crowd.

'Not a move, you Yankee villain, or I'll end it here!' Smeaton yelled. Rumstick fell silent, his eyes on the deck.

'Take him below, you men,' said Dibdin, 'and put him in irons. And see you make them secure. Mr Appleby, go below and see that Rumstick is secured so he don't think he can take French leave of us.'

Four men escorted the silent Rumstick below, with Appleby following behind. Biddlecomb watched him disappear down the hatch and felt sick with apprehension. 'There will be a trial, will there not?' he asked Wilson, who stood beside him. 'There'll be some kind of hearing . . . ?'

Wilson just shook his head. 'McDuff had it right, mate. Rumstick's a dead man.'

278

CHAPTER 20

Rough Justice

Capt. James Pendexter stared out the aft window at the *Icarus*'s wake, just visible in the growing dawn, and he giggled as mirth once again overwhelmed him. He was giddy with relief, consumed by an excitement and an anticipation that he had not felt since the boat had first taken him across Boston Harbor to his first command. He thought for a moment on how long ago that was and was surprised to realize that not even six weeeks had passed. It was the great anxiety oppressing him that made him feel as if he had had the *Icarus* for years. But now he had the means to remove that anxiety, like a surgeon plucking a musket ball from a wound.

It was ideal, absolutely ideal, and McDuff had provided the means for the extraction, as Pendexter had planned, but in a way quite different from the original strategy. But that did not matter. Now he could root out the whole problem, both of the damned Jonathans, with one pull.

He moved his gaze from the wake and looked down at his desk, now quite tidy since he had, in a fit of exasperation, tossed most of the papers out of the stern window. The only thing that lay there, beside

279

the ink and the pens, was the leather-bound copy of the Articles of War. They reminded him, with a twinge of uneasiness, that what he was about to do was not entirely legal. But again, neither was flogging and disrating the gunner, who held a warrant, and no odious consequences had come about due to that action. No, there was only one real law, one that superseded even the Articles of War: Pendexter was the lord and master over this vessel. At sea, when there was no appealing to higher authority, it was his duty to do whatever was required to maintain discipline.

And then he recalled that higher authority was to be found in Barbados, five or six days away. He considered entering that harbor again, considered facing the admiral with a request for a court-martial. 'No time for that,' he told himself, 'no time. This must be done quickly or the lesson is lost on those villains on the lower deck.'

Through the open skylight Pendexter heard the piping of 'up hammocks' with the subsequent rush and stamp as the watch below fled to the weather deck, their rolled hammocks under their arms. Much of the urgency of that morning ritual was lost with McDuff's absence. The bosun was still in his cabin, confined to his cot. Though the cook and Dibdin had set his jaw as best as they were able, McDuff still groaned constantly and clutched at the bedclothes with his fists. Pendexter had an idea of how much pain was required to make a hard man like McDuff behave that way.

Overhead the stowing of the hammocks was complete, and Pendexter could hear the men making ready to scrub the lower deck. This was the moment

280

he had planned for, and as he stood and gathered up the Articles of War, he felt a twinge of fear in his stomach. In the next two hours he would reestablish total control over his brig and gain the respect and fear of the men, as was proper for a commanding officer. If all went well. He swallowed hard, checked his uniform in the mirror, then strode purposefully out the door.

Bloody Wilson and Isaac Biddlecomb carried their wooden buckets of seawater down the main scuttle and forward across the lower deck. They dropped to their knees just aft of the manger boards and applied their stiff brushes to the smooth planks.

'So what's to happen to him?' asked Biddlecomb in a voice quiet enough that only Wilson could hear.

'It's a hanging offence, what he done, striking an officer, especially as he broke his damned jaw. But a death sentence has to come from a court-martial, a captain can't order it.'

'And what's required for a court-martial?'

'You needs five captains, post captains, not lieutenants just called captains like Pendexter, so he's safe until we gets back to Barbados, or Boston. Even then it can take a long time to get five captains together, if the fleet's out.'

'So there is a chance. There'll be a trial.'

'He ain't got a chance, Isaac, all he's got is time. Rumstick broke McDuff's jaw right in front of every officer and man on board. It don't matter the circumstance, Rumstick'll hang. Or be flogged around the fleet.'

'What is "flogged around the fleet"?'

'You don't want to know.'

281

Biddlecomb did indeed want to know and was about to say as much when Longbottom's bosun's call came wailing down the after scuttle.

'All hands to witness punishment! All hands to witness punishment!' he shouted between blasts from the call.

'Punishment?' asked Biddlecomb, suddenly filled with foreboding.

'Let's see who's in for it now,' replied Wilson as he stood and hurried to the ladder, Biddlecomb close behind.

'But it can't be Rumstick! You said there had to be a court-martial!'

'I don't know! Ask the bloody gunner about court-martials on this bucket,' Wilson replied as he disappeared up the ladder.

Biddlecomb emerged on deck, blinking in the sun. Most of the men were already assembled aft, standing in a ragged group and glaring up at the quarterdeck.

The officers stood in their usual order along the leeward side. Pendexter was pressed against the forward rail, stiff and expressionless, the Articles of War tucked under his arm.

'Bring up the prisoner,' he called, his voice as stiff as his posture, and the cry was echoed below.

The men shifted uneasily, some clearing their throats, others standing on one foot then the other and casting around with furtive glances. The atmosphere was charged, volatile, as if just a spark would make the *Icarus* explode.

The after scuttle burst open, like the curtain on a stage, and Rumstick stepped out, manacled hand and foot, Longbottom prodding him from behind. Dried blood was caked around his mouth and he walked with a limp. Biddlecomb imagined that Longbottom had taken advantage of Rumstick's chains to inflict a beating he would not otherwise have dared to give.

The low muttering of the watching men rose in volume to a level that could no longer be ignored. 'Silence, fore and aft!' Smeaton yelled from behind Pendexter's back, causing the captain to start. The brig fell silent again.

Pendexter met Rumstick's gaze, held it for a moment, then cleared his throat and flipped open the Articles of War. 'No person in or belonging to the fleet,' he began, reading through the Article that concerned itself with striking an officer, and ending with 'upon pain of death or such other punishment as the circumstances of his case shall require.'

'That doesn't say anything about a court-martial,' Biddlecomb breathed to Wilson by his side.

'He left it out, didn't he. Bloody convenient.'

'Ezra Rumstick, as you call yourself,' Pendexter continued, closing the Articles, 'in plain view of the officers and men of this vessel you struck the bosun, Mr McDuff, and broke his jaw. This case is clear, there is no need for debate. The men of the *Icarus* will see that justice is swift and terrible under my command. Ezra Rumstick, I sentence you to one thousand lashes, punishment to commence now. Mr Longbottom?'

A murmur rose again, and this time, despite Dibdin's repeated calls for silence, it diminished but did not die.

'A thousand lashes?' Biddlecomb whispered. 'He can't live through that!'

'Is that so? He ain't supposed to, dumb arse. He's

283

being flogged to death,' replied Wilson, who after a pause added, 'There's nothing you can do, mate. I'm sorry. If you try, you'll be next.'

Biddlecomb watched the now familiar ritual as Longbottom unshackled Rumstick and ripped the shirt off his back. Rumstick did not struggle, did not make a sound as the bosun's mate lashed him to the capstan, the marline pulling and distorting his flesh. Biddlecomb felt that he would be sick, felt he would begin to weep. He wanted to explode, wanted to cry out, but he stood there, silently watching, like the others.

Longbottom pulled the cat-o'-nine-tails out of the red baize bag and ran the nettles through his fingers as he sized up his target. He stepped up behind Rumstick, poised, wating for the order to 'do his duty.'

'One moment, Mr Longbottom, if you please,' said Pendexter, and Longbottom looked up at him, his expression one of disappointment. 'The bosun has been injured by this man's cowardly act, and you cannot deliver one thousand lashes by yourself. We must find someone to aid in the punishment.'

Pendexter looked over the crowd, as if searching for the best candidate, and Biddlecomb wondered whom he would pick, what unfortunate would be made to flog his shipmate to death.

'You there. Biddlecomb. Step up, there. You shall deliver the first five hundred strokes.'

He said the words in an even voice, and his face was as composed as a card player's, a good card player's. Or was it? Was there a hint of amusement? Of triumph? Biddlecomb was stunned by the order, he felt suddenly dizzy. He could not do it, of course.

Would not. And then he would be flogged . . . that was it, that was it all along! He had not been selected randomly, nothing of the sort. Flog your friend to death or join him. And Pendexter knew he would not flog Rumstick to death.

Longbottom pushed through the crowd and grabbed Biddlecomb's arm, pulling him into the space reserved to swing the cat, and thrust the whip into his limp hand. Longbottom was grinning now, aware as Biddlecomb was of the trap that had sprung.

'Do your duty,' said Pendexter. 'Captain Biddlecomb.'

Biddlecomb stared at Pendexter. *Captain* Biddlecomb? Where had that come from?

And then he recalled his note, the note he had given to Bolton. I hope there ain't anything in it you don't want old Pendexter to read, Wilson had said. That son of a bitch. That was what started all this.

'Do it, Isaac!' said Rumstick in a harsh whisper, turning his head in an attempt to see his friend. 'Do it, or he'll do you up next! That's what he wants!'

The murmuring behind grew louder, loud enough to intrude on Biddlecomb's thoughts. He stared up at the quarterdeck. He needed time, more time, to think this out.

'Biddlecomb, do your duty now, or you shall be flogged as well for disobeying a direct order.'

So there it was, out in the open now. Biddlecomb heard a shuffling of feet from behind. The muttering and coughing seemed louder, seemed like a physical thing that occupied space on the deck.

And then Biddlecomb realized, with an insight that startled him and jerked him erect, that this was the

285

moment, the instant for action, and that it would never come again.

He turned toward Longbottom and kicked down hard on the bosun's mate's knee and Longbottom collapsed shrieking to the deck. Then he ran aft, seeing the startled faces from the corner of his eye, and jumped the two steps up to the quarterdeck.

Pendexter and Smeaton shrank back as from a leper, surprise and fear in their faces. Biddlecomb raised the cat above his head and brought it down with full force across Pendexter's face.

The blow spun the lieutenant around, and as he fell, Biddlecomb kicked him hard in the ribs and sent him sprawling into the scuppers.

'Icaruses, to me!' Biddlecomb shouted as he lashed out at Smeaton. He caught the first officer in the motion of drawing his sword. The cat struck him on the shoulder and threw him off-balance, and Biddlecomb drove his fist, clutching the handle of the cat, into the surprised man's face, and he too went down.

'To me!' he shouted again, looking over his shoulder at the brig's men, who stood watching, immobile with shock. He turned back. Dibdin was jerking a belaying pin from the starboard rail and at the same time pulling young Appleby out of the way, shielding him with his body.

Now there was a sound from behind, and Biddlecomb turned to face Longbottom, limping up the steps, a capstan bar in his hands. He brought the cat down across Longbottom's face, opening his cheek up with half a dozen lacerations, the force of the blow throwing the bosun's mate to the deck. He turned again. Dibdin was advancing now, and Pendexter pulling himself from the scuppers. Biddlecomb could not hold out half a minute against the two of them, and Smeaton was stirring as well.

'Come on, lads, have at it!' Biddlecomb heard Bloody Wilson shout, and then there was a great yell and the brig's company swarmed aft, pouring up the steps and over the rail, streaming past Biddlecomb as they drove the officers aft and piled upon them. Biddlecomb caught the look of terror in Pendexter's eyes as he disappeared beneath the press of men. Fists and belaying pins rose and fell as the crew clustered above their victims.

Biddlecomb sagged against the rail, watching the scene like a dream unfolding in a troubled sleep. He could not let the men kill the officers. He leapt up on the pinrail, steadying himself with the shrouds, looking down on the mob. 'Stop it! Stand down!' he shouted, and one by one the men let up from their beating and stepped back.

Appleby, with Dibdin shielding him, leaned against the taffrail, apparently unharmed. Pendexter and Smeaton had born the brunt of the attack, and their faces were streaked with blood, their clothes torn, and their cocked hats trampled on the deck. They stared at the retreating men, but did not attempt to stand.

'Listen here, you men,' Biddlecomb began, anxious to take command of the situation, and the *Icarus* as well. 'We have taken the ship! She is ours!'

The men burst into a wild, frenzied cheering as months of fear and anger were released in one purging cry.

Rumstick, freed from his bonds, stepped up to the quarterdeck and stood on the deck beneath Biddlecomb.

287

'You've been hard used by these officers,' Biddlecomb continued as the cheering subsided, 'but we must not stoop to their level. We must not murder them.'

'Blackheart Pendexter was going to flog Rumstick to death! He flogged the gunner and stopped our tot!' shouted a voice in the crowd, and Biddlecomb was suddenly afraid that he would lose control of the men.

The after scuttle burst open and two waisters stepped out, a breaker of rum in their hands. 'Here's rum, lads, and more where this come from!' one of the men shouted, and before Biddlecomb could speak another word the men swarmed back down to the waist and down below. Biddlecomb and Rumstick, Wilson and Barrett, were left alone on the quarterdeck with the brig's former officers.

'Weren't nothing you could do,' said Rumstick, and Biddlecomb knew that he was right. There was no force anywhere on that desolate spot of ocean that could prevent the debauchery from taking place.

288

CHAPTER 21

Bacchanal

The *Icarus*, hove to for all hands to witness punishment, rode easily over the Caribbean swells, though no hands aboard were giving a thought to her operation or for that matter to anything else, save their consumption of the rum in the spirit room. Biddlecomb looked out over the orgy developing on the waist. Five minutes ago he was flailing a cat-o'-nine-tails around the quarterdeck. Five minutes before that he was looking at the certainty of grisly death. He wondered what the next five minutes would bring.

Bloody Wilson appeared with an armload of weapons. Biddlecomb took a pistol and cutlass. He felt like a pirate.

'The rest of the arms I locked up, but it won't serve if that lot decides they wants weapons,' Wilson said. 'Bloody lock on the spirit room didn't last too long.'

'Let's hope they're too drunk to find the arms chest,' said Biddlecomb, leading Wilson aft. By the taffrail Rumstick and Barrett stood guard over the former officers, holding them at bay with their own swords.

'Biddlecomb!' spat Pendexter. 'I will see you hang for this! I'll kill you with my own hands!'

'Indeed. Well, I suggest you wait awhile, as I am now the only thing preventing that drunken mob from tearing you apart.' Biddlecomb turned to Rumstick. 'We had best stow them down in the bread room.'

Biddlecomb grabbed Smeaton by the collar and jerked him to his feet. Rumstick did likewise with Pendexter. They were far from steady, and neither was able to stand fully erect.

'Mr Dibdin,' Biddlecomb addressed the master, who stood to one side, still shielding Appleby, 'you have always been a gentleman and a good officer. I wish you would join us.'

'I'll have no truck with mutiny, sir. Lieutenant Pendexter may have no business commanding a king's vessel, but he is the commander, all legal and proper, and I must recognize that. I still hold the king's warrant.'

'Very well. I'll see you are treated with the same respect that you showed the men.' Biddlecomb turned to Pendexter and Smeaton and said, 'The same, I fear, shall apply to you. Now, Rumstick, get them below.'

Appleby pushed past Dibdin and ran up to Biddlecomb, grabbing the sleeve of his coat. 'Please, sir, let me come with you! I don't have to be a midshipman, I can go forward, just let me come with you!' he pleaded. 'I've been used awful hard, just like you.'

'Do you realize the implications of this? If we're caught, we shall surely hang.'

'And you shall be caught, depend upon it,'

290

Pendexter said, then broke into a coughing fit as Rumstick pushed him along.

'I don't care, sir. I'm desperate. Please let me come with you!'

'But what about your family in England? Your parents?'

Appleby's eyes met Biddlecomb's and held them. He drew himself up to his full, if insubstantial, height. 'Bugger my parents, beg your pardon, sir,' said Appleby with a determination in his voice that Biddlecomb had not heard before. 'And bugger His Majesty's navy.'

Biddlecomb smiled, he could not resist. 'Of course you can come. You're a fine officer, Mr Appleby. But now I want you to go to the gunroom and lock yourself in your cabin. I'll call for you when you're needed.'

Appleby smiled as well. 'Thank you, sir!' He saluted smartly, and then, as if afraid that Biddlecomb would change his mind, turned and fled below.

With the officers stowed in the bread room and Barrett left on guard, the mutineers made their way to the great cabin. Biddlecomb threw open the door and the three men stepped inside.

Rumstick took in the surroundings and nodded his approval. 'Damn fine lash-up Mr Pendexter has here.'

Biddlecomb withdrew a bottle of wine from the rack and held it up to the light, letting out a low whistle as he read the label. 'Will you gentlemen join me?' he asked, reaching for the corkscrew.

'Blackstrap? Fine, what the hell,' said Rumstick.

'Blackstrap? You don't use the term *blackstrap* when talking about . . . never mind,' Biddlecomb sighed as he handed the crystal glasses to the sailors. They looked like doll's dishes in their huge and callused hands.

On the deck above the shouting and laughter was increasing, and now one voice could be heard above the others, bellowing out a forecastle song, a favorite among the man-of-war's men.

> *A topman and an afterguard through*
>   *London did stray*
> *Says the topman to the afterguard,*
>   *'I think we best pray*
> *For all the blessings of all sailors,*
>   *and the mischief of all men,*
> *And whatever I do pray for you must*
>   *answer . . .'*

And the drunken men roared out the answer, a lusty *'Amen!'* and the singer coughed and choked and then began, in a shaky voice, on the next verse.

Biddlecomb raised his wine into the light, ran the glass under his nose, then slowly drew in the first swallow, his eyes closed. The wine seemed to melt into his palate, buttery and dry, and suddenly he was very far away, back at Stanton House, nestled in the big chair in the sitting room, savoring the bounty of Stanton's wine cellar. Virginia was there as well, with her tousled hair and her tan face and that flash of a smile, like whitecaps on the sea, looking girlish and at the same time very much a woman.

Bloody Wilson cleared his throat and recalled Biddlecomb to the present. 'Faith, you interrupt the first pleasure I've had in two months,' Biddlecomb said.

292

'Come on, Isaac, this ain't a garden party, we have work to do,' said Rumstick.

'Philistine,' said Biddlecomb as he selected a chart from the rack against the wall and spread it out across the table, then scanned along the line of daily fixes until his finger rested on the most recent. He picked up the parallel rule – brass inlaid with gold and enamel in a design that Biddlecomb guessed to be the Pendexter coat of arms – and the dividers and measured off the estimated drift, based on the wind and his considerable knowledge of the local currents, and plotted the dead-reckoned fix on the chart.

'You know how to navigate?' Wilson said, more of a statement than a question. Biddlecomb looked up at him and saw that his face showed confusion and admiration, as if he had discovered that Biddlecomb could speak fluently in a foreign tongue.

'Isaac's been master in merchantmen and mate before that for these seven years and more,' said Rumstick with a touch of pride.

'But you was a foremast jack when we pressed you.'

'It's a very long story. Suffice to say that I can navigate.'

> *First I'll pray for those navy officers,*
> *those blackhearts from hell,*
> *Who owe us three years' wages, prize*
> *money as well,*
> *But it's 'We shan't pay you now, Jack, try*
> *next voyage again,'*
> *May the devil double, triple damn them,*
> *Says the afterguard . . .*

293

And again the raucous cry of '*Amen!*' came loud through the skylight, and rather than diminish, the hooting and screaming continued, rising and falling like waves.

'I think we should consider running for Narragansett Bay. I know those waters and it's the safest place we shall find,' Biddlecomb began, but Rumstick cut him off.

'Isaac used to run molasses into Bristol. Late at night.'

'You was a smuggler,' said Wilson.

'The tariffs were unfair, imposed with no American representation in Parliament, contrary to the self-government Americans have enjoyed for . . .' said Biddlecomb speaking loud to be heard over Rumstick's laughter.

'You got patriotism pretty damn fast, didn't you, Isaac?' he said.

'And it serves me well. Now, if our luck holds, the revelries will run their course before a British patrol happens upon us. In that case, once the men are reasonably sober, we shall select officers and lay a course to fetch Long Island. If the wind holds, we can hope to be there in a fortnight, and then we're safe and free.'

'And you can continue your fight for liberty, Isaac,' Rumstick added.

> *Next I'll pray for the bosun with his*
> *rattan cane.*
> *Who calls out, 'All hands!' then serves*
> *us out pain,*
> *He starts many a bold fellow, then*
> *beats him again,*

294

May the devil double, triple damn him,
Says the afterguard . . .

Biddlecomb heard the words through the skylight. Something bothered him, made him feel a vague alarm. And then he remembered.

'Sweet mother of Jesus!' he cried, leaping to his feet and striking his head on the deck beams. 'The goddamned bosun!' He leapt over the table, his head already throbbing, and pushed past the startled sailormen.

'Isaac, what in hell . . . ?' shouted Rumstick, but Biddlecomb was already out the door and halfway across the gunroom. He burst through the scuttle onto the weather deck, and the roaring of the men seemed, incredibly, even louder.

The scene that confronted him was like none that Biddlecomb had ever witnessed, though he had often imagined that pirate havens in Nassau would have looked much like this, when the takings were good.

A few of the men were still standing, but most, by far, were either sitting or lying on the deck in various states of intoxication. The foretopmen, as a group, seemed to have retained a modicum of their senses, but the waisters were far gone, exceeded only by the cook and Jack in the Dust, his assistant, who were lying in the leeward scuppers and alternately vomiting.

Biddlecomb approached Paul Harland, who sat on the step to the quarterdeck.

'Isaac!' he said, his words slurring, but only a bit. 'Fancy me sitting on the step to the quarterdeck! Fifteen years I been in the king's service and I ain't never sat on the step to a quarterdeck!'

295

'I am glad for you, truly, but tell me something. Has, ah, the bosun been on deck?'

Harland grinned broadly and swayed a bit more than was necessary to compensate for the roll of the ship. 'Aye, he and Longbottom, bloody Longbottom, they both been here, and didn't we all dance to a merry tune together.'

'And now?'

'They ain't here now.'

Biddlecomb stepped back to where Wilson was standing. 'What do you think became of them?'

'You don't want to know,' Wilson said, and this time he was right.

Biddlecomb rested the heavy telescope against a ratline on the main topgallant shrouds and slowly swept the horizon again. He knew from experience that the light at dawn could play tricks on a lookout, and he had to be certain before he made his discovery known.

The horizon was empty, a sharp orange line against the pale blue sky, as he swept along, and then . . . there it was again. A sail, Biddlecomb had no doubt now, a topgallant sail. It was too far to make out the details, but the fact that it was a topgallant told him a great deal.

It could be a merchantman with a captain bold enough to carry topgallants all night, but he knew of only a few merchant captains other than himself who made that their practice at that time of year. Or perhaps the captain was cracking on at first light, which was more likely. But Biddlecomb did not believe that was the case either. He did not believe that the sail was anything but a man-of-war.

296

He swiveled around and looked down to the deck below. An hour before, with men strewn about fore and aft, it had looked like the aftermath of a terrible battle, a battle in which the Icaruses had been soundly defeated. But now the men were up and moving and had already discovered that the rum was gone, though fortunately they had not discovered that Rumstick had poured great quantities into the bilges. Sober or not, Biddlecomb needed the men to start cracking on all the sail that the *Icarus* would carry.

Bolton was there, sitting on the quarterdeck steps, ingratiating himself with the mutineers, a man whose loyalty was solidly grounded in expedience. Biddlecomb considered hanging him, right then. It would be infinitely satisfying and he was certain that no one would try to stop him. But the time was not right. He was trying to prevent the Icaruses from taking vengeance; he could not indulge that luxury himself. Later, he told himself. Later.

Biddlecomb slung the telescope over his shoulder and grabbed on to the topgallant backstay and rode it down to the deck. He did not tell the others that he believed the strange sail to be a British man-of-war, nor did he have to. Just the mention of the distant topgallants elicited the response he had expected.

'It's the *Cerberus*, the bloody frigate *Cerberus*!' Harland exclaimed. 'This here's her patrol area. Oh, Christ, but she's fast as the wind!'

Biddlecomb had no doubt that Harland was right, but now was not the time for the men to dwell on it. 'Hands to sheets and braces!' he shouted, and the formerly paralytic men raced to the lines with

297

startling alacrity. 'Stand ready to set topgallant sails! Mainmast, let go and haul!'

The main yards swung around and the *Icarus* gathered way once again, and Biddlecomb was glad to see that all hands had obeyed his orders. No one seemed to question his ascension to the captaincy. 'Hands aloft to cast off gaskets! Studdingsails aloft and alow!' he called. 'Come on, then, go!' The Icaruses poured into the rig and raced aloft, driven by anxiety now mixed with hope.

Rumstick stepped up to the quarterdeck and stood beside Biddlecomb. 'What's your plan, Isaac? We can't outrun that damned frigate.'

Biddlecomb glanced around. 'I know, and I have no plan. I'm making this up as I go.'

'No matter. With that lot laying around drunk we was dead for certain. At least now we have a fighting chance.'

Biddlecomb felt the deck heel farther as the *Icarus* spread her canvas to the wind. He glanced astern. The strange topgallants were just visible from the deck, and Biddlecomb had only the faintest hope that she was not the *Cerberus*.

He felt like a fraud, an utter fraud. It had been simple enough to assume command, but now that he was there, he did not have a clue as to how he would elude the frigate. He looked over at Rumstick, who had gone forward to supervise the setting of the studdingsails. He at least was back to his former self, changed like one who has undergone a religious conversion. He smiled and shouted orders, cajoling and encouraging the men. They were fighting back, and for Rumstick that was like aqua vitae to a midwife. But arranging their escape was not his responsibility.

298

Biddlecomb looked astern in the direction of the *Cerberus*, down the length of their own deepening wake. By nightfall they might all be prisoners crammed in her hole. But if they were captured, it would not be for a lack of effort on his part. From that moment, and until the *Cerberus* ran them down, the *Icarus* was his command.

CHAPTER 22

Cerberus

'Deck, there!' shouted the lookout from the top of the main topgallant mast. Biddlecomb looked up at the seaman clinging with one hand to the shrouds as he held the telescope in the other. With the *Icarus* running before the following sea, he was getting a wild ride so high above the deck.

'Deck, aye!' Biddlecomb returned the hail.

'She's the *Cerberus*, for certain! No mistaking the drop of them topsails!'

Well, that's that, thought Biddlecomb. Until that moment he had still entertained the hope that the strange sail could be a merchantman on the same course as the brig. Now he knew for certain that his worst fears were correct.

From his position on the weather side of the quarterdeck, he looked down along the waist to the foredeck where the men were coiling down the running gear, and from there his eyes ran aloft to the spread of canvas above. The *Icarus* was carrying everything that would draw, including a water sail and a spritsail topsail set flying. For the past hour Biddlecomb had overseen the setting and trimming and hauling and checking away, and now he could

300

comfort himself with the fact that the *Icarus* was moving as fast through the water as she was physically able.

'On deck!' the lookout cried again.

'On deck, aye!'

'Frigate's setting studdingsails, aloft and alow!'

And therein lay the rub. Biddlecomb could make the *Icarus* go as fast as she was able, but he could not make her go faster than the frigate.

'Wilson, Barrett, Rumstick, step up here, please!' he called out, and the three men left their jobs and stepped up to the quarterdeck.

Wilson was grinning broadly despite their possibly fatal predicament. 'God, but it's nice to see this old gal driven hard, the way she likes it!'

'Israel, have you ever stood as officer of a watch?' Biddlecomb asked.

'Bless me, yes, sir, in many a prize I helped bring to port, and I was rated master's mate for a time, before some unfortunate business in Gibraltar.'

'Good. And you, Wilson?'

'Well, not exactly, no. No.'

'It's no matter. Rumstick, I know you're a greenhorn, but you'll have to do.' Biddlecomb stepped up to the break of the quarterdeck. 'Listen up, you men!' he shouted. The last of the running gear was hung on its pin and all faces turned aft. 'These men will be the ship's new officers: Israel Barrett shall be first officer, Bloody Wilson is second, Mr Appleby is rated midshipman, and Rumstick is bosun. Mr Hickman of course is gunner.' Biddlecomb saw heads nodding fore and aft. The men he had picked were popular and competent and he had not expected dissent. Biddlecomb was taking it for granted that he

301

was to be captain, and he was happy to see the others were as well.

'You will obey them as you would any officer,' Biddlecomb continued. 'You will call them "Mister." The *Icarus* is still a man-of-war and must run as such if we have any wish to live past the next ten hours. Is that understood?'

'Aye,' called out a lone voice, and then as one the rest of the men shouted, 'Aye!' and nodded their approval. For all their professed hatred of tyranny, these men wanted desperately to be led, and never so much as in a crisis. And Biddlecomb knew it.

'Very good. Carry on,' Biddlecomb said, and realized that the men had nothing to carry on doing, which was not good. They could not be allowed to sit idle and fret as the *Cerberus* ran them down. It might occur to someone that Biddlecomb did not actually have a plan. He turned to his newly appointed officers.

'Gentlemen, what would be the next thing one might do aboard a man-of-war in the present circumstance?' he asked in a low voice.

'Well, sir, I reckon we'd clear for action,' Barrett suggested.

'Clear for action! Exactly! Mr Barrett, make it so.'

Barrett stepped up to the quarterdeck rail. 'Clear for action!' he roared, and the men burst into activity, dashing to carry out their assigned functions.

Biddlecomb turned his attention to the activity on deck. Men scrambled here and there, locating and laying out the gear needed to fight the brig. It seemed more confused and disorderly than was quite necessary, though having never seen any vessel other than the *Icarus* clear for action, Biddlecomb admitted that he could not be certain.

Rumstick, at home in the bosun's position, was on the foredeck seeing to the laying out of the running gear and sending men aloft to rig chain slings on the yards. Biddlecomb wondered how Rumstick knew to do that.

Bloody Wilson stepped over to the foreshrouds and began to lay aloft. Biddlecomb called him aft.

'What's the duty of the second officer at quarters?' Biddlecomb asked.

'Standing around with his thumb up his arse, it always seemed to me.'

'Then that's what you should be doing.'

'I can't leave my mates to do all the work.'

'Number four- and six-gun crews seem to be arguing over some point, and it appears that the gun captains are about to come to blows. Please go remedy the situation, Mr Wilson,' and Wilson turned and raced off to prevent the old feud from erupting.

Alone at the weather rail Biddlecomb forced himself to turn and look aft, something he had hitherto been avoiding.

The *Cerberus* was closer now, much closer, her courses and lower studdingsails clearly seen without a glass, and on the rise Biddlecomb caught a glimpse of her hull, black and buff, the row of gunports stretching along her side. What was her captain thinking, standing on his quarterdeck and watching the brig as Biddlecomb was watching him? Fast as the wind, Harland had called her, and he was hardly exaggerating.

At last the brig was cleared for action, the guns run out and their crews standing by, sponges and

303

rammers and handspikes in place, the water buckets and smoldering tubs of slow match in perfect rows along the deck.

'Cleared for action, sir,' Barrett reported. 'Twenty-six minutes.'

'Twenty-six minutes? Very good, Mr Barrett.'

Barrett looked embarrassed. 'It's a bloody disgrace, sir. A first-rate can clear away in ten.'

'Humph,' said Biddlecomb, and then after a pause added, 'We'll work on that time once we're clear of the frigate.'

'Shall we set the boat adrift, sir?'

'Uh, why would we wish to do that?'

'Horrible lot of splinters they throws off, sir, if they gets hit with round shot.'

Of course. Biddlecomb had heard tales from Barrett and other veterans of naval combat concerning the horror and frequency of splinter wounds. 'No. We may need the boat in the future. Besides, I don't intend to get into a shooting match with the frigate. I fear we wouldn't get the best of it.'

'Indeed we would not, sir.'

The two men turned their attention forward. The only sounds now were the vessel working and the bow crashing into the swells, and in that quiet every man aboard heard the single gunshot, several miles to windward. Biddlecomb turned in time to see the gray smoke swirl away from the frigate's bow.

'Bloody hell, they're firing on us!' someone shouted forward, and the deck erupted in frantic speculation.

'Silence!' Rumstick shouted, and the deck fell silent again and Biddlecomb was thankful that the men were recognizing authority.

'Sir! Sir!' Appleby called, leaning on the taffrail, the telescope to his eye. 'Frigate is signaling, sir.'

Biddlecomb turned to the men on deck. 'The frigate was firing to draw our attention to signals, nothing more.' He then turned to the midshipman. 'Mr Appleby, how long has the frigate been signaling?'

Appleby looked at Biddlecomb, then down at the deck. His face was quite red. 'I don't know, sir.'

'Quite a while, wouldn't you imagine, if they felt compelled to draw our attention to their signal?'

'Yes, sir.'

'What signal are they making?'

'I don't know, sir.'

'God damn your eyes, you worthless runt!' Barrett exploded. 'Look it up in the signal book, or by God I'll run you up to the yardarm before the *Cerberus* gets the chance!'

Appleby swung the telescope back toward the frigate, then tucked it under his arm. He reached for the signal book, dropping the telescope, dropped the signal book while reaching for the telescope, then collected both and began thumbing through the pages. 'Private recognition signal, sir,' he said at last.

'Do you know what the proper reply would be?' asked Biddlecomb.

'Aye, sir. Our number, along with the response that's written here,' Appleby said brightly, happy to have an answer ready.

Biddlecomb considered the facts that were before him in hopes that this exercise would inspire a plan. The *Cerberus* would overtake them, and shortly, that was a fact to be considered. He could masquerade as French, or Dutch, but they would not be fooled by

305

that, there was too much about the ship that was clearly British. If he convinced them there was fever aboard, they might stay away, but no, the *Icarus* had flashed out studdingsails too fast to be a vessel crippled by fever.

And why had the *Icarus* flashed out studdingsails? If the men could recognize the frigate, then the men of the *Cerberus* would recognize the brig. Why were they running? That was the question that the captain of the *Cerberus* would be asking himself. Why were they running? And then, like a far-off cry, barely heard, an idea came to him.

'Mr Appleby, make our number and the proper reply,' he ordered, wondering how long he had been standing there in silence while the others waited. The midshipman bent the flag to the halyard and hoisted away. 'And the Union Jack on the ensign staff . . . Mr Barrett, a moment, please.'

Barrett stepped across to the weather side.

'Do you believe that they recognize us?'

'I should think so. *Icarus* has been on and off this station for years. I'd be surprised if they didn't.'

Biddlecomb considered this. 'So the captain of the *Cerberus* must know Pendexter?'

'That I couldn't tell you, sir.'

'But you just said the *Icarus* has been here many times.'

Barrett looked confused. 'Aye, that she has, but I don't know if Pendexter has.'

'Why would Pendexter not be with his own brig?'

Barrett's face brightened with understanding. 'Bless you, sir, Pendexter just got command in Boston, just before you was pressed! He ain't never

306

taken the *Icarus* to the West Indies. Of course you wouldn't know that.'

That was the final piece of information that Biddlecomb needed. Now he had a plan, tenuous as it might be, on which he could act.

'Mr Appleby, step over here, please,' he said, and the midshipman trotted up to the weather rail. 'If we were pursuing an enemy and wished to convey that to the *Cerberus*, what signal would we hoist?'

Appleby considered this. ' "Enemy in sight"?' he asked in the apparent belief that Biddlecomb was quizzing him.

'Perhaps. Would there be a way to tell the *Cerberus* where this enemy was?'

'Well, sir, there's "Enemy to windward" or "Enemy to leeward" or—'

'Enemy to leeward! That's it! Do you know that hoist?'

'Not offhand, sir, though I was going to study the signal book this dogwatch, I swear it.'

'Never mind that. Look up the signal in the book.'

'On deck!' the lookout cried.

'On deck, aye!'

'Frigate's signaling again!'

'Mr Appleby, please see what the frigate wants now,' said Biddlecomb.

For long and frustrating minutes Appleby alternated staring at the frigate and the signal book as he read and translated the hoist, and Biddlecomb decided that either the system of signals in the Royal Navy was absurdly overcomplicated or Mr Appleby had not been as attentive to learning his duty as one might wish. He suspected that the truth, as is so often the case, lay somewhere in between.

307

'*Cerberus* acknowledges our number, sir,' said Appleby at last, 'and signals, "Heave to, captain to repair on board." '

'Mr Hickman!' Biddlecomb shouted down to the waist. 'Fire the bow chasers if you will, two shots apiece.'

'Two shots apiece, aye,' Hickman replied, then turned and walked quickly to the bow.

Biddlecomb turned back to Appleby. 'Please signal, "Enemy in sight to leeward." ' Appleby looked at him, confused, and then he grinned and nodded his head.

'I see what you are up to, sir! I've smoked it!' Laughing, he pulled the flags from the bag at his feet and bent them to the halyards.

At that moment the larboard bow chaser roared out. Biddlecomb stepped over to the break of the quarterdeck and looked out toward the bow. The men were grinning and watching the bow chaser's crew sponge out and load. Hickman shoved the slow match into the touchhole of the starboard chaser and it roared out as well, and the men grinned more broadly. Have they smoked my trick? he wondered, and decided that no, they had not. They just liked to fire the guns.

Biddlecomb watched as the last two rounds were fired, watched the arch of the balls as they flew a mile ahead of the brig and plunged into the sea, and just as the starboard gun was being sponged out for the second time, Mr Appleby spoke.

'*Cerberus* signaling, sir.' As Biddlecomb turned, Appleby was already thumbing through the signal book. Biddlecomb tried to hide his impatience, and he wondered if Appleby understood, as he did,

308

that the reply flying at the frigate's yard meant the difference between possible escape and certain execution.

'Frigate replies, "Continue chase," sir,' Appleby reported, and he was smiling. 'They believed you, sir.'

Biddlecomb glanced back at the *Cerberus* and then up at the sun, almost directly overhead. The frigate would be up with them in five or six hours, and the sun would set two hours after that. Five or six hours of waiting, then ten minutes of excitement, and then they would all escape or they would all hang.

CHAPTER 23

The Net Is Cast

Waiting. It was the bitter enemy of morale, and it seemed to be the most common undertaking on board any ship. Biddlecomb had waited before – waited for over a month for the wind to blow fair before he could leave Kingstown, waited two weeks for the trades to fill in in the horse latitudes – but that couldn't compare to the anxiety of just a few hours of waiting for a powerful enemy to slowly and inexorably run one down.

It was worse for the men who stood at their stations with no idea of what Biddlecomb's plan could be, or if he had one at all. But Biddlecomb knew that if they did know and had five hours to discuss it among themselves, it would be ruinous to discipline, and to his plan as well, such as it was. So he let them stew, driving them to trim sail when it was needed, though with a following wind it rarely was.

Two bells struck, two bells in the afternoon watch. Biddlecomb turned and looked down their wake, leading straight back to the *Cerberus*. Both vessels were sailing north by west; for the *Icarus* it was the way to Rhode Island, but Biddlecomb could not be

310

certain if the *Cerberus* had been on that heading initially or if she had altered course when she sighted the brig. Not that it mattered to any large degree.

The frigate was hull up now, and her long black and buff sides and row of gunports could be seen easily without a glass. When Biddlecomb did look through the glass, it revealed more minute details: the straining sails, all she would carry, and the foaming white wave at her bow and the spray that she flung back along her deck. Biddlecomb felt his stomach twist. She looked every inch like the merchant of death that she was, and she was right in their wake.

'Mr Wilson,' Biddlecomb said to the new second officer, who had relieved Barrett, man-of-war fashion, at noon. 'I believe we should pipe the men to dinner. They can eat by watches, an hour below for each watch.'

'Aye. Shall we serve it out cold, then?'

'Why cold?'

'Well, the galley fire was flung overboard when we cleared for action. Always is.'

'Oh. Well, then, have the cook stoke up the fire once again and feed the men a proper meal. I want the larbowlines eating in one bell.'

The cook did stoke the fire, and half an hour later the larbowlines below and the former officers in the bread room and Biddlecomb and Wilson aft were gnawing lukewarm salt beef and dried peas. Biddlecomb had not realized how hungry he was, but the sight of the salted meat made his mouth water, a rare reaction indeed when confronted with meat five years in the cask. He set to it with a will, and soon his jaw ached with the effort.

311

'You saw to it that Pendexter and the others in the bread room were fed?' he asked Wilson after tossing his bone overboard.

'Aye, they're fed,' Wilson said, and broke into a grin.

'Why are you smiling? Did you do something to their food?'

'No. It's just, well, I'll warrant Pendexter or Smeaton ain't eaten much salt horse before, them gentry types, and I'm wondering how they likes it.'

Biddlecomb imagined that Pendexter would not have much of an appetite, and the salt 'horse' would not whet what appetite there was. No matter. He felt morally obligated to give his prisoners food, not to make them eat.

Eight bells and the first of the dogwatches began, but no watch was changed as every man aboard the *Icarus* was already on deck, already at his station. The wind had freshened during dinner, and the seas had increased with it, so that now the brig, straining under an excess of canvas, bashed her bow into the waves, sending a shudder through her fabric that could be felt all the way aft, and flinging spray as high as the fore top. The conditions were now very much in *Cerberus*'s favor; the chop did not slow the larger vessel, and the fresh breeze drove her now noticeably faster than the *Icarus*. But that was fine, that was what Biddlecomb had counted on. If the wind had died away, then there would have been no hope at all.

Biddlecomb looked down along the waist at the grim-faced men who manned the guns. Here and there a man stood on his toes or leaned out of a gunport trying to see how close the *Cerberus* had

312

come, but mostly they just stood. They did not speak, and their eyes did not meet, and Biddlecomb knew that each was contemplating his imminent death.

Biddlecomb looked aft once more. Their pursuer was less than a mile behind, quickly overhauling them. The signal to continue chase still flew from her main yard. I wonder whom they think they're chasing, he thought. Mr Appleby caught his eye and smiled and Biddlecomb smiled back, wondering as he did if Appleby ever bothered to wash his uniform.

His uniform! Biddlecomb felt his stomach tighten and panic rush over him. How could he be so stupid? He hoped to masquerade as a commander dressed like Jolly Jack Tar?

'Wilson, Barrett, come with me! Hurry!' he yelled as he dived down the scuttle and into the blinding darkness of the gunroom. He heard the others behind him.

'What is it, Isaac?' Wilson asked.

'We need damn uniforms! Why didn't I think of it? The captain of the *Cerberus* expects to see officers on the quarterdeck! Wilson, rummage through Smeaton's cabin there, find one of his uniforms – it should fit you. Mr Barrett, I am afraid I must demote you to sailing master for the time being. We should have one on deck, and Dibdin's uniform will serve. I'll see what Pendexter has.'

Biddlecomb hurried into the great cabin. It was undisturbed since he had last been there, but now the *Cerberus* was so close that she fairly filled the aft windows. Biddlecomb pulled his eyes from the awful sight and began tearing through Pendexter's sea chests, flinging nightshirts and boat cloaks aside. He

313

pulled out a red silk gown, pausing briefly to wonder at its presence, then continued to dig. At last he found the chest that contained the uniforms, carefully stored. He pulled out the one on top and tore off his own filthy clothes, making a mental note to fling them overboard rather than put them on again.

Silk stockings, breeches, shirt, waistcoat, neckcloth, and coat, he dressed himself. The clothes fit him quite well, just a bit tight in the shoulders and arms. He caught a passing glance in the mirror mounted on the bulkhead. I look quite the thing, he thought, and if there was ever any doubt about my hanging, being caught wearing Pendexter's uniform should satisfy it. He pushed his feet into Pendexter's shoes and stepped out into the gunroom.

Barrett was twitching his neckcloth in place. He looked quite presentable in Dibdin's uniform. The same could not be said for Wilson, who was squeezed into Smeaton's coat, the seams straining as he bent over, trying to pull shoes over his splayed feet.

'Is the shoes necessary?' he asked.

'Yes. Here, let me help.'

The shoes were at last forced on Wilson's feet, and the three men stepped out on deck again. 'Remember, gentlemen, we are officers aboard a king's ship, giving chase to the enemy. I shall stand alone at the weather rail. As the *Cerberus* passes down our side, act, well, like officers. Don't do anything. Mr Barrett, why don't you stand at the helm, where Dibdin usually stands?'

The three men took their places on the quarterdeck, like actors taking the stage. 'Mr Rumstick, lay aft, please!' Biddlecomb called.

Rumstick trotted up to the quarterdeck.

314

'Ezra, those main topmast shrouds, they haven't been set up lately, have they?'

Rumstick glanced aloft. 'No, they'd be slack as a South Street whore but for this following wind. I was planning on setting 'em up tomorrow. If I'm still alive, I mean.'

'It would seem most of the weight in the topmasts is being born by the backstay, wouldn't it?'

Rumstick glanced over at the backstay. 'Aye. Starboard backstay seems to have most of the load.'

'Just as I thought. Good.'

As resigned as he was to his course of action, Biddlecomb's stomach knotted when the *Cerberus*'s jibboom drew level with the quarterdeck. He could see the frigate's officers across the hundred yards of water that separated the two vessels. He put the telescope to his eye and trained it toward the frigate's quarterdeck.

The captain of the *Cerberus* was a short, stout man, and as Biddlecomb stared at him through the glass, he stared back through a glass of his own. Biddlecomb felt suddenly exposed being thus scrutinized, like the dream where one suddenly realizes one is naked.

On the leeward side of the frigate's quarterdeck stood a cluster of officers, a dozen in all, and greatly divergent in age. The few guns on the weather deck were manned and run out.

The captain lowered his glass and called to someone behind him. A midshipman broke from the group of officers and ran over to the binnacle box, snatched up the speaking trumpet, handed it to the captain, then hurried back to the leeward rail.

Biddlecomb lowered his glass as well, and he was

315

startled to see how far the frigate had overlapped the *Icarus* in those few moments. He looked down into the waist of the brig. All hands were silent now, staring out across the water at the frigate. The tension was like a fog that hung over the deck. Rumstick caught his eye and Biddlecomb nodded.

'Ahoy, *Icarus*!' the *Cerberus*'s captain called out, his voice distorted by the speaking trumpet.

'Mr Appleby, the trumpet if you please.'

Appleby snatched up the trumpet and dropped it with a crash, then scooped it up and brought it to Biddlecomb. The midshipman's face was ashen and his hands trembled. 'Here, sir, sorry, sir.'

Biddlecomb put the trumpet to his lips. 'Ahoy, *Cerberus*!'

'Where is Captain Bleakney?' the captain of the frigate called back, his voice edged with agitation. Biddlecomb realized that he did not know where Bleakney was.

'Made post into *Fowey*,' Wilson supplied.

'Made post into *Fowey*!' Biddlecomb repeated through the trumpet.

The captain of the *Cerberus* seemed to pause to digest this information. 'Who are you? Who is this "enemy" you are chasing?' The quarterdecks of the two ships were nearly even now.

'Comdr James Pendexter! We're pursuing a Yankee, quite a large ship, one of these rascals that fancies himself a privateer! The bastard fired into us! He's too fast for us! Can your lookout still see him?'

'No,' the captain replied with no hesitation.

'I'm surprised! We just lost him!' Prizes must be few and far between in time of peace, Biddlecomb

316

imagined, and the hope of one should be enough to take a frigate captain's mind away from other matters.

The captain spoke again, but Biddlecomb never heard the words. From the corner of his eye he saw Rumstick, perched on the starboard channel out of sight from the *Cerberus*, slash with a boarding ax at the starboard main topmast backstay. It parted like a thread, and the thunderclap of the topmast breaking off at the cap drowned out all but the Icaruses' surprise and alarm. Men ran toward the bow and aft to the quarterdeck to avoid the rain of gear; blocks, brace pennants, running rigging, and broken sections of spars poured down on the deck. The mast hung, half-broken, as if unsure what to do, then broke entirely and crashed toward deck, tearing the fore braces and breaking the main spring stay before it came to rest four feet above the deck, hanging from a few tenacious lines. The topgallant mast hit the foredeck and snapped like a twig.

The *Icarus* swung up into the wind, totally crippled, her rig in shreds. Biddlecomb stepped up to the quarterdeck rail. 'Is anyone hurt? Any injuries?' He waited, and from different areas of the deck, some now hidden from view by the wreckage, came the cries of 'All's well.'

Biddlecomb turned back to the quarterdeck. Appleby was staring in awe at the destruction, his fear quite forgotten.

'Mr Appleby, I would imagine that the frigate is signaling. Please see if I am correct.'

Appleby nodded and raced to the rail, the glass to his eye. The *Cerberus* was now two ships lengths past them and moving away fast. More significantly they were making no effort to take in sail. Biddlecomb was

317

gambling on their being more interested in a fat prize than in aiding a crippled brig. As he watched, the signal flags that he had expected broke out at the main yard.

A moment later Appleby read, 'Do you require assistance?' from the signal book.

'Reply, "Negative. Continue chase," ' said Biddlecomb.

'Uh, sir?'

'Yes, Mr Appleby?'

'I don't think it would be quite the thing, a commander telling a post captain to continue the chase.'

'Good thinking. Just the "Negative," then, if you please.'

Appleby sent the flag aloft, and Biddlecomb waited the tense moment for the reply, resisting his urge to tear the signal book from Appleby's clumsy hands.

' "Acknowledge, and good luck," sir,' said Appleby, grinning, and Biddlecomb grinned as well. He looked up at the frigate. The *Cerberus* was half a mile to leeward now, and the faster she ran downwind, the more impossible it would be for her to claw her way back. Biddlecomb was overwhelmed by the most delicious sense of relief he had ever experienced.

And then Barrett was before him, saluting. 'What orders, sir?'

'Well, we shall have to get this wreckage cleared away and some sort of topmast sent up. I would like to be under way again before dawn, but that may be asking a bit much.'

'Dawn? Odds my life, sir, we'll be under way with topmast and topgallant sent up in two hours. The

318

men ain't forgot everything that Bleakney taught them.'

'Two hours? That seems a bit fast.'

'You just watch how we does things in the navy, sir,' said Barrett, stepping up to the break of the quarterdeck. 'All hands to clear away this wreckage! Knot and splice what you can save, we'll be sending a new topmast immediately. Pass the word for the carpenter.'

Biddlecomb was surprised, pleasantly, with Barrett's ease in assuming command, but he was more surprised by half with the way the Icaruses fell to the task of clearing away the broken spars. Like ants swarming over a pile of spilled sugar, there seemed to be men everywhere, casting off standing rigging, short-splicing, long-splicing, laying shroud gangs aside for the new masts, reeving off new running gear. There was little talking, and no shouting, but still the efforts of the crew seemed coordinated and planned.

'I am impressed already, Mr Barrett,' Biddlecomb ventured.

'Captain, when Bleakney had the Icarus, we would send the topmasts down before breakfast. We'd unbend fore and main topsails, switch them, and set them again in five minutes.'

'To what purpose would you switch the topsails?'

'Drill, sir, all drill. Every man learns his job so's he can do it in the dark, in a gale, or with the iron flying around his ears.'

The sun seemed to hang inches above the horizon, and the western sky was vibrant with reds and oranges as the last of the shrouds on the new main topmast were set up and the main topsail yard swayed

319

aloft. The only voice heard aboard the *Icarus* belonged to Wilson, who coordinated the efforts of the men. Rumstick stepped up to the quarterdeck and over to the weather rail where Biddlecomb stood alone.

'We rove off the running gear first,' Rumstick reported, 'and we're sending the yard up with sail bent. I reckon we can send the topgallant gear up while we're under way.'

'Excellent. A famous effort, getting things squared away with this speed.'

'In faith I wish I could take credit, but these men are trained like I've never seen. You never would have guessed it from the sullen way they was with Pendexter and McDuff, but they're something. None of your dally and griping like the merchant service.'

'You'll recall we don't have seventy-five men on a brig in the merchant service, either,' Biddlecomb pointed out, wishing he did not sound so defensive.

'I'll own that. But I tell you, Isaac, this don't make me overconfident about our war with England. We may have the will, but we don't have the training and experience that them Brits do.'

'Indeed? I hadn't thought of that,' said Biddlecomb in an icy tone.

'That's well! Belay all!' Wilson's voice carried over the deck. He turned and walked back to the quarterdeck. 'Main topsail yard's crossed, and we can set in five minutes. Lookout says he ain't seen the *Cerberus* this hour and more, and she was still running away to leeward when he lost sight of her.'

'Very good, Mr Wilson. We shall set all plain sail when you are ready, full and by, and get the main

320

opgallant gear up once we are under way. You have lone an excellent job, I might add.'

'Thank you, sir. Some of the men were talking, and, well, what you done to fool the *Cerberus* . . .'

Biddlecomb knew that he could not endure the entimentality of the lower deck. 'Thank you, Mr Wilson, you don't have to elaborate.'

Ten minutes later the sun dipped below the horizon and the *Icarus* gathered way, sailing full and by on a heading that would take her, for the next twenty-four hours, as fast and as far from the *Cerberus* as she could sail before she turned north by west again.

'Mr Barrett,' Biddlecomb called out from the quarterdeck. 'We'll send up the topgallant gear and stand down to watches. I believe we can carry just plain sail for tonight. And I think perhaps we shall splice the main brace as well, if there is any rum left.'

The men cheered loud and long. 'Three cheers for Captain Biddlecomb!' a voice shouted, and was followed by three lusty huzzahs. Biddlecomb smiled at the utterly predictable reactions of the lower deck. Mr Barrett, you have the watch till midnight. Call me if there are any problems whatsoever. I'll be in the great cabin.' And with that he disappeared below, suddenly wanting very much to be alone.

The *Icarus* was pitching more now, sailing hard on the wind, and Biddlecomb had to brace himself as he sat in the chair behind Pendexter's desk. It was good to be in command again, good to know that the nightmare was all but over. The *Icarus* was a good ship, and they were bound away for Rhode Island. He had never failed to enter Narragansett Bay undetected, never failed to make it home. Except the

321

last time, he corrected himself. But now he knew that the *Rose* was there, and he could avoid her. It was a threat, but the bay was his home, and the *Rose* was only one ship. The *Icarus* charged on through the night, safe at least until dawn, and Biddlecomb felt suddenly and deliciously sleepy.

Capt. James Wallace sat in the great cabin of the *Rose* and stared out of the salt-stained window toward the town of Newport. He was thinking about Isaac Biddlecomb, as he often did, though he knew that doing so made him angry. It was incredible what Biddlecomb had done; escaped from a marine patrol and stolen the *Rose*'s longboat in the process. And since then, nothing. No sign of the boat and no word from his various sources scattered around the bay. It was as if Biddlecomb had been swallowed up by the sea, but that, Wallace knew, was too much to hope for. Besides, if Biddlecomb was to die, Wallace wanted to be the one to facilitate his death.

The *Rose* was anchored in the small harbor amid merchant vessels of various descriptions, the lion lying down with the lambs, as it were. The snow on shore had largely melted, and only a few gray patches remained in the shadows of the brick warehouses. At the turn of the tide the *Rose* would be under way bound for Long Island Sound to see what illegalities the colonials were attempting there. But that was not for five hours, and before that time he had a great deal of paperwork to do.

He pulled his gaze from the town beyond the great-cabin windows. On his desk were the logs of the ship's consumption of beef and pork and dried peas and gunpowder and shot, all waiting Wallace' ttention. He wished at times that he were the type of captain who could pawn off all such accounting asks to his clerk, but he was not.

On the top of the pile was a dispatch from Admiral Graves in Boston. Wallace picked it up and examined t; it had been delivered only five minutes before and was still cold from being in the courier's pouch. Wallace liked dispatches from Graves. Though the admiral could be more active for Wallace's taste, still he believed in suffering no treason to go unpunished. Wallace and Graves were alike in their belief that the smoldering rebellion should be stamped out swiftly nd mercilessly.

Wallace broke the seal and unfolded the dispatch, reading the familiar writing of Grave's clerk.

Aboard the flagship *Preston*,
February 16, 1775

Sir:

As regards your letter of December, last, I am inclined to agree with you concerning the need to quickly suppress what can only be considered a treasonous rebellion among His Majesty's American subjects.

While we enjoy a period of relative peace, there seems no reason that sufficient naval power cannot be brought to bear to quickly stamp out this uprising. Acting upon your suggestion that the colony of Rhode Island seems to now be as much a focal point of these troubles as Boston, I have dispatched the frigate *Glasgow* and the sloop *Swan* and a bomb ketch to reinforce the vessels you have

323

already in place. I am expecting the frigate *Cerberus* from the West Indies and will send her first to New York and then later to join you. With such a force in place I am in no doubt that the Narragansett Bay can be as effectively blockaded as is Boston.

Your obedient, humble servant,
Adm. Samuel Graves
Commander, North American Station,
Boston

Wallace stared at the letter and considered the implications of the admiral's decision. Fewer smugglers were getting into Narragansett Bay these days, far fewer, but even one was too many. Now even those few would be stopped. He would throw a net across the bay that would catch anything coming in or out. Biddlecomb would be his, if he ever made the mistake of trying to slip into Narragansett Bay by sea.

And Wallace had every hope that he would, because Biddlecomb was a seaman and Rhode Island was his home, and if he was not dead, then he would sooner or later be back on the bay. The thought made Wallace's bad temper burn off like a morning fog, and the faintest trace of a smile was on his lips as he opened the ledger.

CHAPTER 24

Dead Calm

Biddlecomb came slowly awake, and as he did, he became aware that he was in a bunk. What bunk? He had not slept in a bunk in some time, only a hammock. And then he realized that he was in Captain Pendexter's bunk, in the great cabin. And someone was shaking him.

'Captain Biddlecomb? Captain Biddlecomb?' a voice was saying. It was Israel Barrett.

'Israel?' Biddlecomb said, now fully awake. 'Is there a problem?'

'No, sir. But dawn is in one glass, and I wondered, did you wish to clear for action?'

'Clear for action?' Biddlecomb thought for a moment. 'Why would we wish to do that?'

'Well, sir,' Barrett began with his usual patience, it's custom on men-of-war to clear for action before dawn, so's we's ready for whatever's there when the sun comes up.'

'That makes a great deal of sense. Why did Pendexter never do so?'

'It ain't always done in times of peace. Most especially not when the old man don't like his sleep disturbed.'

325

'Well, the *Icarus* at least is hardly at peace now Yes, I believe that we'll clear for action.'

Barrett nodded and stepped out of the sleeping caboose, but Biddlecomb called after him. 'Israel?'

'Yes, sir?'

'Do you never get annoyed by the fact that I know nothing about running a naval vessel?'

'Bless you, sir, the men thinks you should be an admiral, after the way you fooled the *Cerberus*. For me, if you can navigate and hold this rabble together too, then as for the rest it don't bother me at all, sir not at all.'

It was still quite dark when Biddlecomb arrived on deck, and the air was cool and damp as it often is on a winter night in the Caribbean. He stepped up to the quarterdeck, and as his eyes adjusted to the light, he saw Barrett move away from the weather rail, leaving it clear for him. Rumstick leaned against the bulwark in the waist. It was lovely and quiet with the brig plunging ahead, lively and fast. Biddlecomb felt loath to disturb the moment.

'Clear for action, please, Mr Barrett,' Biddlecomb said in a quiet voice. Barrett stepped up to the quarterdeck rail and shouted, 'Clear for action!' and the lovely quiet was gone. Rumstick, apparently waiting for that moment, sprang to the scuttle with shouts of 'Clear for action!' and 'Hands to quarters! He sounded to Biddlecomb as if he had been in the navy all his life, but then everything that Rumstick set himself to do he did with confidence and he did well. It was good to see Rumstick full of life again, and no the morose fellow that had been pressed.

It took the Icaruses ten minutes and forty-five seconds to clear for action, and the job was performed

326

with less confusion than Biddlecomb had ever seen aboard the brig. An hour later the sun was up, and the lookout aloft reported an empty sea stretching in all directions.

'Tell me,' Biddlecomb asked Barrett as they stood alone at the weather rail, 'would it not be beneficial to fire the great guns occasionally? To train the men in their firing?'

'It would, I own, but the navy only allows each captain a small amount of powder and shot for drill. Bleakney used to buy powder from his own pocket.'

'I think the least of our worries now is that the navy will be angry with our wasting powder, so what say we drill with the great guns after breakfast? But for now, let's send hands to the braces and head for home.'

Through the night the *Icarus* had sailed close-hauled, almost due east, sailing a course as nearly opposite that of the *Cerberus* as she could. Now Biddlecomb swung the bow off the wind, and once again they settled down on their heading, north by west, the long jibboom pointing toward Rhode Island, far over the horizon.

When the last of the men had eaten, they were again called to quarters, and for three hours they worked the guns, churning the sea around them frothy with the falling iron. It was clear that the men enjoyed the drill, and they were glad to hone skills that had gone dull.

'Secure from quarters, Mr Barrett,' Biddlecomb said at the end of the three hours. 'I believe we'll do this again tomorrow. Now please send someone below to the bread room and fetch the prisoners on deck.'

327

Ten minutes later the scuttle doors burst open and an armed seaman appeared, followed by Pendexter, Smeaton, Dibdin, and another armed seaman. The prisoners' faces were covered in three days' growth of beard, and their clothes were crumpled and filthy, but beyond that they seemed hale. Dibdin had been offered his parole and had accepted and so was free to roam the ship, save when they were at quarters. He shunned the quarterdeck, choosing instead to lean against the leeward rail forward.

Pendexter and Smeaton, to whom no parole had been offered, stepped aft to the weather rail of the quarterdeck where, Biddlecomb knew, they hoped to antagonize him. He hated having them aft, but it was too cruel to leave them in the bread room the whole day, and he was afraid to let them mix with the men; afraid that the men would harm them and afraid that they might shake the men's determination with threats and promises of leniency. Biddlecomb had no illusions concerning the tenuous nature of his command.

'My God, James,' Smeaton said, 'the rogue is wearing your clothes, I believe!'

'So he is, the rascal!'

Biddlecomb had flung his own filthy slops out of the great-cabin window and indulged himself in Pendexter's finery. He felt foolish now, like a boy caught in a minor theft. He knew that his face was flushed and it made him angry. 'It seems I could not stop at simply taking your brig and your naval career away from you, sir, I had to take your clothes as well.'

'I suppose we should have expected no less, John, from such unconscionable villains as these colonials,'

328

replied Pendexter, quite ignoring Biddlecomb, but Biddlecomb would not rise to the bait.

'Thinks he's a gentleman because he has stolen a gentleman's clothes, no doubt,' said Smeaton. 'You would do well to burn them when you get them back.' Biddlecomb wanted to grab the cocky bastard and slap him, but he twisted his hands together behind his back and checked his anger before he spoke again.

'Lieutenant Pendexter, Lieutenant Smeaton, as you know, the weather side of the quarterdeck is reserved for the captain of the vessel. I would appreciate it if you would remove yourselves to the leeward side.'

At this Pendexter turned and faced Biddlecomb. 'I am the captain of this vessel,' he said, his tone like ice.

'Please remove yourselves or I shall have you forcibly removed,' said Biddlecomb, and taking their cue, the two armed seamen took a step toward the two lieutenants.

Pendexter and Smeaton glowered at Biddlecomb, hesitated, and then, opting for the least humiliating of their choices, deserted the weather rail and marched aft.

For three days the *Icarus* carried the faithful southeasterly trade winds with her as she ran her westing and northing down. The breeze blew across the deck at a steady fifteen knots, and the sails – all squares, studdingsails, skyscrapers, and ringtail – maintained an unvarying shape, a gentle curve that neither flogged nor strained the spars. The running gear was idle during that time; braces, bowlines, sheets, and halyards remained fixed to their belaying pins

329

as no sail trim was required in that perfect weather.

The Icaruses greeted each morning at quarters, and each sunrise revealed an empty ocean all around them, and only the increasing chill in the air told them that they had made northing during the night and had not remained fixed to one spot.

Spirits were high aboard the ship, and it was easy for Biddlecomb to guess why. The weather was fine, the discipline was easy, and for the men the voyage had taken on the qualities of a yachting holiday with the daily amusement of firing cannon. If there were decisions to be made or plans to be considered, then they knew that Biddlecomb, who had so ably fooled the *Cerberus*, would take care of them.

And so Biddlecomb alone felt the anxiety inherent in so fragile a joy. One flaw in the wind, one strange sail on the horizon, one challenge to his command, and their yachting holiday could end in their grisly death. He alone was responsible for getting the *Icarus* home through the cordon of British cruisers that ranged the entire American seaboard. He alone knew of the likelihood of loosing the wind at their present latitude. The burden of his knowledge was making him short-tempered and resentful of the men's high spirits. He had never imagined the pressures of commanding a man-of-war on a hostile sea.

And then, just past midnight on the fourth day, as he had known it might, the wind went away. Biddlecomb came awake and lay in the darkness, feeling the motion of the brig. She was no longer plunging ahead. She was wallowing, and through the open skylight came the sound of slatting canvas.

Bloody Wilson was leaning against the quarterdeck

330

rail, staring up at the slatting sails, when Biddlecomb appeared on deck. He wrapped his arms around his chest to defend against the cold of the northerly latitude. 'Well,' he said, stepping up beside Wilson and looking aloft, 'we carried the trades even further north than I had hoped.'

Thirty-six hours later it was still the current that accounted for any progress that the *Icarus* made, as not a breath of wind was felt, and the sea, heaving up and down with the long swell, was smooth and oily on its surface. The galley leavings thrown overboard and the discharge from the heads stayed tenaciously alongside, and soon the vessel was wallowing in its own filth.

And now, at least, Biddlecomb's anxiety was shared by every man aboard. They moved silently and sullenly about the deck, murmuring to themselves, unwilling to speak out loud. They looked at the slatting sails and whistled softly, and when they thought that Biddlecomb was not watching, they stuck their sheath knives in the mainmast, but neither of those remedies seemed to summon the wind. Harsh words and rebukes flashed here and there, interrupting the uncomfortable silence. All this made Biddlecomb more anxious still.

Wilson stepped aft, having set the men to work wetting down the sails, more to keep them busy than in any real belief that it would help.

'Mr Wilson, you have the deck.' Biddlecomb needed to be alone, he needed to think. 'I am going below. Call me if . . . if anything happens.' Then he disappeared through the scuttle.

The chart on the great-cabin table showed the eastern seaboard of America and east to the

331

Windward Islands. A pencil mark on the paper, roughly in line with the colony of Georgia but nearly seven hundred miles offshore, represented Biddlecomb's best deduced reckoning of where they were on the earth. He rubbed his bloodshot eyes with his knuckles. His head was throbbing and he could feel the sweat running down his back.

He looked up at the chart again and with a sigh told himself that he could not put off a sun sight any longer. He flipped open the mahogany box that sat on the desk and withdrew Pendexter's quadrant. He had long admired the instrument, it was one of the finest he had ever seen. It was quite out of place in Pendexter's bumbling hands. Pearls cast before swine, he thought, and headed for the deck again.

He stepped through the scuttle and up to the quarterdeck and stopped short. Pendexter and Smeaton were there. Biddlecomb had intended to pass the word that they were not to be let on deck that day. He was not in the mood to endure their gibes. But he had forgotten to give the order, and Wilson had brought them up, and Biddlecomb did not want to admit to a mistake and order them below again. He frowned and stepped up to the rail, avoiding the lieutenants' eyes.

'Oh, look at this, James,' said Smeaton, standing with Pendexter by the taffrail, 'the rogue has your quadrant.'

'No doubt he thinks I shall navigate for him, perhaps after he has tortured me a bit.'

Biddlecomb squinted up toward the sun, almost directly overhead. It was hot, and the glare off the glasslike surface of the sea made his head pound harder. 'I do not need you to navigate for me, sir,' he

332

said at last, flipping the filter in place. 'But perhaps you could help me in one thing. Pray, what is the index error for your quadrant?'

Pendexter hesitated. 'I most certainly will not—'

'You don't know, do you?' interrupted Biddlecomb. He felt his patience coming to an end, like an angry man with the urge to insensibly beat an inanimate object. He wanted to hurt the Englishman, he wanted his words to cut. 'Do you know what an index error is, at all?'

'Why, I . . .'

'I thought not. I used to watch you, you know, as you pretended to take a fix. I'll wager you always took Mr Dibdin's fix and plotted that, never could come up with one on your own. Am I right?'

Biddlecomb could tell from Pendexter's flushed face that he was indeed right.

'Have no intercourse with this criminal, James,' said Smeaton, and the two men turned their backs to Biddlecomb.

Biddlecomb fixed the sun in the telescope and brought it down to the horizon. 'Mark!' he said, and Appleby, watch in hand, scribbled down the time.

'We must make a list,' Pendexter began again in an overloud voice, 'of those men who are guilty of mutiny and those that were unwilling participants. It will help in deciding who shall be hung.'

'You two will remain silent or you'll go back to the bread room directly,' Biddlecomb said. 'I've no patience for your foolishness today.'

'Tensions seems a bit high today, John,' said Pendexter.

'The rogue has lost his wind, and I dare say is in danger of losing his command,' Smeaton sneered.

333

Biddlecomb turned to the two men and was nearly overcome by his desire to beat them. He could flog them or pummel them with a belaying pin before the cheering crew. It might be a good thing to restore morale. He held their unwavering eyes until the feeling passed. 'Pray, gentlemen, what do you hope to achieve by aggravating me thus?'

'It was never our intent to aggravate you,' said Smeaton. 'We were having a private conversation. If you choose to eavesdrop, like a scoundrel, there's little we can do.'

'This man is a murderer and a coward,' Pendexter interrupted. 'Don't speak to him further. I hope we never hear his voice again until he is screaming for mercy at his execution.'

'It is your own execution, sir, which grows nearer by the moment!' Biddlecomb said in a voice that carried clear to the bow.

'That would be a most convenient way to settle the matter, wouldn't it?' asked Smeaton. 'I would expect it from a villain and a coward such as yourself. I'm surprised that you haven't murdered us yet. Were you a gentleman, we could settle this like gentlemen.'

'I don't require your approval, sir, or that of any arrogant English bastard, to think myself a gentleman,' said Biddlecomb, speaking softly, barely in control.

'A gentleman you say? Then perhaps . . . But, no, you have nothing to gain.'

Biddlecomb was aware of the silence around him and knew that all hands were watching the confrontation.

'Say your piece, Smeaton.'

334

'Let us settle this like gentlemen. An affair of honor. I am calling you out.'

Biddlecomb knew then that he had been had, been led into this like a child lured with candy. He, the manipulator, had himself been played like a flute. He had never fought a duel in his life and knew little about it. To refuse would mean losing face before the men, and the fragile discipline aboard the *Icarus* would be torn apart. To accept . . . Biddlecomb thought of Smeaton's beautiful dueling pistols and the ease with which he could hit a bottle bobbing in the sea fifty feet away.

'Very well then. An affair of honor.'

'If I kill you, which I shall, then I imagine that your mob will murder me, though I expect they will eventually do so in any case. But I should like your assurance that nothing will happen to Captain Pendexter.'

'Neither of you will be harmed in the event of my death,' said Biddlecomb, suddenly disquieted by the likelihood of that event.

335

CHAPTER 25

An Affair of Honor

'There are formalities, certainly, that we must attend to?' Biddlecomb asked, stalling. He needed time, just a moment, to think.

'I shall choose a second, if you wish, and you may do so as well. If you feel it's necessary.' Smeaton's tone was taunting.

'Come on then, Biddlecomb, just bloody kill him!' someone shouted from the waist, and a murmur rose from the watching men. Biddlecomb glanced around. Wilson and Barrett looked on with undisguised anxiety. In the waist Rumstick leaned against the fife rail, arms folded, watching.

'Don't be afraid of that buggerer!' another shouted.

Smeaton was grinning. 'It seems your "crew" is anxious for some blood sport. Will they turn on you if you don't kill me?' Then, turning to the midshipman, he said, 'Appleby, go fetch my pistols.'

And then Biddlecomb recalled one of the few things that he did know about the etiquette of dueling. 'Hold a moment, Mr Appleby. I am the challenged party, I choose the weapons. Is that not true, Smeaton?'

336

'Well, yes, it is. I assumed . . .'

'And that was your mistake, Smeaton.' Biddlecomb turned to the two armed seamen who guarded the prisoners and pulled the cutlasses from their shoulder straps. 'We'll fight with cutlasses. Good English cutlasses.' He passed one of the weapons to Smeaton, who accepted it, holding it tentatively by the handle.

'Really, if we are to fight like gentlemen—'

'The cutlass is an honorable weapon. However, if you care to withdraw your challenge . . .' Biddlecomb took a practice lunge and parry, then held the cutlass above his head and stretched his arms. He was becoming accustomed to the weight of the weapon in his hand.

'Never in my life would I withdraw a challenge. Very well, let's have at it,' said Smeaton, his tone now somewhere between determination and resignation. He pulled off his heavy blue uniform coat and Biddlecomb did likewise. Biddlecomb was more optimistic now. At least with the cutlasses he had a chance.

'We'll fight in the waist where there's more room,' Biddlecomb said, stepping down from the quarterdeck and walking down the larboard side. The men had abandoned any pretense of work and stood ringing the deck and crowding the shrouds for a view of the fight. Biddlecomb could hear wagers being placed. This was indeed a mean-spirited mob, ready to turn on anyone who showed weakness.

'Mr Wilson,' Biddlecomb shouted to Bloody Wilson, who had the watch aft. 'This is an affair of honor between gentlemen, is that not the case, Mr Smeaton?' Smeaton nodded and Biddlecomb

337

continued, 'As such, no action will be taken as a result of the outcome. If I am killed, so be it. You are responsible for seeing that no harm comes to Smeaton or Pendexter.'

'Run the blackballing bastard through, Isaac, do it now!' someone shouted.

'Aye,' replied Bloody Wilson.

Smeaton stepped down to the waist, holding his cutlass above his head and stretching his arms as Biddlecomb had done, with a practiced ease. He dropped his arm and lunged at the air, parried, and lunged again. Biddlecomb could see that he was no stranger to swordsmanship. It was possible that he was as good with a blade as he was with a gun.

'Are you quite ready, Smeaton?' Biddlecomb asked.

Smeaton still appeared confident, though much of his jauntiness had deserted him. 'Quite ready, Brother Jonathan.'

'Pendexter, you may give the word to begin,' Biddlecomb called out, and the two men went on guard, the tips of their cutlasses wavering in the air, facing each other on the silent deck.

'Begin!' shouted Pendexter.

The two blades sounded unnaturally loud as they came together. Biddlecomb advanced hard on Smeaton, hoping to unbalance him with the fury of his attack, but Smeaton turned away thrust after thrust, parried, and thrust himself.

Biddlecomb lunged at Smeaton's chest and Smeaton knocked the blade aside, exposing Biddlecomb's chest as a target. Smeaton thrust, but Biddlecomb was ready and brought his hilt up against Smeaton's blade and slid it along until their

338

hilts were locked. He stepped inside Smeaton's cutlass and with his left hand shoved him hard in the chest.

Smeaton staggered back, slamming up against the mainmast fife rail. Biddlecomb lunged for Smeaton's chest, but Smeaton was fast and leapt to the deck, and Biddlecomb's cutlass found only air. The blade severed the main topgallant sheet and the point embedded itself in the mast.

Smeaton scrambled to his feet as Biddlecomb struggled to free the weapon from the mast, then lunged just as Biddlecomb pulled the cutlass free and swung it back in an arc, deflecting Smeaton's blow. The duelists staggered away from each other. Biddlecomb's arm felt rubbery from the impact of the blades, and his breath was short. But he could see that Smeaton was breathing hard as well, and that his face and shirt were drenched with sweat. He realized that Smeaton was in fact a very good swordsman. Then Smeaton gulped air and attacked again.

Biddlecomb was surprised by the fury of the onslaught, stepping back, just able to turn away the thrusts and feints. But that was fine. Smeaton would tire himself out. He hoped that Smeaton was half as tired as he was now.

Smeaton lunged awkwardly for Biddlecomb's waist and Biddlecomb parried the blow hard, spinning Smeaton half around with the force, then lunged. Smeaton leapt back, but not fast enough, and the point of Biddlecomb's cutlass pierced his white shirt, and a blossom of red spread across the cloth.

Then Smeaton began to advance again, ignoring the cut, driving Biddlecomb back step by step. But Biddlecomb could see the signs of fatigue and knew that a minute more of this and Smeaton would have no speed left. He parried left and right, letting Smeaton do the work. He stepped back again, and his heel caught fast in a ringbolt on the deck.

In the same instant that he felt his heel catch, Biddlecomb knew that he was going to fall. His arms shot out for balance and he caught a glimpse of Smeaton's weary smile as he lunged at Biddlecomb's chest. But Biddlecomb was falling away and Smeaton's cutlass just pierced his skin as Biddlecomb fell flat on his back.

His head made an audible thump on the planking, and then Smeaton was above him, a wild grin on his face, as he brought his cutlass back over his head, like a man chopping wood. Biddlecomb wondered vaguely how Smeaton could have made so foolish a mistake as he crashed his boot up hard on Smeaton's crotch.

Smeaton roared in pain and surprise, nearly hitting Biddlecomb on the head as he dropped his cutlass. Still on his back, Biddlecomb brought his feet up to Smeaton's chest and kicked out, sending Smeaton sprawling across the deck. Biddlecomb leapt to his feet, his cutlass still in his hand, moving carefully, anxious not to make his opponent's mistake, anxious to kill the man. Smeaton was lying on the deck, his face contorted with fear, shaking his head slightly, and Biddlecomb paused. And then he remembered Haliburton, remembered his body drifting down through the water, the smug look on Smeaton's face. Now it was Smeaton's turn to die.

He drew back the cutlass for a final thrust, then paused as a sound, one sound, permeated the haze in his mind. It was flogging canvas.

340

Biddlecomb froze, his eyes locked on Smeaton, who lay groaning in a fetal position, and listened. The sails flogged again and Biddlecomb felt the *Icarus* move under him, not the dead wallowing of the brig becalmed but a genuine reaction to a breeze. The sails were filling and spilling wind with a chorus of snapping sounds. He looked out to sea and felt the breeze on his face and saw the ripples on the water stretching away to the horizon. He lowered his cutlass and continued to stare, stupid with fatigue.

'Hands to the braces, sir?' It was Rumstick, and his voice sounded far away.

'Yes. Yes, by God! Hands to the braces!' Biddlecomb shouted, and the silent deck came alive with laughing and whooping men running to brace the yards around. All of Biddlecomb's hate was blown away by the blessed wind. 'And send someone to long-splice that main topgallant sheet.'

The sails flogged once more, then filled, and the ship rolled to leeward and maintained that angle, held over by the pressure of the wind in the sails. Biddlecomb could hear water gurgling down the brig's side as she gathered way.

'I'm sorry, Smeaton,' Biddlecomb said to the figure on the deck, 'but I shall have to kill you another time.'

For two days the *Icarus* charged north like a runaway coach. Studdingsails were flown until something broke, and only then were they taken in. The hourly log showed ten and twelve knots through the water, but Biddlecomb's noon sights showed him much greater progress over the ground. That and the

341

unique aquamarine color of the sea told him that the ship was solidly in the grip of the Gulf Stream.

They were heading for Rhode Island. Boston was shut up and New York was indifferent at best to the cause of liberty, and they had no knowledge of what dangers awaited at the other ports along the eastern seaboard. But Rhode Island, Rhode Island was Biddlecomb's home, a smuggler's paradise, and Biddlecomb knew how to lose a ship in the islands and shoals of Narragansett Bay. True, the *Rose* was there as well, but she was only one ship, and in the minds of Biddlecomb and Rumstick and the others, it was a case of better the devil you know. Rhode Island was the safest place they could be in a world that was, for them, anything but safe.

The weather began to change rapidly as they ran north, and soon the cool days and cold nights were replaced by cold days and freezing nights. But this did not dampen the men's spirits, being as it was such a tangible measure of their progress. Even the abuse of Pendexter and Smeaton would not have angered Biddlecomb in his current state of exhilaration, though they now refused to emerge from the bread room except to visit the head.

On the morning of the third day, as the Icaruses cleared the brig for action, Biddlecomb found himself stamping his feet and blowing steaming breath through his hands. His dead reckoning put them somewhere off New Jersey or New York, but he would have to wait for a noon sight to be certain. In any case they were close to home now, very close to home.

The activity on the deck settled down, and Barrett stepped up to the weather rail to report. 'Cleared for

342

action, sir. Eight minutes, fourteen seconds.' It was all routine by now.

In the gray predawn light Biddlecomb could see the men at their stations, stamping their feet and holding hands under armpits in their effort to keep warm, and he realized how inadequate their clothing was.

'Mr Barrett, does the brig have anything like a slop chest, at all?' he asked.

'Aye, and well stocked too. With the purser left in Boston, Pendexter never thought to issue nothing.'

Biddlecomb wished he had been informed of this earlier, but he did not say as much. 'Detail some men to bring it up on deck, and get all of Smeaton's and Pendexter's and the purser's clothing up here as well. We shall distribute them to the hands.'

Ten minutes later all thoughts of what the rising sun might reveal were lost as the men reveled in their bounty. Normally an issue from the slop chest carried with it a concern for how much would eventually be deducted from already meager pay, but now the men took with happy abandon. Rumstick personally stopped four fistfights from breaking out, three of them over plugs of tobacco.

So concerned were the men with the free slops, and so concerned were the officers with an equitable and nonviolent distribution, that the lookout's voice, when he did at last sing out, came as a surprise.

'On deck!'

Biddlecomb looked up. This too was a part of the routine: the cry, the response, the negative report. 'Deck, aye!' Biddlecomb shouted, thinking of how cold the lookout must be.

'Sail to leeward, sir. Hull down. Looks like a ship.'

343

Biddlecomb was so unprepared for this that he had to think about the words. But of course there would be a ship. After so many days of empty sea one had to expect a ship eventually. And besides that, they were now closing with one of the busiest ports in America.

The *Icarus* was silent again, and the men's new clothes, those articles that were not being worn, were discreetly tucked away as the ship waited for further news from aloft. From the quarterdeck Biddlecomb could now see the lookout high aloft on the main topmast crosstrees, the big signal telescope pointing aft.

'On deck!' the lookout cried again, and not waiting for a reply continued, 'She looks like a frigate, sir, close-hauled, sailing . . . southwest!'

Biddlecomb considered this. They were sailing in nearly opposite directions. No doubt the stranger was one of His Majesty's ships, bound away on some vital mission.

'She's hauling her wind, sir!' the lookout cried again, his voice a bit higher. All heads were turned aloft now. 'She's coming up in our wake!' The lookout paused, and his voice cracked when he spoke again. 'Sweet mother of Jesus! It's the *Cerberus*!'

344

CHAPTER 26

Cat and Mouse

Biddlecomb moved his telescope down the wake and up to the horizon, and there, in perfect line with the brig, was the *Cerberus*. The cut of her topsails and topgallants, just visible above the horizon, was unmistakable, so long had he spent looking at them in the Caribbean.

As he held the frigate in his glass, his anger and frustration overwhelmed him. It was the most absurdly bad fortune, as if fate were conspiring against him, as if God were punishing him for McDuff's and Longbottom's deaths, as if the *Icarus* were cursed. He muttered profanities like a chant and fought down the urge to hurl the glass to the deck. He cursed himself and he cursed the *Icarus* and Pendexter and the *Cerberus* and the god who had made them all.

And then like a wave passing under a ship his anger subsided and reason insinuated itself once again. When they had first seen the *Cerberus*, over a week ago, she had been on the same course as the *Icarus*; she too must have been bound away for New England. Where she was heading now, sailing south Biddlecomb could not guess. Not that it mattered; the *Cerberus* was sailing south no longer.

345

Thoughts swirled around like sediment and settled again. Did the *Cerberus* recognize them? That was a certainty. Did the *Cerberus* suspect that something about the *Icarus* was amiss? They had come about and seemed to take up chase the moment they had sighted the *Icarus*, so, yes, it would appear that they were suspicious, and that meant that there would be no fooling them again.

'On deck!' the lookout cried from aloft.

'Deck, aye!' Biddlecomb returned the hail.

'Frigate's setting studdingsails, aloft and alow!'

There was an end to any doubts; the *Cerberus* was chasing them, and doing so in earnest. There could be no harm now in showing flight. Biddlecomb turned and looked up at the canvas that the brig was carrying. The wind was buffeting his back and the wisps of hair that had escaped his queue streamed forward and whipped him in the face. The *Icarus* was carrying topgallants over single-reefed topsails and studdingsails. Biddlecomb considered shaking out the reefs and setting topgallant studdingsails as well.

He looked down along the deck. The men were no longer stamping to keep warm, and the steam from their breath was instantly carried away with the wind. They were counting on him to fool the frigate once more, and once more he had not a clue as to how he would do it. He wondered how long he had been standing silent while the men were waiting for orders. Indecision on his part would not help the men's morale.

'Mr Wilson,' he called down to the waist. 'Please have the watch on deck shake out the reef in the topsails and studdingsails. The watch below can have

346

breakfast, then we'll see if she'll bear topgallant studdingsails as well.'

Wilson turned and relayed the orders to the men, and Biddlecomb could sense their relief. They moved quickly and cheerfully, confident no doubt that Biddlecomb had the situation well in hand. He had fooled the *Cerberus* before, had he not? He would do it again. He wondered if any of them understood the real danger that they were in. Rumstick did, he was certain, but perhaps he was the only one.

He turned to stare at the frigate again as half the crew went below for breakfast and the other half went aloft to shake the reefs out of the sails. The frigate's topsails and topgallants were clearly visible now, and Biddlecomb was aware of a peculiar sensation as he watched them bobbing on the horizon. But for the overcast sky and the frigid air they might be right back in the Caribbean, being chased as they had been a week before.

'On deck!' the lookout cried.

'Deck, aye!' Biddlecomb replied.

'Frigate's signaling, sir!'

I should imagine they are, Biddlecomb thought. He turned to Appleby.

The midshipman was already thumbing through his signal book. 'Frigate's making our number, sir, and signaling, "Heave to." '

That was what Biddlecomb had expected. 'Very well.' The captain of the *Cerberus* would not fall for the same ruse again, nor, Biddlecomb imagined, any other ruse. But other considerations made the ledger balance. They were not on the high seas now, with no place to run. They were off the coast of America, in Biddlecomb's home waters. If there was any spot

347

on earth where Biddlecomb could win a game of cat and mouse, it was here. If only the *Cerberus* did not close with them before he closed with the coast.

'Sir,' said Appleby, interrupting Biddlecomb's thoughts, 'what reply shall I give *Cerberus*?'

Biddlecomb looked out at the frigate and pictured the irascible little captain standing alone at the weather rail, staring at the *Icarus*. 'There is no need to reply.'

Five minutes later the *Cerberus*'s signal flags came fluttering down, and no further signal was hoisted. Neither did the frigate alter her course or take in an inch of canvas, and Biddlecomb knew that this time the *Cerberus*'s captain would not be satisfied until he had a boarding party on the brig's deck.

Noon came, with the sun sulking low in the northern sky and just visible through the gray cover of clouds. Biddlecomb flipped one filter on Pendexter's quadrant and stepped up to the break of the quarterdeck.

'Beg pardon, sir,' said Barrett, emerging from the scuttle, 'but the prisoners says they'd like to come on deck.'

'I think not, we don't need that aggravation today.'

Ten minutes later Biddlecomb drew a mark on the chart that lay spread across the great-cabin table and smiled for the first time since dawn. The *Icarus* was not off the coast of New Jersey at all, but crossing the latitude of New York City, and Biddlecomb imagined that they were not above one hundred miles offshore. If the wind and the spars held, they would sight Montauk Point and Block Island by sunset, and then Biddlecomb could lose his pursuer in the dark, running close inshore.

'Montauk Point,' Biddlecomb said the words to himself, softly, like a prayer. Montauk Point meant Point Judith, and that meant Narragansett Bay, and home. Biddlecomb felt the first stirring of hope and confidence in his breast.

'If . . .' Biddlecomb reminded himself. There were many factors to consider. There would be a half moon tonight, rising just after sunset. That was in their favor. But they had to reach Montauk Point before the *Cerberus* overtook them. Actually, before the *Cerberus* was within cannon shot, close enough to inflict crippling damage. Biddlecomb picked up the dividers and walked off the miles to Block Island, then figured the rate at which the *Cerberus* was overtaking them. If none of the tophamper carried away, then it would be close. Very close.

Biddlecomb stepped up to the quarterdeck again, into the bracing cold. The reefs were out of the sails, and the topgallant studdingsails were straining in the gale. Forward, Rumstick had the men rigging the spritsail topsail, ready to sway the light yard out under the jibboom.

Ten minutes later the strange sail was set and drawing, and Rumstick ambled aft to the quarterdeck.

'We're close to home, Ezra, just abeam of New York,' Biddlecomb informed him. 'Now if only the Royal Navy will let us get there.' The two men turned and looked aft at the frigate. Her courses were visible now. She had gained at least three miles on them since dawn.

'They ain't far from long cannon shot,' Rumstick observed.

'Indeed not. But those bow chasers don't point

349

straight ahead. They'll have to turn to bring them to bear, and I doubt they'll want to lose the distance doing that. My guess is that they'll wait till they've really closed with us to open fire.'

'You're already sounding the right naval captain, Isaac.'

'So I have been told. In any case we shall be in Rhode Island Sound in four hours.'

'Of course the frigate will be right up with us in three.'

'You're an optimistic sod. Recall, however, that by that time the sun will be setting, which will aid us much if we haven't yet been beaten into splinters. But for now let's begin jettisoning everything we can.'

'Not the powder and shot, please. We'll get a bigger welcome in Providence if we bring in quantities of powder and shot.'

'Very well, keep the powder for your damned revolution. But all water and food goes over the side save rations for one day. In any event we won't need more than that.'

The brig's company turned to with the enthusiasm of men laboring to save their lives. Hatches were broken open and barrel after barrel of rancid salt pork and salt beef and dried peas were swayed out of the hold and dropped into the sea. The hogsheads of water were started and drained into the bilges, and the pumps made their cacophony of squeaking and banging as a river of fresh water cascaded down the deck and burst from the scuppers. By the next cast of the log the *Icarus* had picked up half a knot of speed, and the lightening was still going on.

Biddlecomb looked aft once again. Streaming away

350

at regular intervals in the brig's wake was a line of barrels, and he imagined that the *Cerberus* would now be bumping into the first of them. He looked up at the frigate. She was hull up now, noticeably closer, and Biddlecomb wondered when she would try her first ranging shots.

He put his glass to his eye. The frigate's bow wave was just visible, as was the ghastly figurehead with its leering canine faces. Cerberus, the mythological gatekeeper of hell, inviting them in. And above that the black barrels of the bow chasers, thrust out from the side, not quite pointing at the *Icarus*. The real teeth of Cerberus.

A burst of gray, like a cloud, shot from the frigate's side, and Biddlecomb imagined for a instant that they were firing their great guns at the empty sea. But the cloud did not dissipate and Biddlecomb realized that it was a jet of water. The frigate had started her water casks as well. If they were willing to jettison their water, then they were very eager to catch the *Icarus*, and that would make that event much more likely.

'Captain Biddlecomb?' Rumstick stepped up behind him. 'All the food and water's over the side, and bosun's stores and carpenter's stores and spare spars as well. That's about all we can jettison.'

Biddlecomb jerked his thumb in the direction of the *Cerberus*. 'They've started their water.'

Rumstick looked at the frigate and nodded his head. 'We could jettison the guns,' he said at last. 'My friends in Providence aren't as desperate for them as they are for powder.'

Biddlecomb considered that. 'No. We may need the guns.'

351

'They won't do us a bit of good against the frigate.'

'No. But the *Cerberus* may not be our only enemy tonight.'

The *Cerberus* was not more than a half a mile astern when she began to fire her bow chasers. It was quiet, and Biddlecomb's back was to the frigate, when all at once he was assaulted by the sound of screaming metal and torn and flogging canvas, and trailing behind, the distant sound of the frigate's bow chaser. Biddlecomb jumped clear off the deck in surprise. There was a hole in the mainsail ten feet above his head.

'Jesus Christ!' Biddlecomb shouted, whirling around as he did. The *Cerberus* was turning to starboard, coming back in line with the *Icarus*, having fallen off to bring the gun to bear. If they had lost any ground by turning, Biddlecomb could not tell.

The *Cerberus* turned until her bowsprit was once again in line with the *Icarus*, then continued to turn, presenting her larboard gun with a target. Biddlecomb watched, transfixed, as the gun fired. He heard the ball shriek overhead, but faintly, and he knew that the shot had gone wide. And now the *Cerberus* was turning again and her starboard bow chaser was running out.

Biddlecomb looked over the larboard side. Long Island stretched out low and gray on the horizon, and he could just make out Montauk Point and Block Island beyond. The sun was an hour from disappearing, and the cloud cover was breaking up. A winter afternoon like so many he had known in those waters.

The *Cerberus* fired and another hole appeared in the mainsail.

He had lost. He had driven the brig as hard as she could be driven, but the *Cerberus* had run them down. He was so close! In an hour he could round Montauk Point, shaving it closer than the *Cerberus* would dare, and find shelter behind Long Island. By the time the frigate followed them, night would have fallen and it would have been easy work losing them in Long Island Sound. But he did not have an hour. The next shot, or the next, would bring down the top-hamper, and even if the bow chasers did not cripple them, the frigate, with twice the brig's weight of iron, would be alongside in twenty minutes.

The *Cerberus* fired, but Biddlecomb did not see where the shot landed.

'Wilson, Barrett, Rumstick, step over here, please,' he called out, and the three men stepped up to the weather side. 'We must face the truth, we cannot escape. The *Cerberus* is simply too fast. I'm sorry. We had best figure what we'll do when we're taken.'

353

CHAPTER 27

Montauk Point

The three men stood looking at Biddlecomb, grim-faced and silent.

'I'll do what the crew wishes,' Biddlecomb continued. 'We can fight or surrender. But if we're taken, I want you three to make like you're foremast jacks, it may go easier for you.'

'Maybe they don't want us at all,' said Rumstick, 'maybe it's the Admiralty wanting to ask Pendexter why he's such a horse's ass.' He was smiling, but the joke fell flat.

'Barrett, I want you to go . . .' Biddlecomb said, his voice trailing off as an idea materialized.

The *Cerberus* fired and the starboard main topmast studdingsail collapsed in a flogging heap. 'Harland! Get a gang aloft to clear that away!' Rumstick shouted.

'Perhaps there is one trick left,' Biddlecomb said slowly, 'not much of one, but it is a chance,' and the others leaned closer as Biddlecomb outlined his idea.

Ten minutes later Pendexter and Smeaton emerged on deck, escorted at gunpoint by Israel Barrett. Biddlecomb, standing in the waist, was ready to greet him.

354

'Ah, gentlemen, your servant,' he called. 'Step over here, please.'

They stepped over grudgingly, motivated largely by Barrett's prodding with the pistol.

'Are you going to hang us now? I take it that that shoreline is America,' Pendexter said.

'Hang you? Never in life. Here is your sword back, and your boat cloak and cocked hat,' Biddlecomb said, handing the items to Pendexter. 'Here, Smeaton.'

Appleby stood at the bulwark holding Smeaton's sword and the pistols. Biddlecomb took them from the midshipman and handed them to the former first officer.

And then Smeaton did a surprising thing. He flung the sword and the pistols into the sea. Biddlecomb watched as the ripples they made were left astern.

'Why did you do that?'

'I know you're about to murder us, Biddlecomb. Why else would you force us up on deck? I'll not have you give me back my things, then murder me and steal them again, you coward!'

Biddlecomb could not imagine why he would want to do such a thing, or why Smeaton would even think he would. 'Suit yourself.'

The *Cerberus* fired and a hole appeared in the main topsail. Pendexter spun around, leaning over the bulwark and staring aft.

'Oh, so this is it!' he said, and his face broke out in a wide smile. 'You're about to be run to earth, and now you're returning my command! Well, forget it, you Yankee bastard. I shall see you kick out your life at the end of a halter!'

Biddlecomb felt the rage seething up again, and he

355

marveled at this man's ability to elicit that emotion. Pendexter possessed an uncanny sense for finding just the words that would make him furious. After all of the cruelty, after all of Pendexter's arrogance and his utter failure at command, after driving decent men to commit the heinous crimes of mutiny and murder, after all that madness, Pendexter could still stand there with his pompous attitude and call Biddlecomb a Yankee bastard.

That was the end. Biddlecomb felt the anger raging inside and knew he was about to strike the aristocratic whore's son down, first with words and then with the flat of his cutlass. And then Pendexter spoke again.

'You should know, Biddlecomb,' he said in the same tone that he might address a servant, lifting his chin slightly, 'that my father is Lord Pendexter and my uncle is Admiral Graves, commander in chief in the colonies. What you have done here can never be forgiven.'

And with those words all of the anger was out of Biddlecomb, like the wind from a luffing sail. Those few words told Biddlecomb the whole story: coddled from childhood, promoted due to influence, given a command he was not ready to receive, put in charge of men he did not understand. They had been setting him up for this fall since he was born, and they thought they were doing him a favor. Pendexter was not a man at all, he was a frightened boy. The thoughts of vengeance were gone, and in their place was something approaching pity.

'My God, but you are one sorry bastard. Yes, I am giving you a command, of sorts. Your second command. God help you to handle it better than

356

your first. Step down there, sir.' Biddlecomb indicated a section of grating hanging two feet above the water, suspended from a whip at the main yard-arm and held against the side of the brig by a line belayed at the pinrail.

Pendexter looked down at the grating. As the brig rolled, the water washed over it and twisted it around. 'I most certainly will not go down there.'

'I have no time to waste.' As if to reiterate the point the *Cerberus* fired again. Biddlecomb pulled the cutlass from Barrett's shoulder strap and prodded Pendexter with the point.

'Ow! God damn your eyes!' Pendexter shouted. Biddlecomb prodded again and Pendexter clambered over the side and settled down on the grating.

Biddlecomb turned the cutlass on Smeaton, pressing the point into his shoulder. 'You next.' Without a word Smeaton clambered over the side and settled down next to Pendexter.

'There's a lanyard there for you to clap on to,' Biddlecomb pointed out.

'Here, Captain.' Wilson hurried up and handed Biddlecomb a gun's rammer with a white shirt fluttering like a flag from the end.

'Excellent,' said Biddlecomb, handing the flag down to Pendexter. 'Take this.'

'What am I supposed to do with this?'

'Whatever you wish. Now, listen, you men,' Biddlecomb addressed the hands at the fall of the whip, 'when the grating swings outboard, we'll cast off the whip on a larboard roll.'

'What in hell!' shouted Pendexter from over the side. 'I insist—'

No one ever had a chance to find out what

357

Pendexter insisted. As the *Icarus* rolled to starboard, Biddlecomb cast off the line and the grating swung away from the side, like a pendulum hanging from the main yard.

'Now!' Biddlecomb shouted as the ship began to roll to larboard. The men cast loose the whip, and the line shot up the mast and through the block. The grating splashed down in the sea, twirling like a leaf in a stream. Pendexter shouted with outrage. Seconds later he and Smeaton were out of sight from the waist.

The men of the *Icarus* took up a rousing cheer, yelling and hooting and shouting insults and waving to their departing officers.

Biddlecomb stepped up to the quarterdeck where Rumstick and Wilson and Barrett stood clustered around the taffrail, watching the strange raft bobbing astern.

'That were excellently well done, Isaac!' said Rumstick, slapping Biddlecomb painfully on the back.

'Let's see if it works,' Biddlecomb cautioned, and the four men looked astern again.

The *Cerberus* completed her swing to starboard and let loose with the bow chaser. Biddlecomb saw the ball skip once on the sea, then again, just abeam of the *Icarus*, before it disappeared. They were shooting low, shooting for the rudder. Or the quarterdeck.

'That couldn't have missed them two by much,' Barrett said.

Apparently it had not, for Smeaton was now standing on the raft, frantically waving the white flag. The *Cerberus* was a quarter mile from him now, swinging to larboard to bring the next bow chaser around.

It occurred to Biddlecomb, as he watched the two

358

figures on the grating dwindle astern, that he might now be responsible for the deaths of two more men. If the *Cerberus* did not see the grating, then they would run it down, and even if they did, they might well opt to ignore it and continue the chase. Once night fell, the raft would be lost and Pendexter and Smeaton would not live long on the winter sea. Were the lives of two lieutenants worth more to the captain of the *Cerberus* than catching this brig that had eluded them before? That question would be answered in the next few moments.

Biddlecomb focused his telescope on the frigate's quarterdeck. He could make out individual figures, patches of blue standing here and there. And suddenly the quarterdeck was a flurry of activity, the blue patches running in every direction. Biddlecomb took the glass from his eye. The frigate was still turning to larboard. The bow chaser fired and the ball whistled overhead, but the frigate did not check her swing. Her courses flogged and were hauled up to the yards, and the studdingsails collapsed and disappeared. The main yards swung around and the sails came aback.

'She's heaving to,' Biddlecomb said softly. The *Cerberus* was stopping to pick up the unknown officers on the raft.

'She's heaving to!' Rumstick shouted down the deck, and the men began cheering louder than Biddlecomb had ever heard before.

Biddlecomb put the glass to his eye. A boat lifted off the booms and swung out over the frigate's side. He looked west to where the sun was setting over Long Island. Half an hour more and they would be beyond their enemy's grip.

It did not take the *Cerberus*'s men ten minutes to

359

launch the boat, retrieve Pendexter and Smeaton, and sway the boat aboard again, but in that time the *Icarus* had gained half a mile on the frigate.

'That was nice work, launching and recovering that boat,' Biddlecomb said, a touch of smugness in his voice, 'but I doubt they can make up the distance they lost.'

And then the *Cerberus* erupted in smoke as she fired her full broadside at the *Icarus*. The shriek of the round shot was deafening. Wood and metal fragments flew as the balls struck the hull. Forward a man screamed in agony and then was silent, and his cry was replaced by a rending, shattering sound from overhead.

Biddlecomb looked aloft. The main topgallant mast leaned forward, swaying with the roll of the brig. Then the weather backstay parted and mast and yard, sail and studdingsails, fell forward. The yards on the foremast jerked and swung wild as the falling wreckage tore away the braces.

'God damn me for a fool! Why didn't I see that coming!' Biddlecomb shouted. 'Wilson, Rumstick, get some men aloft and clear that wreckage, just cut it away, and reeve off new running gear, fast as you can. Barrett, supervise the waisters.'

The three men ran forward and Biddlecomb turned aft. The *Cerberus* was under way again, resuming the chase of her now crippled prey. But her momentum was gone, and she would have to set her courses and studdingsails again, and after taking in sail as fast as she had, the gear would be in disarray and the sails would not be set with the usual alacrity. He turned his back to the frigate. Staring at her would not help.

The seamen aloft cut the topgallant sail free from the yard, and Biddlecomb watched it flutter away, the heavy canvas born easily by the gale. Biddlecomb heard a splash forward and the shattered topgallant mast appeared in their wake, followed by the topgallant yard. Rumstick was already seeing the spare mast and yard readied for swaying aloft.

Biddlecomb looked up at the *Cerberus* and realized that the light was quickly fading. The starboard bow chaser fired, its muzzle flash brilliant in the twilight, but Biddlecomb did not see where the ball fell.

He turned and looked to the west. The sun was gone, leaving only a red tint on the gray and black sky overhead. And there was Montauk Point, just abeam.

'Hands to braces, what braces we got left!' Biddlecomb shouted. 'Larboard, three degrees,' he told the helmsman.

The *Icarus* began to swing toward Montauk Point. Biddlecomb would shave the land, closer than most would dare. He looked astern for the last time. The *Cerberus* was nearly lost in the gloom.

He had won. He had eluded *Cerberus*. He had now only to sail the gauntlet of Narragansett Bay and he was home, and with that thought he wondered if he had flanked the keeper of the gate only to charge straight into hell itself.

361

CHAPTER 28

The Gates of Hell

The moon crept higher and higher, and in the pure, cold air it illuminated the *Icarus* and Rhode Island Sound to a surprising degree. Block Island had disappeared astern an hour past, and for the moment the lookouts could see nothing on the horizon but water, and that was all that Biddlecomb wished to see.

Overhead the main yards swung around and the sails filled and the *Icarus* gathered way once more. Biddlecomb looked over the larboard side. The *Icarus*'s gig, carrying Dibdin, Bolton, and two others whose loyalties had changed once again, was pulling away from the brig. In ten hours they would be in Newport.

Biddlecomb remembered how Bolton had screamed as three men dragged him down into the gig, and the memory made him smile. Bolton had thrown in entirely with the mutineers, he was as guilty as any of them, and it was with pleasure that Biddlecomb handed him back to the Royal Navy. Dibdin, he knew, would make certain that Bolton's cooperation was brought to light. Biddlecomb doubted that it would be above a week before the

362

former steward was choking out his life at the yard-arm.

'You're a strange one, Biddlecomb,' Dibdin had said as the two men stood in the waist watching Barrett supervise the preparation of the gig. 'I thought that when you was first brought aboard. You're no foremast jack, are you?'

'I was once, a long time ago. Sixteen years. The last time I sailed this way I was master of a merchant-man.'

'Sixteen years ain't so long to go from the lower deck to the quarterdeck, especially not at your age. Most men don't do it in a lifetime.'

'I was lucky.'

'You held this rabble together, which is more than two commissioned lieutenants and three warrant officers could do. How is it you came to be pressed as a common seaman?'

As the gig rose from the chocks, Biddlecomb told his story that began in those same waters aboard the little *Judea* so many months ago, and the further he went in relating the tale, the angrier he became; angry with himself for his stupid mistakes and angry at the circumstances that had ruined his carefully structured life, and above all else angry at the British, whom, he realized, he had come to regard as the prime movers of his misfortune. He stood in silence for a moment, allowing his bitterness to subside.

'It occurs to me, as I tell you this, that I've been quite ill-used by the British navy,' Biddlecomb said.

'Bah!' replied Dibdin. 'Every damned sailor thinks his lot is the hardest. I've known men would beg to have it as easy as you've had it.'

363

The sound of footsteps coming aft woke Biddle-comb from his reveries. 'Beg, pardon, sir.' The seaman who had been standing lookout at the bow was standing before him and saluting. 'I sees the loom of land, broad on the larboard bow.'

'Thank you. That was well seen,' said Biddlecomb by way of encouragement, though he himself had spotted Point Judith ten minutes before. 'Pass the word for Mr Wilson.'

Wilson appeared on the quarterdeck a minute later. 'Mr Wilson, we'll clear for action, but quietly, no yelling. Pass the word to the men,' Biddlecomb instructed.

'Aye, sir.' Wilson disappeared forward, and less than a minute later the men poured up through the hatches and cleared the brig for action. The evolution had an unreal quality as the men moved quietly about, whispering orders and laying their tools down softly and easing the guns inboard with a minimum of sound.

Twelve minutes later Barrett stepped up to the quarterdeck. 'Cleared for action, sir. It took a bit longer, on account of our having to be quiet.'

'That's fine, Mr Barrett.' Biddlecomb stepped up to the larboard rail and leaned low to peer under the foresail. Point Judith was clearly visible off the larboard beam, and ahead and to starboard he could see the rugged shore of Rhode Island standing out against the stars. He looked down at the water rushing along the ship's side. They were making a good eight knots. He relished the brig's speed and her handiness. 'Make your head north by east,' he said to the helmsman.

Point Judith passed astern and the *Icarus* ran

364

across the entrance to the West Passage. Biddlecomb peered under the foresail again, past the starboard bow, allowing his eyes to relax and scan the dark shore. He saw a flash, he was certain, a line of gray in the blackness, the sea breaking along Brenton Reef and Castle Hill. 'You see those breakers?' Biddlecomb asked the helmsman.

'Aye,' the helmsman replied, a note of uncertainty in his voice.

'Steer to leave them to starboard, but just to starboard. Stand in as close as ever you can. There's plenty of water there, so don't be afraid.'

It was all so familiar; the breakers at Castle Hill, dimly seen in the dark, the spray swept back over the deck, the familiar entrance to Narragansett Bay. And it was all so different; the line of guns down either side of the deck, the crowd of men standing anxiously beside them.

Then Biddlecomb felt the anger well up in him again and bury him like a breaking wave rolling over him in the dark. Rhode Island was his home, and yet he had to come crawling back in the night, like some low thing, terrified of his master's hand. For five years he had been doing this, and at last he was sick of it. The British had taken from him his ship and his fortune, and now they had taken his home. Neither Narragansett Bay nor any other port in America would be safe for him until the British were forcibly driven from the water. He realized that, and he was ready to start driving.

'God damn them all to hell!' he said out loud as the anger washed him away. He slammed his fist down on the caprail. The pain was good, the sensation of striking something when he could not strike

365

the enemy. But anger alone would not drive the British out, and anger would not get the men of the *Icarus* to safety.

He looked over at Mr Appleby. The midshipman was staring at him, wide-eyed, as were the helmsmen. Biddlecomb smiled despite himself, realizing that he must look quite the lunatic, cursing and beating the rail with no apparent provocation.

Conanicut Island was just visible in the moonlight on the larboard side, the trees standing out against the sky and the rocks shining wet along the shore as Biddlecomb turned the *Icarus* north. On the starboard side and two miles distant, Newport Harbor opened up, revealing the constellation of lights on the anchored ships and in the town beyond.

And then the lights were lost from sight, one by one, as Goat Island and Rose Island came between the brig and the shore, and it was dark and quiet again. It was a beautiful night, and running before the wind made it seem less cold. Biddlecomb's thoughts began to wander to Bristol, and William Stanton, and Virginia Stanton. He thought of the way she looked, handing them the pistols from beneath her cloak, that glimpse of bare ankle as she stormed out of the sitting room, clad only in her nightgown.

He shook his head and admonished himself for his dreaming. We're not in Providence yet, not even close, he thought, and forced himself to consider the next question: whether to pass Prudence Island to the east or west.

He looked over at Gould Island, now less than half a mile away. They were right in the middle of the channel, in good, deep water, with Conanicut Island

366

passing down their larboard side and Gould Island to starboard.

The western side of Prudence Island was a maze of shallows. It was true that the British were less likely to be there, for good reason, but there was also the greater likelihood of running the *Icarus* hard aground. Biddlecomb pictured the brig stranded high on a falling tide, the launch and the gig gone, surrounded at first light by boatloads of marines. No, he would take the longer but deeper east side. That course allowed them more routes of escape if the *Rose* was spotted. The only real danger lay in becoming trapped in the relatively narrow passage between Prudence Island and Rhode Island. If they could make it through there, then they would be all right.

Biddlecomb stared at Gould Island slipping past the starboard side. He could make out the individual trees, straight as ship's masts, their tops swaying in the wind. They moved together, rhythmically, like dancers. Except . . .

Biddlecomb looked again, straining his eyes.

'Sir?' Wilson was beside him with a question, but Biddlecomb held up his hand for silence. There it was again. It wasn't a tree at all. It moved, rather than swayed, gliding past the tall pines, disappearing and reappearing again.

'There's a ship on the other side of the island,' Biddlecomb said softly.

'Are you certain?' Wilson asked, peering into the dark.

'Yes. It's sailing nearly the same course as we are. We'll meet as we pass the island. Please clew up the foresail and have the men stand in readiness at the starboard guns. And quietly as you can.'

367

Wilson nodded and hurried forward, giving orders in a harsh whisper, and Biddlecomb considered the strange sail. It could, of course, be anything, even a smuggler such as he once was. If that was the case, then the stranger would be anxious to avoid any contact, particularly with a vesel that was ostensibly a British man-of-war. Biddlecomb looked forward. They would pass the far end of Gould Island in just a few moments. Then they would know. He felt the telltale signs of fear and excitement in his stomach and his feet.

And then they were past and Biddlecomb could see the strange vessel clearly as it too moved beyond the shelter of the land. It was ship-rigged, but small. If it was a naval vessel, Biddlecomb imagined it would be what they called a sloop of war. It was sailing under topsails and foresail, and moving fast even with that reduced canvas.

'You were right,' said Wilson, returning to the quarterdeck. 'Do you think they've seen us yet?'

'I do not know.'

Across the water a voice cried out in surprise, 'Hey!' and was followed by the sound of running feet. Snatches of loud conversation were carried on the wind.

'They see us now,' Biddlecomb observed. 'If they're a man-of-war, and they fire on us, we'll give them a broadside then crack on all she'll carry to get away, do you understand?' Biddlecomb addressed Wilson, Barrett, and Rumstick, who were gathered now on the quarterdeck. The three men nodded. 'Good. Wilson, go forward and pass the word.'

Wilson ran forward once again and the *Icarus* fell silent. Biddlecomb tried to imagine the discussions aking place on the other ship, less than a quarter mile away. They had not put up their helm and fled upon seeing the *Icarus*, and that did not bode well.

Biddlecomb could feel the tension like a physical presence on the deck. The quiet was distracting and unnerving. And then the strange ship broke the silence.

'You there, the brig!' The voice was loud and distorted by a speaking trumpet. 'What ship is that?'

Biddlecomb snatched up the speaking trumpet. 'This is Capt. James Pendexter, of His Majesty's brig *Icarus*. Who are you? Identify yourself immediately.'

There was a pause as the two vessels sailed on, the sloop closing with the brig, and then the voice spoke again. 'This is Commander Smith, of His Majesty's sloop of war *Swan*. To whom am I speaking?'

'I've told you once already, sir! I am Capt. James Pendexter of the brig *Icarus*!' said Biddlecomb in a tone of exasperation. The sloop of war *Swan*. Another vessel of the British navy was polluting his home. Here was the enemy now, not a cable length away.

'Heave to immediately. Heave to or we shall fire into you!' said Commander Smith.

The two vessels sailed on, silent, and Biddlecomb could see that the *Swan* was setting topgallants and heading to cross the *Icarus*'s bow. He was considering coming about, spinning the brig on her heel, and running for the shelter of Gould Island when the *Swan* fired her forwardmost gun. The muzzle flash was blinding in the dark night, and the deck beneath Biddlecomb's feet shuddered as the ball struck the *Icarus*'s side.

369

The fear and rage poured into Biddlecomb, filling him up, like the sea through a sprung plank. They had made it this far, they would not be stopped now. He clenched his fists, feeling as if he would burst, feeling the need to lash out. He heard his own voice yell, 'Fire!' and the night was shattered with a roar and flash as the *Icarus*'s starboard battery went off. Biddlecomb saw fragments flying from the *Swan*'s side, heard a man screaming across the water. Biddlecomb realized that he was smiling.

'Set the foresail!' he shouted, coming to his senses, and hands peeled away from their stations at the guns to attend to the sail.

And then the *Swan* fired her larboard battery, the full broadside, in one horrible rain of iron. The bulwark five feet in front of Biddlecomb blew into splinters, and the hull jerked from the impact of the round shot. But now the Icaruses were running their guns out again.

'Fire!' Biddlecomb shouted, and another broadside hurled across the water.

'Sir, you might want to order "fire as you bear" and just let them have at it,' Barrett advised, and Biddlecomb saw the wisdom of this.

'Mr Wilson, fire as you bear!' he shouted just as the *Swan* exploded in another broadside. The fore topmast stay parted and collapsed and two gunports were smashed into one. A seaman fell screaming, impaled on a four-foot splinter, and was dragged out of the way by his mates.

The foresail tumbled down and was sheeted home and Biddlecomb felt the *Icarus*'s speed increase. They were pulling ahead of the *Swan* now and might even cross her bows and rake her. He could not allow a

370

hase clear to Providence, he had to cripple her and ose her.

For an instant the two vessels and the intervening water were brilliantly illuminated as both broadsides fired together, and in the flash Biddlecomb saw that the *Swan* was setting more sail as well. With her ship rig and longer waterline she would be faster than *Icarus*. It would not be easy to shake her.

He coughed as the gun smoke filled his lungs, and tears streamed from his eyes. It was so hard to think in the noise and the smoke and confusion.

Biddlecomb tried to block out the screams and the smoke and gunfire and concentrate. Where were they? Tactics would do them no good if they were hard aground. He looked over the larboard side. Conanicut Island was still abeam and ahead, and he could just make out the west side of Prudence Island. He would have to turn east and try to cross the *Swan*'s bow if he hoped to make the east passage.

The gunfire was continuous now, and the weird light reminded Biddlecomb of a terrific lightning storm. Iron and splinters whistled through the air, and the *Icarus* shuddered again and again with the impact of round shot. The smoke made Biddlecomb's eyes ache.

'Make your head east-northeast!' Biddlecomb shouted to the men at the helm. They nodded and pushed the tiller over, and Biddlecomb saw the bow begin to swing. He looked over at the *Swan*. The sloop was not altering course, rather it was closing with the *Icarus*. Biddlecomb imagined that Commander Smith would try to come alongside and board. That would never do, they were certain to be outnumbered.

371

Biddlecomb took his bearings again. He con sidered the navigational hazards in that area. Ther was Prudence Island, of course, and Dyer Island, an Halfway Rock . . .

Biddlecomb felt suddenly sick with fear. Halfwa Rock! Of all things, how could he have forgotte that?

'Steady as she goes!' he yelled at the helmsmen a he leapt down to the main deck and raced forward jumping over wounded men and clumps of falle rigging, and made his way to the bow. He mounte the bowsprit and peered forward, but his night visio was quite destroyed by the gunfire, and he could no make out any details beyond the jibboom.

The *Swan* fired, three guns at once, and in th flash Biddlecomb thought he saw the marker. Witl his eyes fixed in that direction, he waited for the gun to fire again.

The *Icarus*'s guns, numbers three and five, wen off together, and Biddlecomb saw it clearly: a two fathom pole with a white flag streaming from the top a quarter mile ahead. There was still time to avoid it And then another thought struck him.

He made his way aft again, searching the wild decl for Rumstick. He found him at the main mast reeving off a new forebrace.

'Ezra!' Biddlecomb shouted. 'I want hands read at the braces. Take a gun crew if you need to. The must be ready to brace up, larboard tack, when w turn. Quickly now, go!'

Rumstick nodded and raced away, shouting order as he went, and Biddlecomb stepped up to th quarterdeck. The helmsmen stood like statues a the tiller, only their heads moving as their gaz

372

alternated from the compass up to sails and then over to the *Swan*.

'Listen here, you two!' Biddlecomb shouted above the din. 'On my command you'll turn hard to larboard, do you hear, hard to larboard!'

'Hard to larboard on your command, aye,' said the helmsman on the weather side.

'Good. Watch for my signal.' Biddlecomb clambered up into the main shrouds, a few feet below the maintop where he could peer over the foreyard and past the bow of the ship, trying to ignore the whistling round shot and musket balls that pelted the spars around him.

Along the deck Biddlecomb saw men standing by at the braces, Rumstick racing fore and aft to see that all was in readiness. A section of the bulwark shattered, and the man at the main-topsail brace was tossed across the deck like a rag doll, but Rumstick was there and snatched up the brace himself.

The two vessels were less than a hundred yards apart now, and the *Swan* was rapidly closing the gap, men crowding her side, ready to leap aboard the *Icarus*. Biddlecomb looked forward. In the light of the nearly continuous fire he could see the marker, line on the starboard bow and a cable length ahead. He guessed that the *Icarus* was making nine knots, the *Swan* slightly more.

Together they raced down on the buoy, one hundred yards, fifty yards, and Biddlecomb hoped fervently that the marker was in the right place and had not drifted. Thirty yards, twenty-five yards, the *Swan* was closing rapidly on their starboard side.

'Turn, now! Hard a-larboard!' Biddlecomb shouted, and waved his arm, and the two helmsmen

373

pushed the tiller over. The *Icarus* heeled hard as she came broadside to the wind, sweeping through the turn. Biddlecomb tightened his grip and looked aloft as the brig heeled. The yards were bracing around together, the sails full and straining.

'Amidships!' Biddlecomb shouted, and the helmsmen pushed the tiller over.

Biddlecomb looked aft. The *Swan* was coming up in the brig's wake, swinging wide as she followed the *Icarus* around. The sloop's yards braced up and the ship heeled hard to starboard, building momentum on a beam reach, her speed climbing beyond ten knots, when she piled up on Halfway Rock.

374

CHAPTER 29

Bitter End

Biddlecomb was staggered by the destruction. The *Swan*'s foremast bent like a bow, then snapped ten feet above the deck. The mainstays, designed to prevent the mainmast from falling backward, now served to pull it forward, and in succession the main topgallant mast, the main topmast, and the mizzen topmast snapped like dry twigs and crashed to the deck.

The sloop was smothered by sails and fallen wreckage. A gun fired blindly from the larboard quarter, and then it was quiet again and the most obtrusive noise that Biddlecomb could hear was the ringing in his ears. The wreck shifted, and Biddlecomb imagined that it was filling with water and settling. The *Swan* was shattered, a total wreck, and Halfway Rock was the only thing preventing it from sinking.

Capt. James Wallace of His Majesty's frigate *Rose*, watching from the break of the quarterdeck, was equally staggered by the *Swan*'s destruction. It was not the first time he had seen a ship reduced to wreckage, but this was so sudden and so complete.

375

And more to the point, this was a ship under his command, being destroyed, he had to assume, by an American. His face was expressionless and he uttered not a word as he watched the *Swan* wreck itself on Halfway Rock.

Lieutenant Leighton, behind him and at the lee ward rail, knew no such stoicism. He had been swearing intermittently for ten minutes, since the running fight began. The ships had been just visible to them, two miles distant, but as the gunfire grew steady, they had had a spectacular view of the battle. Wallace turned to order his first officer to be silent but Leighton spoke first.

'Studdingsails aloft and alow, sir?' The *Rose* was close-hauled under plain sail, and Leighton asked the question as if the answer were obvious.

'No. Clew up the courses and topgallants. I'm going to wear ship. We'll spin on our heel and dip behind Dyer Island. We'll heave to and wait for the brig to come to us.'

Leighton was visibly taken aback, but he issued the orders firmly, with not a second's pause.

'But what if she's bound for sea, sir?' Leighton continued to protest even as the sails were hauled up to the yards. 'We'll lose her!'

'If she was bound for sea, she would have been heading for sea during the fight. If we show ourselve now, she *will* head for sea, and we'll lose her among these damn islands.'

'But what if she goes around the west side o Prudence Island?'

'She won't,' Wallace said, surprised and not a little annoyed by the extent of the lieutenant's questions 'The shallows are too tricky.' With that Wallace

376

urned his back on the lieutenant, turned his attention back to the brig now sailing directly away from the frigate, barely visible in the moonlight.

The Yankees had become increasingly bold, hiding their livestock from him, depriving him of provisions, and firing at the *Rose* from the shore. But this was the end. He would butcher this Yankee, whoever he was, who had destroyed the *Swan*. Wallace ground his teeth together. He will wear ship, Wallace thought. He will turn and come to me.

A lantern appeared on the *Swan*'s deck, then another, and in the light Biddlecomb could see the crew scurrying about, axes in hand, as they cleared the wreckage away. It was a useless effort, but perhaps they wanted the great guns clear, fearing that the strange brig would come about and rake them as they lay stranded.

That thought made Biddlecomb realize that the *Icarus* was sailing in the entirely wrong direction, and if he did not come about soon, they would be blown up the west side of Prudence Island. 'Prepare to wear ship!' he shouted, then turning to the helmsmen said, 'Put your helm down.'

The *Icarus* began to turn, and the yards braced round as her stern swung through the wind.

'Hold her there. Steady as she goes,' Biddlecomb said to the helmsmen, and the brig steadied up on her new course, the wreck of the *Swan* now broad on the starboard beam. They closed quickly and Biddlecomb could see her men scrambling for cover. He hoped that they would not fire at the *Icarus*.

The *Swan* came abeam of them, one hundred yards to leeward, and the men of the *Icarus* watched

377

silently as they passed, as if witnessing a funeral. The sloop fired once, her aftermost gun, and here and there were flashes of small-arms fire, but no shot struck the *Icarus*.

And then they were past. The *Swan*'s guns would no longer bear and the distance was too great for small-arms fire. Biddlecomb saw the lanterns reappear on the sloop's deck, and the men resumed clearing the wreckage.

'Mr Rumstick,' Biddlecomb called out, surprised at the fatigue in his voice. 'Please see the decks cleared of all wreckage and squared away. And set some men to reeving off new running gear. Mr Wilson, detail a party to attend to the wounded.' Biddlecomb turned to the helmsmen. 'Steady as she goes. I'm going forward for a moment.'

'Steady as she goes.'

Biddlecomb stepped down to the waist and made his way forward, past knots of men clearing wreckage away and flinging it over the side. He stepped past the shattered bulwark and his foot slipped out from under him. He felt himself going down, would have fallen had not a seaman standing nearby grabbed him.

'Careful, sir, there's blood still on the deck and it's slick as a kipper,' the seaman warned.

'Thank you,' said Biddlecomb, and spotting Rumstick, called out, 'Ezra, come to the bow with me.'

The two men walked forward together. 'Harland's dead. Cannon fell on him,' said Rumstick. 'I'll own it's better he didn't live long.'

Biddlecomb stepped up on the bowsprit and looked forward. Their way was clear as far as he could

378

see. The bay looked tranquil in the moonlight. 'There's Dyer Island. We'll see Bristol in half an hour.'

The two men stood on the base of the bowsprit, drinking in the smells of the pine trees and the brackish water of the bay and the wood smoke carried faintly on the wind. Overhead the familiar stars of that northern latitude, those brilliant enough to outshine the moonlight, were eternal and comforting. Biddlecomb felt his anger subside, purged by the destruction of the *Swan*, and in its place he felt an overwhelming joy at being back in Narragansett Bay, at regaining his freedom and shedding the burden of the *Icarus*. Soon he would be back in Bristol, his beloved Bristol.

He watched the dark shape of Dyer Island slip astern, then shifted his gaze north along the shoreline, pausing as he caught yet another shape that stood out from the land.

'Rumstick, what do you suppose—'

The night exploded in a broadside, twelve heavy guns going off as one, the noise and flash staggering. Biddlecomb was thrown to the deck by the impact of the metal. He heard men scream. Overhead a spar cracked and broke.

'Isaac! Isaac, are you hurt?' Rumstick was above him, lifting his head.

'No, no, I'm fine.' Biddlecomb's mind was focused on the image he had seen in the muzzle flash, a fraction of a second frozen in his mind like a painting: a full-rigged ship, illuminated by the light of her broadside. 'It's the *Rose*, Ezra. It's that goddamned frigate *Rose*!'

Biddlecomb pulled himself to his feet and

379

stumbled aft, Rumstick at his heels. 'Larboard guns, fire at will!'

The first of the *Icarus*'s guns went off just a Biddlecomb regained the quarterdeck, and it wa followed by another and another as the men fell to loading and firing as quickly as they could. Biddle comb looked aloft. The main yard was shattered in it slings, the thousand pounds of wood held up by the lifts and main topsail, but Biddlecomb knew that it would not hold for long.

'Rumstick, send some men aloft there, just lash that yard up it so it doesn't come down and knock u on our heads!' he shouted, and Rumstick nodded and headed forward.

The last of the *Icarus*'s guns fired just as the *Rose* unleashed her terrible broadside again. Number seven gun upended and crashed to the deck, its crew scattering, barely avoiding the falling barrel. Round shot hit the foremast, tearing a section away.

The *Rose* was underway now, abeam of the *Icaru* and gathering speed. She would be much faster than the brig; Wallace could remain alongside and batte them to kindling if he chose. Biddlecomb knew that he had to shake the frigate off, but he was in a channel, with Prudence Island to larboard and Rhod Island to starboard. There was no place that he coul run that the frigate could not follow.

The *Rose* fired again, her broadside increasingly ragged but her accuracy not diminishing. The binnacle box exploded and Biddlecomb was knocked to the deck again by a fragment of wood. He pulled himself back up. The helmsman was dead, his neck torn open by splinters. The tiller lolled over to larboard and Biddlecomb could feel the brig turning

380

He jumped to the tiller, slipping in the helmsman's blood, then grabbed the wooden shaft and pushed it amidships.

Barrett appeared at his side, blood streaming down his face. 'Let me take the helm, sir.'

'You're wounded, Israel.'

'It ain't nothing.' Barrett took the tiller and Biddlecomb stepped forward.

The larboard section of the main yard broke free and came crashing down, swinging on the lift that remained attached at the yardarm, and inflicted as much damage as the *Rose*'s broadside. Two guns in the larboard battery lay on their sides, and a five-foot section of deck was stove in. The yard swung back inboard, crushing the quarterdeck rail.

Biddlecomb opened his mouth to shout orders, but Rumstick was already there, racing aft, a cutlass held over his head. He hacked at the lift and it parted, and the yard crashed down on the edge of the hole it had created, widening it, then toppled over and splashed into the bay. The main topsail flapped uselessly, like wash on a line.

Biddlecomb looked down the length of the deck and past the bowsprit. The *Rose* was crossing in front of them, from starboard to larboard, and as her forwardmost gun came to bear, it fired, and then the next and the next, and so on down the line, a rippling broadside, the shot flying the full length of the *Icarus*'s deck.

The destruction was horrible, ghastly. The crew of number-one gun was killed to a man, grapeshot tearing through the close-packed, toiling men and tossing them aside like bloody rags.

The *Rose* had crossed their bow and Wilson was

381

leading the men to the larboard battery in hopes of getting a gun to bear.

Biddlecomb looked toward the land on either side. He could turn and try to run into Mount Hope Bay. 'Barrett!' Biddlecomb shouted aft, but before he could give the order the *Rose* fired again. The hull shuddered, a deep, profound shudder, and above the sound of the guns came the rending, cracking sound of splitting wood.

Biddlecomb turned and looked toward the bow. The jibboom was gone and the bowsprit shattered. The foremast swayed drunkenly, shot clean through at the fife rail, supported only by the rigging.

'Rumstick, get the sail off her!' Biddlecomb shouted. 'Cut the sheets, cut them away!'

Rumstick pulled his cutlass and slashed at the sheets, but it was too late. The mast leaned to larboard, farther and farther, until the starboard shrouds could bear no more but parted, one after another, and the hundred-foot foremast plunged over the side, still bound to the brig by the maze of rigging. The fife rails and bulwarks were crushed, and the foresail blanketed half the deck. Blocks and line and sections of shattered spars rained down on the men, who ran in all directions to escape.

Then the main topgallant mast and yard plunged to the deck. Biddlecomb saw the yard crush a man's skull, then break into fragments. He felt his stomach tighten and was afraid that he would be sick. It seemed incredible to him that he was still alive.

In the unnatural empty space left where the foremast had stood, Biddlecomb could see the *Rose*, two cables ahead, putting her helm up and wearing round to deliver another broadside, crossing their bow again, now from larboard to starboard. The *Icarus* was slewing around to starboard, pivoting on the foremast that dragged alongside, all steerage gone.

'Barrett, come here,' Biddlecomb yelled. Barrett abandoned the useless tiller and stepped over to him. 'Wilson, Rumstick, lay aft!' Biddlecomb shouted, and as he did, he realized that he did not know if his friends were alive or dead.

Wallace watched the brig's foremast lean forward and collapse, surprised that it had lasted that long. But the main would shortly follow; once one mast was gone, the other was never far behind. The *Rose*'s guns, now firing more or less at will, continued to reduce the brig to flotsam. The slaughter they were visiting on the Americans had a cathartic effect on him; he felt relieved and even a bit euphoric as more and more of the fury that had been building for the past six months was released with every lethal shot from the *Rose*'s great guns.

'Mr Leighton, I am not at all satisfied with the performance of number-five gun. Please make a note for the gunner,' he called out across the deck.

'Aye, sir,' replied Leighton, and Wallace could hear his footsteps as he crossed over the quarterdeck. 'Sir?' the first officer asked in a voice as low as could be heard over the din. 'Sir, shall I ask them if they strike? They've no hope now, and they must know it.'

'No,' said Wallace, and his tone did not invite questions of any kind.

'Aye, sir,' said Leighton, retreating back to the leeward side.

They would love the chance to strike, Wallace thought. But surrender meant prisoners and trials,

383

public outcry, and treasonous editorials in the colonial papers. It meant soft, stupid judges who could be influenced by the mob, and military decisions made for political expedience. It meant more of the wrongheaded action that had already let the rebellion get this far. It meant a chance for escape, like that damned Biddlecomb had escaped. 'Mr Leighton,' he called, and the lieutenant stepped over to him once again. 'Send word to the gundeck that their rate of fire has dropped below what is acceptable.'

To Biddlecomb's relief the two men appeared, stepping over the battered break of the quarterdeck.

'We're lost, now. There's no hope. We can't steer and the boats are gone. I shall strike the colors.'

Wilson spat on the deck. 'They don't give a damn if you strike or not, mate, they'll finish us either way. If they wanted you to strike, they'd have asked by now.'

'Bloody Wilson's right,' said Barrett, and as if to emphasize the point, the *Rose* began her next rolling broadside, shot after shot striking home. The larboard quarterdeck rail collapsed, showering the men with splinters, and more iron screamed overhead. Biddlecomb flinched, shielding his face from the flying wood, then looked up again.

Wilson was not there, the space he had occupied was empty, and Biddlecomb looked at it, stupid with fatigue, wondering where Wilson had gone.

And then he saw him, flung up against the larboard rail, half-sitting, his stomach ripped open. His blood already covered the deck where he lay, his mouth was

384

slowly opening and closing, and his eyes were wide as if he was surprised by this turn of events.

'Wilson!' Biddlecomb cried. In two steps he crossed to the rail and knelt beside the foretopman. He felt Wilson's warm blood soak through his breeches, saw it pulsing out of the wreckage of Wilson's abdomen. 'Damn it to hell, damn it to hell, no . . .' Biddlecomb said softly, over and over, like a litany. He felt Wilson's hand on his shoulder; there was no strength there, Wilson just rested it on his coat, and Biddlecomb looked into his friend's eyes.

'So . . .' Wilson said in a strangled voice, and then the life that was in Wilson's eyes was gone and his hand slipped from Biddlecomb's shoulder. Biddlecomb looked down at the deck. Tears streamed off his cheeks and made little round marks in the blood pooling around his knees.

The gunfire from the *Rose* was continuous now, and Biddlecomb could feel through the deck the constant vibration of the round shot striking the hull.

'God damn their eyes, why don't they stop!' Biddlecomb cried in despair. He stood up and looked over the nightmare scene. The carnage on the deck was like nothing he had ever seen; half his men had been slaughtered, mutilated, and still the frigate fired.

'I don't know what in hell is keeping us afloat. Habit, I guess,' said Rumstick, his voice tinged with fear despite an effort to maintain an even tone. Biddlecomb noticed for the first time how low the *Icarus* was riding in the water, badly holed and filling fast. Only a third of her battery was still intact, and of those guns only two would bear on the *Rose*, but those two were still being served, the gun crews running them in and out, firing more out of defiance

385

than any hope of inflicting damage. But the magazine was flooded, and once the cartridges on deck were used up, there would be no more.

Biddlecomb stared forward, unseeing, reaching deep inside himself, reaching down to that place where he had found courage before, found the courage to lay out on a topsail yard to shorten sail on a howling black night, found the courage to maintain the deck as storms had torn ships to pieces around him and other men had cowered below, found the courage to live after his mother had died and to go on after his father had bled to death in his arms.

And then his mind was working again, working with clarity, sifting through the options available to him. The Icaruses were still fighting back, but that would do no good. They could not abandon ship; there were no boats left and the men would not survive ten minutes in the cold water, floating on wreckage. They could plead for quarter, and if it was granted, then they would go to prison and then be hung or, worse, much worse, flogged to death. No, there were only two real possibilities: find some way to get off the *Icarus* or stay there and die.

And what if they were to stop fighting, simply stop? If Wallace thought they were all dead, what would he do? He would either continue to pound the brig until it sank, or he would stop the cannonade and take possession of what was left of her. He would heave to, put a boat in the water, and send a boarding party across to take possession. Biddlecomb felt the stirring inside, felt the soles of his feet tingling. Wallace would send a boat.

* * *

386

The men were firing faster now, Wallace noted with some satisfaction. They were no doubt tired, but still the rate of fire had increased after he had made his displeasure known. He stared across the water at the dark hulk that was the brig. It was difficult to see; the muzzle flash of the guns below nearly blinded him; but he was fairly certain that the brig was lower in the water and the mainmast was listing to starboard and on the verge of toppling. It would not be long now.

Number-seven gun roared out, and then there was a pause in the firing. On the gundeck below, Wallace heard the sound of wooden wheels rolling across wooden planks, the next gun running out, and he realized that the Americans had not returned fire, not for several minutes. Were they trying to strike? He had not heard anyone hail the frigate. Were they all dead or wounded, 100 percent casualties? He had never heard of such a thing, but again he had never doled out such a beating as this.

He began to feel a nameless discomfort where before there had been only bloodlust. This was madness, what he was doing, and contrary to all accepted rules of warfare. He had known that from the start of this slaughter, but it had not bothered him then as it was starting to now. He imagined Admiral Graves, sitting behind his desk, shaking his head in that annoying manner and saying in his peevish voice, 'Really, Captain, I fail to see why you did not take the brig. Was it quite necessary to sink it, a perfectly good vessel? I am not altogether pleased with your judgment on this.'

Another of the *Rose*'s guns fired and then another, and Wallace thought he saw more of the brig's bulwark collapse. 'Mr Leighton, pass the word to cease firing. We shall heave to, main topsails aback.'

'Cease firing, aye, aye, sir,' said Leighton, the relief evident in his voice as he passed the word to a midshipman, then called for sail trimmers to their stations. The *Rose* swung up into the wind and the main topsails flogged then filled aback, and the frigate stopped in the water, the shattered brig now fifty yards off her starboard quarter.

'Give me the speaking trumpet, please,' Wallace said to no one in particular. He held out his hand and the trumpet was placed in it and he said, 'Thank you,' without bothering to see who had handed it to him. He put the trumpet to his lips and paused. He did not want to do this, not at all, but he had no choice. It was his duty.

'Ahoy there! Ahoy, the brig! Do you strike?' He put the mouthpiece of the speaking trumpet against his ear and trained it toward the brig. The mainmast was creaking, groaning as the brig rocked in the swell, and the sound, amplified by the speaking trumpet, was mixed with the low sound of human agony, the too familiar moaning of wounded and dying men. But there was no answer to his hail.

'Ahoy, the brig! Do you strike?' Wallace called again, and again there was no answer. He stared at the wrecked vessel as his vision became more accustomed to the dark. Was it possible that everyone was wounded or dead? It was possible, though unlikely. Was it a trick, and if so, what did they hope to accomplish? Even if someone was alive over there, he could not have much fight left in him. It was time to act.

388

'Mr Leighton,' Wallace said, and the lieutenant stepped across the quarterdeck and saluted. 'We'll send a boarding party to see what's happened over there. Clear away the . . .' He almost said 'the longboat' before he remembered that they had no longboat. They had not had an opportunity to replace their largest boat since it was stolen by Biddlecomb. Biddlecomb. Wallace felt again the anger and the humiliation of having his prisoner escape and take the Rose's boat with him.

'Clear away the barge. Barge crew to be fitted with pistols and cutlasses. Send . . .' Wallace considered the number of marines that he could fit in the barge. He would have sent thirty in the longboat.

'Send fourteen marines with them,' he said at last. Ten men in the barge crew and fourteen marines. That should be quite sufficient to subdue any resistance, particularly as it seemed no resistance would be offered.

'Aye, aye, sir,' Leighton said, and then asked, 'Shall I take charge of the boat?'

'No.' Wallace knew just the man to zealously carry out this duty. 'Mr Norton,' he called down the deck, 'you will take charge of the boarding party.'

The Icarus's shattered main yard had left in its wake a great hole in the weather deck, and through that rent Biddlecomb could see the stars overhead and the main shrouds as they strained to hold the crippled mast upright. The wounded men, the five that they had located who could not walk but were still alive and still had a chance to remain so, had been moved to the gangway, just forward of the hole, and their moaning seemed much louder now. Farther aft the mainmast groaned with each roll of the ship, and the water of Narragansett Bay poured into the battered vessel and lapped around the ankles of the men huddled in the tween decks.

Biddlecomb looked over the massed crew, barely visible in the dim light. There were just over thirty left, less than half of the *Icarus*'s original company. Their faces were dark and streaked with sweat and powder smoke, and their hands moved nervously over the muskets and pistols and cutlasses that they held at the ready. Barrett was there, his face streaked with blood, a cutlass in his hand. He looked very old. Appleby stood beside him, his jaw set, his hands trembling. This was the final, forlorn hope, and each man knew that full well.

There was a shuffling overhead, the muted sound of someone crawling across the deck, and then Rumstick appeared in the hole. He stepped down onto the chests piled on the deck and then down onto the deck itself. 'She's hove to,' Rumstick said sotto voce. 'It sounds like they're putting a boat over the side, but I couldn't tell for certain.'

'If they're hove to, then they'll come take a look. It only stands to reason,' Biddlecomb said with an assuredness that he did not feel.

'You men—' he began to say when the *Icarus* lurched to starboard, the hundreds of tons of water that filled her sinking hull shifting, threatening to roll her over. Men flailed their arms in an attempt to maintain balance as the ship rolled. A cutlass dropped to the deck. In the dark a voice shouted, 'Son of a bitch!' Biddlecomb could see wide eyes staring around the dark space. The fear was a tangible thing; not the fear of the coming fight but the fear that the

Icarus would roll over entirely and take them all down with her.

As Biddlecomb opened his mouth to speak again, the low groaning of the mast overhead grew suddenly louder, higher, the sound of rending wood filling the tween decks. The brig rolled farther as the mast collapsed; they could feel the water surging around their feet. 'God damn it!' a man shouted, his voice high-pitched with panic. He flung his pistol aside and clawed his way through the waiting men, scrambling desperately for the hole and the deck above.

'Stay down, you idiot!' Rumstick hissed through his teeth, grabbing the man by the shirt and pulling him back into the tween decks.

'The ship's capsizing!' the man said, his voice starting at a whisper and building before Rumstick punched him in the side of the head. The sound was like a wooden mallet striking a rotten plank. The man went limp.

Biddlecomb heard a tearing sound, low down on the hull, and he knew that the chain plates were ripping from the brig's side. He gritted his teeth. His hand clamped on to his cutlass's grip, and he tried to prepare himself for the death that would come when the brig rolled over, the drowning death that every seaman has with terror contemplated.

And then the mainmast fell, plunging over the side. The *Icarus* came upright again, and Biddlecomb could tell that she was riding higher in the water, relieved as she was of several tons of spars and rigging. A murmur ran through the waiting men, and Biddlecomb did not need to hear the words to understand their sense of relief.

'They better get here fucking quick or there won't

391

be nothing left to board,' Rumstick growled. He grabbed the unconscious man at his feet and hefted him up through the hole in the deck, depositing him with the other wounded men. A voice drifted across the water, as clear as if it were addressing them.

'Right, she looks stable now. Give way.'

The men in the tween decks were silent, completely silent, each man listening to the sound of oars grinding in tholes and the sound of water churned by the oars' blades, getting closer, audibly closer.

'You men know what to do,' Biddlecomb said in a whisper. 'Wait for my signal. Not a sound until then.' He looked around the dark space and grim faces nodded back at him. He looked at Rumstick at his side and towering over him. Rumstick held a cutlass in one hand and a boarding ax in the other. He met Biddlecomb's eyes. His expression was set and determined.

'It's a better way to die than hanging,' Biddlecomb said.

'That it is,' Rumstick said.

Three feet away, on the other side of the hull's planking, the frigate's boat bumped alongside, the sound loud in the narrow tween decks. 'Marines, follow me,' the voice said. 'Weapons at the ready. Shoot anyone who offers any fight, we'll suffer no trouble from this lot. Jones, stay with the boat. The rest of you bargemen up after the marines.' Boots thumped against the hull as the marines clambered up the boarding steps, then thumped overhead as the marines spread out across the deck.

Biddlecomb stepped farther back in the shadows, his eyes fixed on the hole overhead, but nothing was visible there beside the stars. The sound of the marines' boots on the boarding steps was replaced by the lighter sound of the sailors' shoes, and finally no more people were coming aboard and the deck overhead was alive with men searching fore and aft. How many? Biddlecomb could not guess.

There was another voice from forward. 'Nothing but dead un's here, Lieutenant, and them wounded bastards by the gangway.'

'Good.' The first voice again. The lieutenant apparently. 'Send some men to search below. Start at that forward scuttle and sweep aft.'

Biddlecomb felt a stirring among the men. They were ready to go, but this was not the moment. He held up his hand. Not yet. Another minute, when half of the marines were below and half on deck. That was the time.

Boots sounded in the forward scuttle as the marines moved down into the tween decks. 'Spread it out there, spread it out, keep your eyes open,' he heard someone say. The first of the marines stepped aft and Biddlecomb saw his own men looking anxiously around.

'Hey . . . what?' a voice called in the dark, then, louder, 'Hey there!' and the moment was on them.

'Go! Go! Go!' Biddlecomb shouted as he leapt onto the piled sea chests and burst through the hole onto the deck overhead, Rumstick beside him, the rest of the Icaruses at their heels. There were men standing about the deck, sailors and marines, and close by he saw looks of surprise and muskets coming up to shoulders. But the Icaruses were spreading out, facing fore and aft, and their pistols and muskets went off in a great volley, and a half dozen of the boarders fell in heaps among the wreckage.

From over the side Biddlecomb heard a voice shout, 'No! Bloody hell!' and a splash, and he guessed that the unfortunate Jones had opted to swim for safety rather than die for the *Rose*'s boat.

'Get these wounded in the boat! Go!' Biddlecomb shouted, and eager hands grabbed up the wounded men and lowered them over the side.

The boarding party was rallying. They were shooting now, the double flash of flintlock and muzzle erupting here and there around the deck. The man beside Biddlecomb screamed and fell to the deck. Biddlecomb could hear footsteps coming back up the scuttle, and the boarders came at them in an awkward and uncoordinated attack. Dark shapes hurled themselves across the deck, swords flashing in the moonlight, pistols and muskets banging out, men screaming.

The brig, which a second ago had been quiet as a tomb, was now filled with shouts and the clash of steel. A marine, his white crossbelt glowing dull in the fading moonlight, thrust a bayonet at Biddlecomb. Biddlecomb beat the musket down with the flat of his cutlass. The bayonet stabbed into the deck and Biddlecomb drove the cutlass through the startled man's throat. He pulled it out and the marine collapsed, and Biddlecomb slashed right, deflecting a cutlass blow from one of the barge's crew.

They did not have to beat these men, Biddlecomb reminded himself even as he fought off the attacking sailor, they only had to get to the boat. 'Fall back! Fall back! To the boat!' he shouted, and he sensed more than saw his men stepping back, yielding the deck to the boarders, as they moved toward the gangway and the boat below.

394

The bargeman thrust, a clumsy move, and Biddlecomb ran his blade over the man's arm, opening up the flesh, and the sailor shouted and dropped the cutlass. He was out of the fight and Biddlecomb turned, cutlass before him, to face another advance. A blade slashed down and Biddlecomb caught it with his cutlass and turned it away, but the attacker stepped back before Biddlecomb could reach him; a nice coordinated movement. This man was a swordsman.

Biddlecomb shot a look to his left. Rumstick was there, fighting his own fight, standing like a wall between Biddlecomb and any attack on that flank. All but a few of the Icaruses were in the boat.

He turned back to his man. It was an officer, blue coat, white lapels and breeches, a look on his face of confusion, recognition. It was Lieutenant Norton.

'Biddlecomb,' Norton's lips formed the word. The tip of Norton's sword was resting on the deck. With a move like a snake he lifted the weapon and came at Biddlecomb, the light blade moving fast, slashing and probing. Biddlecomb worked the heavy cutlass as best he could, holding off the attack. Norton was good, very good, and there was no sergeant of marines to get in his way now.

There was a flash like lightning from behind Biddlecomb's back and the sound of half a dozen guns going off. The men in the boat were driving the marines from the bulwark with gunfire. It was time to go.

Rumstick was backing down, inching toward the gangway, working the ax and the cutlass, fighting off three men at once. He would have been dead, they all would have been dead, Biddlecomb knew, if the

395

boarders had not been stumbling over each other to get in the fight. He wondered how long it would be before one of the boarders reloaded a weapon and shot them.

'Let's go, Isaac, we got to go!' Rumstick shouted, stepping through the gangway above the boat, now only four feet below the deck of the sinking brig. Biddlecomb knew that he was right, but Norton was coming at him again and he could not climb into the boat and defend himself from that fast blade. His own body was shielding Norton from the Icaruses muskets.

Norton slashed down and Biddlecomb beat the sword aside, using the weight of the cutlass to throw the lieutenant off-balance, then bringing the weapon across and opening up a gash in Norton's side. The lieutenant stumbled back, staring at the blood flowing over his hand, staring at the pistol thrust in his belt.

'Jump for it, Isaac!' Rumstick shouted, sweeping his cutlass at the men around him then leaping for the boat. Biddlecomb was alone on deck now, his back against the shattered bulwark, his eyes locked on Norton. He inched toward the gangway. The men in the boat were keeping the other boarders at bay with a steady musket fire, but that would not last forever. Biddlecomb could see the marines ramming powder and shot down their muskets.

Norton jerked the pistol out of his belt and drew the lock back and leveled the barrel at Biddlecomb's face. 'You son of a bitch!' he shrieked, and Biddlecomb braced for the bullet's impact.

And then the *Icarus* lurched again, rolling to starboard. Biddlecomb grabbed the splintered

396

ulwark to steady himself as around him men were hrown to the deck.

Biddlecomb's eyes met Norton's, and the ieutenant's were wide with surprise and fear, and both nen knew what would happen next. Biddlecomb urled his cutlass at Norton. The lieutenant flinched nd Biddlecomb spun around and launched himelf over the bulwark. Norton's pistol exploded and 3iddlecomb felt the burn of lead tearing through his houlder as he fell, hurtling down, down into the boat.

He heard shouting, screaming, as he plunged into he crowd of men. His head struck something hard. Ie was in great pain, as if his entire body were roken, and for a moment he lay still and felt the lood flowing from his shoulder. He rolled over and e knew he was in the bottom of the boat. Hands rabbed him and pulled him up, and he wanted to ell them to be careful, that there was a bullet in his houlder, but his head was swimming and he could ot speak.

He looked up, up at the great hulk looming over hem, pale, weed-covered, gleaming in the night, and e did not know what he was looking at. He stared tupidly, and it came to him like the answer to a great iddle that it was the bottom, the *Icarus*'s bottom. 'he brig had rolled over at last, capsized by the great lood of water in her hull. 'My God, my God, my God,' he muttered to himself. He could think of othing else to say.

'Give way, all!' he heard Rumstick's voice, and uddenly the great weed-covered hull was moving ast them as the Icaruses leaned on the oars.

'I think they're launching another boat,' Barrett aid.

397

Rumstick snorted. 'Let 'em. They won't catch u
now, and they won't find us once we're in Bristol.
Biddlecomb knew Rumstick was right. 'Hey, yo
forward, see to the captain! Be careful there
you whores' sons!'

Biddlecomb heard shouting from the *Rose*, and th
squeal of blocks and tackle as another boat lifted of
the booms. He turned his back on the frigate. The
cannot catch us now. He stared forward into th
night, toward the darkened town of Bristol.

THE END

**Continued in *The Maddest Idea* –
to be published soon**

Glossary

Note: See diagram of brig for names and illustrations of all sails and spars.

aback: said of a sail when the wind is striking it on the wrong side and, in the case of a square sail, pressing it back against the mast.

abaft: nearer the back of the ship, farther aft, behind.

abeam: at right angles to the ship's centerline.

aft: toward the stern of the ship, as opposed to fore.

afterguard: men stationed aft to work the aftermost sails.

backstay: long ropes leading from the topmast and topgallant mastheads down to the channels. Backstays work with shrouds to support the masts from behind.

beakhead: a small deck forward of the forecastle that overhangs the bow. The crew's latrine was located there, hence in current usage the term *head* for a marine toilet.

beam reach: sailing with the wind abeam.

belay: to make a rope fast to a belaying pin, cleat, or other such device. Also used as a general command to stop or cancel, e.g. 'Belay that last order!'

belaying pin: a wooden pin, later made of metal,

generally about twenty inches in length, to which lines were made fast, or 'belayed.' They were arranged in pinrails along the inside of the BULWARK and in FIFE RAILS around the masts.

bells: method by which time was marked on shipboard. Each day was generally divided into five four-hour 'watches' and two two-hour 'DOGWATCHES.' After the first half hour of a watch, one bell was rung, then another for each additional half hour until eight bells and the change of watch, when the process was begun again.

binnacle: a large wooden box, just forward of the helm, housing the compass, half-hour glass for timing the watches, and candles to light the compass at night.

bitts: heavy timber frame near the bow to which the end of the anchor cable is made fast, hence the term *bitter end*.

block: nautical term for a pulley.

boatswain (bosun): warrant officer in charge of boats, sails, and rigging. Also responsible for relaying orders and seeing them carried out, not unlike a sergeant in the military.

boatswain's call: a small, unusually shaped whistle with a high, piercing sound with which the boatswain relayed orders by playing any of a number of recognizable tunes. Also played as a salute.

boatswain's chair: a wooden seat with a rope sling attached. Used for hoisting men aloft or over the side for work.

boom: the SPAR to which the lower edge of a fore-and-aft sail is attached. Special studdingsail booms are used for those sails.

booms: spare spars, generally stowed amidships on

400

raised gallows upon which the boats were often stored.

bow: the rounded, forwardmost part of a ship or boat.

bow chaser: a cannon situated near the bow to fire as directly forward as possible.

bower: the two primary anchors stored near the bow, designated best bower and small bower.

bowline: line attached to a bridle, which is in turn attached to the perpendicular edge of a square sail. The bowline is hauled taut when sailing close-hauled to keep the edge of the sail tight and prevent shivering. Also, a common knot used to put a loop in the end of a rope.

brace: line attached to the end of a yard, which, when hauled upon, turns the yard horizontally to present the sail at the most favorable angle to the wind. Also, to perform the action of bracing the yards.

break: the edge of a raised deck closest to the center of the ship.

breeching: rope used to secure a cannon to the side of a ship and prevent it from recoiling too far.

brig: a two-masted vessel, square-rigged on fore and main, with a large fore-and-aft mainsail supported by boom and gaff and made fast to the after side of the mainmast.

bulwark: wall-like structure, generally of waist height or higher, built around the outer edge of the weather decks.

bumboat: privately owned boat used to carry vegetables, liquor, and other items for sale out to anchored vessels.

buntlines: lines running from the lower edge of a square sail to the yard above and used to haul the bunt, or body of the sail, up to the yard, generally in preparation for furling.

cable: a large, strong rope. As a unit of measure, 120 fathoms or 240 yards, generally the length of a cable

cable tier: a section of the lowest deck in a ship in which the cables are stored.

cap: a heavy wooden block through which an upper mast passes, designed to hold the upper mast in place against the mast below it. Forms the upper part of the DOUBLING.

caprail: wooden rail that is fastened to the top edge of the bulwark.

capstan: a heavy wooden cylinder, pierced with holes to accept wooden bars. The capstan is turned by means of pushing on the bars and is thus used to raise the anchor or move other heavy objects.

cascabel: the knob at the end of a cannon opposite the muzzle to which the breeching is fastened.

cat-o'-nine-tails (cat): a whip with a rope handle around an inch in diameter and two feet in length to which was attached nine tails, also around two feet in length. 'Flogging' with the cat was the most common punishment meted out in the navy.

cathead: short, strong wooden beam that projects out over the bow, one on either side of the ship, used to suspend the anchor clear of the ship when hauling it up or letting it go.

ceiling: the inside planking or 'inner wall' of a ship.

chains: strong links or iron plates used to fasten the deadeyes to the hull. The lower parts of the chains are bolted to the hull; the upper ends are fastened to the chainwale, or CHANNEL. They are generally referred to as forechains, mainchains, and mizzenchains for those respective masts.

402

hannel: corruption of *chainwale*. Broad, thick planks extending from both sides of the ship at the base of each mast to which the shrouds are attached.

lear for action: the process by which a ship is prepared for an engagement. Also the order that is given to prepare the ship.

lew: either of the two lower corners of a square sail or the lower aft corner of a fore-and-aft sail. To clew up is to haul the corners of the sail up to the yard by means of the clewlines.

lewlines: lines running from the clews of a square sail to the yard above and used to haul the clews up, generally in preparation for furling. On lower, or course, sails the clewlines are called clew garnets.

lose-hauled: said of a vessel that is sailing as nearly into the wind as she is able, and her sails are hauled as close to her centerline as they can go.

onn: to direct the helmsman in the steering of the ship.

ourse: the largest sails; in the case of square sails, those hung from the lowest or course yards and loose footed. The foresail and mainsail are courses.

rosstrees: horizontal wooden bars, situated at right angles to the ship's centerline and located at the junction of the lower and upper masts. Between the lower and the topmasts they support the TOP, between the topmast and the topgallant mast they stand alone to spread the shrouds and provide a perch for the lookout.

ead reckoning: from deduced reckoning. Calculating a vessel's position through an estimate of speed and drift.

eadeye: a round, flattish wooden block pierced with three holes through which a LANYARD is rove.

403

Deadeyes and lanyards are used to secure and adjus standing rigging, most commonly the SHROUDS.

dirk: a small sword, more like a large dagger, worn b junior officers.

dogwatch: two-hour watches from 4 to 6 P.M. (firs dogwatch) and 6 to 8 P.M. (second dogwatch).

doubling: the section where two masts overlap, such a the lower mast and the topmast just above the top.

fall: the loose end of a system of blocks and tackle, th part upon which one pulls.

fathom: six feet.

fife rail: wooden rails found generally at the base of th masts and pierced with holes to accept belaying pins

first rate: the largest class of naval ship, carrying on hundred or more guns. Ships were rated from first t sixth rates depending on the number of guns. Sloop brigs, schooners, and other small vessels were nc rated.

flemish: to coil a rope neatly down in concentric circle with the end being in the middle of the coil.

fore-and-aft: parallel to the centerline of the ship. I reference to sails, those that are set parallel to th centerline and are not attached to yards. Also use to mean the entire deck encompassed, e.g. 'Silenc fore-and-aft!'

forecastle: pronounded *fo'c'sle*. The forward part of th upper deck, forward of the foremast, in some vesse raised above the upper deck. Also, the space enclose by this deck. In the merchant service the forecastl was the living quarters for the seamen.

forestay: standing rigging primarily responsible fc preventing the foremast from falling back when th foresails are ABACK. Runs from under the fore top t the bowsprit.

404

forward: toward the bow, or front of the ship. To send an officer forward implied disrating, sending him from the officers' quarters aft to the sailors' quarters forward.

frigate: vessels of the fifth or sixth rate, generally fast and well armed for their size, carrying between twenty and thirty-six guns.

furl: the process of bundling a sail tightly against the YARD, stay, or mast to which it is attached and lashing it in place with GASKETS.

futtock shrouds: short, heavy pieces of standing rigging connected on one end to the topmast shrouds at the outer edge of the TOP and on the other to the lower shrouds, designed to bear the pressure on the topmast shrouds. When fitted with RATLINES, they allow men going aloft to climb around the outside of the top, though doing so requires them to hang backward at as much as a forty-five-degree angle.

gangway: the part of the ship's side from which people come aboard or leave, provided with an opening in the bulwark and steps on the vessel's side.

gantline: a line run from the deck to a block aloft and back to the deck, used for hauling articles such as rigging aloft. Thus, when the rig is 'sent down to a gantline,' it has been entirely disassembled save for the gantline, which will be used to haul it up again.

garboard: the first set of planks, next to the keel, on a ship or boat's bottom.

gasket: a short, braided piece of rope attached to the yard and used to secure the furled sail.

gig: small boat generally rowed with six or fewer oars.

glim: a small candle.

grapeshot: a cluster of round, iron shot, generally nine in all, wrapped in canvas. Upon firing, the grapeshot

405

would spread out for a shotgun effect. Used against men and light hulls.

grating: hatch covers composed of perpendicular, interlocking wood pieces, much like a heavy wood screen. They allowed light and air below while still providing cover for the hatch. Gratings were covered with tarpaulins in rough or wet weather.

gudgeon: one-half of the hinge mechanism for a rudder. The gudgeon is fixed to the sternpost and has a rounded opening that accepts the PINTLE on the rudder.

gunwale: the upper edge of a ship's side.

halyard: any line used to raise a sail or a yard or gaff to which a sail is attached.

headsails: those sails set forward of the foremast.

heave to: to adjust the sails in such a way that some are full and some aback so as to stop the vessel in the water.

heaver: a device like a wooden mallet used as a lever for tightening small lines.

hogshead: a large cask, twice the size of a standard barrel. Capacity varied but was generally around one hundred gallons.

holystone: a flat stone used for cleaning a ship's decks.

hoy: a small vessel, chiefly used near the coast, to transport passengers or supplies to another vessel.

hull down: said of a ship when her hull is still hidden below the horizon and only her masts or superstructure is visible.

jolly boat: a small workboat.

lanyard: line run through the holes in the DEADEYES to secure and adjust the SHROUDS. Also any short line used to secure or adjust an item on shipboard.

larboard: Until the nineteenth century the term

406

designating the left side of a vessel when facing forward. The term *port* is now used.

leech: the side of a square sail or the after edge of a fore-and-aft sail.

leeward: downwind.

letters of marque: a commission given to private citizens in times of war to take and make prizes of enemy vessels. Also, any vessel that holds such a commission.

lifts: ropes running from the ends of the yards to the mast, used to support the yard when lowered or when men are employed thereon.

limber holes: holes cut through the lower timbers in a ship's hull allowing otherwise trapped water to run through to the pumps.

line: term used for a rope that has been put to a specific use.

log: device used to measure a vessel's speed.

longboat: the largest boat carried on shipboard.

lugsail: a small square sail used on a boat.

mainstay: standing rigging primarily responsible for preventing the mainmast from falling back when the mainsails are aback. Runs from under the maintop to the bow.

make and mend: time allotted to the seamen to make new clothing or mend their existing ones.

marline spike: an iron spike used in knotting and splicing rope.

mizzen: large fore-and-aft sail, hung from a gaff abaft the mizzenmast.

mizzenmast: the aftermost mast on a three-masted ship.

painter: a rope in the bow of a boat used to tie the boat in place.

407

parceling: strips of canvas wrapped around standing rigging prior to SERVING.

partners: heavy wooden frames surrounding the holes in the deck through which the masts and CAPSTAN pass.

pawls: wooden or iron bars that prevent a windlass or capstan from rotating backward.

pintles: pins attached to the rudder, which fit in the GUDGEONS and form the hinge on which the rudder pivots.

post: in the Royal Navy, to be given official rank of captain, often called a post captain, and thereby qualified to command a ship of twenty guns or larger.

privateer: vessel built or fitted out expressly to operate under a LETTER OF MARQUE.

quadrant: instrument used to take the altitude of the sun or other celestial bodies in order to determine the latitude of a place. Forerunner to the modern sextant.

quarter: the area of the ship, larboard or starboard, that runs from the main shrouds aft.

quarter gallery: a small enclosed balcony with windows located on either side of the great cabin aft and projecting out slightly from the side of the ship.

quarterdeck: a raised deck running from the stern of the vessel as far forward, approximately, as the mainmast. The primary duty station of the ship's officers, comparable to the bridge on a modern ship.

ratline: pronounced *ratlin*. Small lines tied between the shrouds, parallel to the deck, forming a sort of rope ladder on which the men can climb aloft.

reef: to reduce the area of sail by pulling a section of the sail up to the yard and tying it in place.

reef point: small lines threaded through eyes in the sail for the purpose of tying the reef in the sail.

rigging: any of the many lines used aboard the ship. *Standing rigging* is employed to hold the masts in place and is only occasionally adjusted. *Running rigging* is used to manipulate the sails and is frequently adjusted, as needed.

ring stopper: short line on the CATHEAD used to hold the anchor prior to letting it go.

ringbolt: an iron bolt through which is fitted an iron ring.

ringtail: a type of studdingsail rigged from the mainsail gaff and down along the after edge of the mainsail.

round seizing: a type of lashing used to bind two larger lines together.

running rigging: see RIGGING.

sailing master: warrant officer responsible for charts and navigation, among other duties.

schooner: (eighteenth-century usage) a small, two-masted vessel with fore-and-aft sails on the foremast and mainmast and occasionally one or more square sails on the foremast.

scuppers: small holes pierced through the bulwark at the level of the deck to allow water to run overboard.

scuttle: any small, generally covered hatchway through a ship's deck.

service: a tight wrapping of spunyarn put around standing rigging to protect it from the elements.

sheets: lines attached to the CLEWS of a square sail to pull the sail down and hold it in place when the sail is set. On a fore-and-aft sail the sheet is attached to the BOOM or the sail itself and is used to trim the sail closer or farther away from the ship's centerline to achieve the best angle to the wind.

ship: a vessel of three masts, square-rigged on all masts.

short peak: indicates that the vessel is above the anchor and the anchor is ready to be pulled from the bottom.

shrouds: heavy ropes leading from a masthead aft and down to support the masts when the wind is from abeam or farther aft.

slings: the middle section of a yard.

sloop: a small vessel with one mast.

sloop of war: small man-of-war, generally ship rigged and commanded by a lieutenant.

slop chest: purser's stores, containing clothing, tobacco, and other items, which the purser sold to the crew and deducted the price from their wages.

snatch block: a block with a hinged side that can be opened to admit a rope.

spar: general term for all masts, yards, booms, gaffs, etc.

spring: a line passed from the stern of a vessel and made fast to the anchor cable. When the spring is hauled upon, the vessel turns.

spring stay: a smaller stay used as a backup to a larger one.

spritsail topsail: a light sail set outboard of the spritsail.

spunyarn: small line used primarily for SERVICE or seizings.

standing rigging: see RIGGING.

starboard: the right side of the vessel when facing forward.

stay: standing rigging used to support the mast on the forward part and prevent it from falling back, especially when the sails are ABACK. Also, to stay a vessel means to tack, thus missing stays means failing to get the bow through the wind.

stay tackle: system of blocks generally rigged from the MAINSTAY and used for hoisting boats or items stored in the hold.

410

stem: the heavy timber in the bow of the ship into which the planking at the bow terminates.

step: the process of putting a mast in place. Also, a block of wood fixed to the bottom of a ship to accept the base or heel of the mast.

stern chasers: cannons directed aft to fire on a pursuing vessel.

stern sheets: the area of a boat between the stern and the aftermost of the rowers' seats, generally fitted with benches to accommodate passengers.

sternway: the motion of a ship going backward through the water, the opposite of headway.

stow: as relates to sails, the same as FURL.

tack: to turn a vessel onto a new course in such a way that her bow passes through the wind. Also used to indicate relation of ship to wind, e.g. a ship on a 'starboard tack' has the wind coming over the starboard side.

taffrail: the upper part of a ship's stern.

tarpaulin hat: wide, flat-brimmed canvas hat, coated in tar for waterproofing, favored by sailors.

tender: small vessel that operates in conjunction with a larger man-of-war.

tholes: pins driven into the upper edge of a boat's side to hold the oars in place when rowing.

thwart: seat or bench in a boat on which the rowers sit.

tiller: the bar attached to the rudder and used to turn the rudder in steering.

top: a platform at the junction of the lower mast and the topmast.

top-hamper: general term for all of the spars, rigging, and sails; all the equipment above the level of the deck.

411

train tackle: arrangement of BLOCKS and tackle attached to the back end of a gun carriage and used to haul the gun inboard.

truck: a round button of wood that serves as a cap on the highest point of a mast.

trunnions: short, round arms that project from either side of a cannon and upon which the cannon rests and tilts.

tween decks: (corruption of *between decks*) the deck between the uppermost and the lowermost decks.

waist: the area of the ship between the quarterdeck and the forecastle.

waister: men stationed in the waist of the vessel for sail evolutions. Generally inexperienced, old, or just plain dumb seamen were designated waisters.

warp: a small rope used to move a vessel by hauling it through the water. Also, to move a vessel by means of warps.

water sail: a light-air sail set under a boom.

wear: to turn the vessel from one TACK to another by turning the stern through the wind. Slower but safer than tacking.

weather: the same as *windward*, thus 'a ship to weather' is the same as 'a ship to windward.' Also describes the side of the ship from which the wind is blowing.

weather deck: upper deck, one that is exposed to the weather.

whip: a tackle formed by a rope run through a single fixed block.

woolding: a tight winding of rope around a mast or yard.

worming: small pieces of rope laid between the strands of a larger rope to strengthen it and allow it to better withstand chaffing. Also the process of putting worming in place.

yard: long, horizontal spars suspended from the masts and from which the sails are spread.

yardarm: the extreme ends of a yard.

THE GUARDSHIP
by James Nelson

'A master both of his period and of the English language'
Patrick O'Brian

With the bounty from his years as a pirate – a life he intends to renounce and keep forever secret – Thomas Marlowe purchases a fine Virginia plantation from a beautiful young widow, Elizabeth Tinling. Soon afterwards, while defending her honour, he kills the favourite son of one of the colony's most powerful families in a duel. But in a clever piece of manoeuvring he manages to win command of the *Plymouth Prize*, the colony's decrepit guardship, and is charged with leading the King's sailors in bloody pitched battle against the cutthroats who infest the waters off Virginia's shores.

A threat from his illicit past appears, however, as an old pirate enemy plots to seize the colony's wealth, forcing Marlowe to choose between losing all – or facing the one man he fears.

Book One of *The Brethren of the Coast* trilogy, featuring Thomas Marlowe.

'Brilliant . . . Readers will gladly be swept along by a wonderful plot'
Publishers Weekly

'A master storyteller'
Sailing

0 552 14838 5

THE BLACKBIRDER
by James Nelson

'A master both of his period and of the English language'
Patrick O'Brian

Thomas Marlowe, former pirate and captain of the Guardship, lives prosperously on his tobacco plantation near Williamsburg with his lovely wife Elizabeth. But when King James, the huge ex-slave who is in command of Marlowe's sloop, kills the crew of a slave ship – a blackbirder – and makes himself the most wanted man in Virginia, Marlowe is forced to go and hunt him down.

Setting off in pursuit of the blackbirder, struggling to maintain control over his crew – rough privateers, set only on plunder – Marlowe follows James's trail of destruction all the way to the shores of Africa. There, in the slave port of Whydah, James and Marlowe face a common threat – and their final showdown.

Book Two of *The Brethren of the Coast* trilogy, featuring Thomas Marlowe.

'A master storyteller'
Sailing

0 552 14842 3

THE PIRATE ROUND
by James Nelson

'A master storyteller'
Sailing

Former pirate and captain of the Guardship, Thomas Marlowe is now a man of property, keeping his prosperous tobacco plantation in Virginia with his beautiful wife Elizabeth. But the Anglo-Spanish war has meant a decline in tobacco prices, and Thomas decides to come to England to trade his wares, little thinking that in the busy streets of London he will meet an old enemy from his pirating days.

Forced to abandon his tobacco and flee, he has to take to sea and finds himself in battle with the ships bound for the Moghul Empire, and in Madagascar he at last comes face to face with his pirate foes.

Book Three of *The Brethren of the Coast* trilogy, featuring Thomas Marlowe.

'First rate action writing'
Publishers Weekly

'A master both of his period and of the English language'
Patrick O'Brian

0 552 14843 1